KEEPING DOWN THE BLACK VOTE

Also by Frances Fox Piven from The New Press

The War at Home: The Domestic Costs of Bush's Militarism

The Breaking of the American Social Compact
(with Richard A. Cloward)

KEEPING DOWN THE BLACK VOTE

Race and the Demobilization of American Voters

Frances Fox Piven
Lorraine C. Minnite
Margaret Groarke

THE NEW PRESS

NEW YORK
LONDON

Requests for permission to reproduce selections from this book should be mailed to:
Permissions Department, The New Press, 38 Greene Street, New York, NY 10013.

Published in the United States by The New Press, New York, 2009
Distributed by W. W. Norton & Company, Inc., New York

LIBRARY OF CONGRESS CATALOGING-IN-PUBLICATION DATA

Piven, Frances Fox.
    Keeping down the black vote : race and the demobilization of American
voters / Frances Fox Piven, Lorraine C. Minnite, Margaret Groarke.
        p.   cm.
    Includes bibliographical references and index.
    ISBN 978-1-59558-354-3 (hc. : alk. paper)   1. African Americans—Suffrage.
2. African Americans—Politics and government.   3. Voting—United States.
I. Minnite, Lorraine Carol.   II. Groarke, Margaret.   III. Title.
JK1924.P68   2008
324.6'208996073—dc22   2008036014

The New Press was established in 1990 as a not-for-profit alternative to the large,
commercial publishing houses currently dominating the book publishing industry.
The New Press operates in the public interest rather than for private gain, and is
committed to publishing, in innovative ways, works of educational, cultural, and
community value that are often deemed insufficiently profitable.

www.thenewpress.com

Composition by dix!
This book was set in Minion

Printed in the United States of America

10   9   8   7   6   5   4   3   2   1

To the sustained courage and optimism of the African American people who launched the voting rights movements that breathed life into the ideals of American democracy. We owe them much.

CONTENTS

FOREWORD

Adam Cohen

The United States is generally regarded as the world's preeminent democracy. The history of voting in this country, however, has not always been a proud one. From the earliest days of the Republic, there has been a raging battle between voting rights and disenfranchisement—and disenfranchisement has always put up a good fight.

It started, of course, with the Founders. They established a republic on the principle that "all men are created equal," but they had a narrow view of who should be able to vote: white, male property owners.

To win the vote for blacks as a matter of law took a civil war, and then the enactment of the Fifteenth Amendment in 1870.

Winning the vote for women took even longer. "Logically, our enfranchisement ought to have occurred . . . in Reconstruction days," Elizabeth Cady Stanton lamented before her death in 1902. "Our movement is belated, and like all things too long postponed, now gets on everybody's nerves." The Nineteenth Amendment, extending the right to vote to women, did not become law until 1920.

The struggles of blacks and women to win the right to vote are the two great enfranchisement narratives in American history, but there is a great deal more to the story.

Other groups have also been systematically excluded from the franchise. There have long been efforts, which continue to this day, to make it difficult for immigrants to vote. In 1840, New York enacted a voter registration law that applied only to New York City, aimed at the growing Irish-Catholic population. In 1921, New York adopted a constitutional amendment imposing a rigorous literacy test, aimed in large part at keeping hundreds of thousands of Yiddish-speaking Jews from casting ballots.

And working-class Americans have often been a target. In the 1800s, New Jersey adopted "sunset laws" that required the polls to close before factories let out for the day. Many states used to deny the vote to "paupers."

In this long, intricate, and unproud history of disenfranchisement, the struggle of black Americans to win the right to vote—not merely in law, but in reality—has been the most difficult. And it continued long after 1870, when the Fifteenth Amendment was added to the Constitution.

Up until the civil rights era, blacks were prevented from voting in a wide variety of ways. There was the explicit, and chilling, violence of Ku Klux Klan night riders and lynching parties who went after black people who dared to try to register to vote.

Medgar Evers, the NAACP Mississippi field secretary who was killed in his driveway by a Ku Klux Klansman, described in his autobiography what happened after he and some black friends tried to vote in the 1940s—after Evers had returned from serving in World War II. They ignored the threats of violence and registered to vote. Then, on Election Day, they went to the polls:

> Not a Negro was on the streets, and when we got to the courthouse, the clerk said he wanted to talk with us. When we got into his office, some 15 or 20 armed white men surged in behind us, men I had grown up with, had played with. We split up and went home. Around town, Negroes said we had been whipped, beaten up and run out of town. Well, in a way we were whipped, I guess . . .

Along with the threat—and reality—of violence, there were electoral schemes like the infamous "white primaries," which prohibited blacks in some states from participating in the Democratic Party nominating process.

The Supreme Court and civil rights protesters wiped away many of these restrictions. In 1944, white primaries were declared to be unconstitutional. In the 1960s, the poll tax and literacy tests were struck down. The Voting Rights Act of 1965 put the power of the federal government behind southern blacks who were being denied the right to vote.

In history textbooks, the story of blacks and the vote often ends in 1965—or a few years later, when its effects were finally felt across the South. The real story of black disenfranchisement continued long after, and continues to this day—as Frances Fox Piven, Lorraine C. Minnite, and Margaret Groarke demonstrate convincingly in this passionately argued book.

I have seen the persistence of black vote suppression for myself over the last six years, reporting and writing about election mechanics for the *New York Times* editorial board. Black disenfranchisement, although more subtle than it once was, is still very much alive.

Today, it is done with laws that achieve this goal by indirection. Felon disenfranchisement statutes, for example, in many cases deny felons the right to vote even after they have served their sentences. Often, these laws were adopted or modified shortly after the enactment of the Fifteenth Amendment with the express purpose of keeping down the number of eligible black voters. Because of the unequal incarceration rates between the races, the effect on black voters today is substantial. Fully 13 percent of black men nationwide are disenfranchised by these laws. In two states, almost one in three black men are.

Another way black voting is suppressed is increasingly onerous voter identification laws. Georgia passed an infamous voter ID law that required people to pay for the ID they needed to vote—a modern version of the poll tax. The racial animus behind the bill was barely disguised. The Georgia legislator who sponsored the bill was quoted in a Justice Department memo saying that if blacks in her district "are not paid to vote, they don't go to the polls."

Voter ID laws are becoming more common, and their racial impact is clear. They are increasingly requiring voters to present government-issued photo ID—something anyone who drives a car has, but nondrivers often do not. Blacks, poor people, the disabled, and the elderly are disproportionately kept away from the polls by these laws.

• • •

Supporters of voter ID laws claim that their purpose is preventing vote fraud, but there are virtually no known cases of people showing up at the polls impersonating another voter. The biggest source of vote fraud is absentee ballots—but legislators who campaign against vote fraud rarely impose any restrictions on them. It is clear that the real goal of voter ID laws is to disenfranchise poor and minority voters—and all too often it works.

Still, when voting rights advocates challenged Indiana's oppressive voter ID law, the Supreme Court upheld it in a terribly reasoned decision. The court did not believe that the law would actually keep eligible people from voting. A week after the decision, twelve elderly nuns who tried to vote in the Indiana were turned away because they lacked valid ID.

Another kind of law aimed at suppressing the black vote is the increasingly tough rules that are being imposed on voter registration drives. Legislatures have begun putting extraordinarily burdensome requirements on registration drives—including enormous fines for small mistakes in the registration process. It is clear that their goal is not reducing the number of mistakes, but rather putting an end to registration drives that sign up poor and minority voters.

The laws have begun to have their intended effect. In 2008, the League of Women Voters temporarily suspended its voter registration work in Florida. The group said that it was afraid that the crippling fines imposed by the state for small mistakes in voter registration efforts could bankrupt it.

There are even more obscure and insidious laws put on the books with the goal of suppressing the minority vote. One of these is a little-known rule for counting provisional ballots known as "right church, wrong pew." Provisional ballots are ballots that election officials are required by federal law to make available to voters if there is some question about their eligibility to vote. They are set aside, and after the election is over, a determination is made about whether the ballot is valid.

Provisional ballots are disproportionately cast by poor and minority voters. Legislators who do not want to see a high turnout by such voters look for ways not to count provisional ballots. The "right church, wrong pew" rule, which several states have adopted, says that when a provisional ballot is handed in at the right polling place but in the wrong precinct within that polling place, it has to be thrown out. Clearly, anyone who cared about voting rights would require that the ballot be taken to the correct precinct and counted there. But the legislators behind "right church, wrong pew" are looking for technicalities with which to take away the vote from people they do not want to see voting.

The list goes on. In the pre-civil rights era, the battle to win the vote for blacks was difficult, but the obstacles were clear. There was nothing subtle about a voting registrar in Wilcox County, Alabama, simply refusing to register black people or a Virginia law imposing a poll tax.

Today, the lines are not as clear. Even if the intent behind a voter ID law is to keep down the black vote, it is wrapped in a package of "voter integrity" that is convincing enough to win the endorsement of the Supreme Court. Even though felon disenfranchisement laws in many cases have had both the purpose and effect of reducing the black vote, they have been difficult to challenge in court and in legislatures.

Of course, not all of the suppression of the black vote is done through laws. A great deal is done by dirty tricks, which remain a fixture of close elections. One old standby is the anonymous flyer that appears in black neighborhoods just before Election Day. Sometimes these flyers say the election has been postponed until a later date. Other times, they try to scare people into believing they may be arrested if they try to vote. In early October 2008, the *Philadelphia Daily News* reported that a flyer was showing up in black neighborhoods in North and West Philadelphia warning that voters with outstanding arrest warrants or unpaid traffic tickets might be arrested at the polls.

The driving force behind disenfranchising blacks was once racism, pure and simple. Now, it is more often partisanship. Republican elected officials often see blacks as reliable Democratic voters and try to keep down their numbers simply to win elections. There is an undeniable political logic, but it is morally wrong. Voting rights advocates need to point out vote suppression where it occurs and to underscore the racial impact when it is there.

They will be joined by people who rely on black votes, of course—in the current political landscape, Democrats. But advocates of fair voting should also have support from people of principle from both parties, or no party at all, who believe that American democracy is diminished by laws that disenfranchise eligible voters.

That is what happened in 1859—and the person of principle was Abraham Lincoln. Massachusetts Republicans had pushed through a requirement that immigrants wait two years after becoming citizens to vote. A group of German Americans asked Lincoln what he thought of the law. As a Republican, mere partisanship should have led Lincoln to support laws of this kind, but he opposed them.

"I am against its adoption in Illinois, or in any other place where I have a right to oppose it," Lincoln wrote in a now-famous letter. "Understanding the spirit of our institutions to aim at the elevation of men, I am opposed to whatever tends to degrade them."

PREFACE

This book was written during the remarkable election campaign of 2008. Because the outcome of the campaign seemed to hang on the mobilization of new voters and on the turnout of minorities, fears ran high that Republican strategies to suppress these voters could lead to a stolen election. And there was voter suppression, in all the forms recounted in the pages that follow. As it turned out, however, the margins by which the Democratic presidential candidate won were large enough to swamp the advantage gained by age-old strategies of purging, caging, challenging, or intimidating voters, or by multiplying administrative obstructions to the vote—for example, by requiring photo identification or by requiring that the data on new voters match the information in error-prone databases.

However, we should not be misled by the success of the Obama campaign to think that voter suppression is no longer a problem in American politics. To the contrary, voter suppression is embedded in enduring features of the American electoral system. As we show in the pages that follow, it is propelled by the logic of two-party competition, which makes blocking the votes of groups likely to vote for the opposition rational—perhaps more rational than the fabled idea that competition propels the parties to mobilize new voters. After all, from the perspective of party operatives, vote suppression yields a smaller and more manageable electorate. And because vote suppression tactics typically target marginal groups with potentially discordant demands, they ease the problem of fashioning a majority voter coalition in a fractious society. Moreover, vote suppression is practically institutionalized in our sprawling and inchoate system of election administration, which generates multiple opportunities for the manipulation and obstruction of voters.

So even after the United States has elected an African American president, the problem—and it is huge—of a system of party competition that creates incentives to dampen turnout, especially among groups that can be more readily marginalized, and an election administrative system that facilitates this remains with us. Proportional representation and multiparty campaigns are not likely in the near future, but perhaps the historic break with the past brought by an African American president will create the opportunity for reform. What we need now, at a minimum, are simple and straightforward national standards for voter registration and balloting and transparent methods of counting the vote.

November 14, 2008

KEEPING DOWN
THE BLACK VOTE

INTRODUCTION

"Keeping down the black vote" is a practice as old as American politics that both reflects and reinforces the subordination of African Americans in our culture and in our economy. In this book we will focus particularly on suppression of the black vote since the passage of the Voting Rights Act in 1965, when blacks finally won formal legal and political recognition of their dignity and citizenship after centuries of oppression. The complex of electoral rules and party maneuvers invented in part to keep down the black vote in the nineteenth century survives in the contemporary period despite the great victories of the civil rights struggle. Or, it might be more accurate to say, the apparatus and tactics of vote suppression flourish *because* of the victories of the civil rights movement, since those victories contributed to making blacks a pivotal bloc in both national and municipal election campaigns. This irony of reform explains why, four decades after what some have termed the Second Reconstruction, the weapons of racially targeted vote suppression remain in the arsenal of at least one of the major political parties.

Just as the political parties have exerted themselves to demobilize black voters, so have blacks exerted themselves, often at terrible cost and always with intense passion, to realize the promise of the vote and all it entails. Black voter mobilizations in turn have typically activated the stratagems of vote suppression we describe in this book. They have also triggered partisan efforts to overwhelm the black vote by fashioning racist appeals to mobilize white voters. These contests have not only poisoned American politics, but they go far toward accounting for the skewed and narrow patterns of electoral participation in the United States.

• • •

Before the twentieth century, most blacks lived in the apartheid South, where they were stripped of the right to vote by means of felon disenfranchisement, literacy tests, poll taxes, difficult or forbidding voter registration procedures, and lynch mob terror. The Great Migration of blacks from the South to the urban North, a migration pushed by the mechanization of southern agriculture, and pulled by the availability of industrial employment, especially during World War II, brought African Americans into electoral politics, and into the urban base of the Democratic Party.

By the 1960s that fact became the basis of two contradictory developments. One was the growth of the civil rights movement, itself largely based in the South, but nevertheless drawing political strength from the new concentrations of black voters in the cities controlled by Democratic organizations. The fervor of the movement also encouraged many southern blacks to brave the obstacles of the electoral process, even while the legislative victories of the movement reduced those obstacles. The second development was the rise of the Republican Party's "Southern Strategy," which took advantage of white fear of and profound distaste for African Americans, and the growing identification of blacks with the Democratic Party, to lure hitherto reliably Democratic whites, both southerners and working-class voters in the northern cities, into the Republican ranks. Barry Goldwater and George Wallace were the brazen spokesmen of the strategy, and every Republican presidential contender from 1964 onward relied upon it.

Once the moral triumphs of the civil rights movement had made the old racist slurs impermissible, new, less obvious racist codes came into vogue in Republican campaign rhetoric. The words denoting blacks became "welfare," "crime," and "illegitimacy," and still other code words pointed to Democratic indulgence of African American needs and demands, such as disparaging references to Lyndon Johnson's Great Society programs, or simply the term "liberal." Or as Republican operative Lee Atwater put it,

> You start out in 1954 by saying "Nigger, nigger, nigger." By 1968 you can't say "nigger"—that hurts you. Backfires. So you say

stuff like forced busing, states' rights and all that stuff. You're getting so abstract now [that] you're talking about cutting taxes, and all these things you're talking about are totally economic things, and a byproduct of them is [that] blacks get hurt worse than whites. . . . And subconsciously maybe that is part of it. I'm not saying that. But I'm saying that if it is getting that abstract, and that coded, that we are doing away with the racial problem one way or the other. You follow me—because obviously sitting around saying, "we want to cut this," is much more abstract than even the busing thing, *and* a hell of a lot more abstract than "Nigger, nigger." [1]

This southern (and northern) Republican strategy of stigmatizing Democrats by their association with blacks is familiar. What is not so familiar is that the strategy is typically accompanied by more surreptitious campaign tactics to suppress voting among blacks, who are now almost inevitably Democrats. These tactics draw upon the apparatus of voter registration rules and balloting procedures that are the crystallization of a long history of vote suppression targeted mainly at blacks, but also at other marginalized groups such as immigrants. The apparatus is not, however, just the residue of history. When the opportunity presents itself, partisan operatives also continually push for the elaboration of new administrative obstacles to the vote. Just as important, party operatives wage under-the-radar war against black voters with concerted tactics of voter intimidation and misinformation. In the contemporary period, this has been mostly the work of Republicans. But not so long ago, when blacks in the cities made their bid to take control of city governments, local Democratic parties were quick to deploy their own battery of vote suppression tactics.

We begin our argument in chapter 1 with a discussion of the logic of competition in a two-party system that drives vote suppression. This analysis will be unfamiliar because the conviction that parties mobilize voters is treated as axiomatic in studies of American politics. We will show why that notion is sometimes right but often wrong, and we will review the major historical episodes which support our view that the logic of two-party competition also drives vote suppression.

In chapter 2, we review the political consequences of the economic and demographic upheavals of the post–World War II period that drove many blacks out of the rural South and into the big cities, setting the stage for the emergence of African Americans as a major voting bloc. This development transformed American electoral politics. Not only did it make possible the rise of the civil rights movement and the eventual dismantling of the southern system of apartheid, but it led both parties to refashion their racial strategies and reshuffle their coalitions in the quest for national power. The once solidly Democratic South became Republican territory, and the Democrats, at least the national Democrats in control of the federal government, reached out to the new black voters in the cities with a battery of Great Society programs.

In chapter 3 we turn to some of the great battles of that era—now only dimly remembered—for political control of the big cities. It was perhaps inevitable that growing numbers of African Americans in the cities and a conciliatory national government would fuel the drive for black municipal power. The late 1960s saw the beginning of a series of fiercely fought races for the mayoralty, in which insurgent black voter mobilizations were countered by the determined efforts of reigning big-city Democratic organizations to suppress the black vote. The most important of these races was the 1983 bid of Harold Washington in Chicago, then the second largest city in the nation, and the domain of the fabled Daley Democratic machine. Washington's victorious campaign was promoted by an insurgent black voter movement that helped reinvigorate the drive for black voting rights everywhere in the nation, and inspired the 1984 presidential bid of Jesse Jackson and the Rainbow Coalition.

While blacks were making progress in gaining local offices, the political upheavals that made those gains possible were contributing to dramatic changes in the configuration of national power. The southern backlash against civil rights victories laid the groundwork for growing support for Republican presidential candidates there and the eventual partisan realignment of the South. In the northern cities, black insurgency also paved the way for the rise of "Reagan Democrats" among the white working class. In 1980, drawing on these new sources of support in a campaign fashioned to exacerbate racial divisions, Ronald Reagan won the presidency.

Chapter 4 describes the remarkable voter registration drive that arose in response to the Reagan regime; the drive's participants went on to campaign for a national reform of voter registration procedures that would make vote suppression more difficult and thus lead to a more inclusive voting universe. The National Voter Registration Act of 1993 was the result. But Republican resistance and Democratic ambivalence in the Congress weakened the legislation, with the consequence that the new law was poorly implemented. And ironically, some provisions of the law were even put to use in subsequent Republican efforts at vote suppression.

Chapter 5 brings us close to the present with accounts of how both parties have tried to manage the problems presented by black voters. Centrists in the Democratic Party explained the string of electoral defeats since 1968 by what they argued was a losing commitment to black issues. Ronald Reagan's crushing victories in the 1980s gave them the upper hand. The race-neutral position promoted by the centrist Democratic Leadership Council was eventually vindicated, for a time, with the election of Bill Clinton.

Especially after the Democrats succeeded in winning back a portion of the southern white vote, the Republicans were also searching for a new strategy, as the story of the fabled Florida 2000 election reveals. The chain of events began with the huge black voter drive in Florida that the prospect of a George W. Bush presidency precipitated. The drive in turn provoked the voter suppression maneuvers that followed. Florida 2000 became virtually a parable of how the black vote is suppressed in contemporary American elections. Much of what went on—the confusing ballots, the abuse of felony disenfranchisement laws, the discarded ballots—is now familiar. The arsenal of vote suppression tactics succeeded in creating an election result that was close enough to be disputed, allowing a Supreme Court with a Republican-appointed majority to deliver the state and therefore the nation to George W. Bush.

Since then, the Republican Party has relied on stratagems like redistricting, highly partisan election administration, and old-fashioned vote suppression to win what continue to be very close elections. In chapter 6 we offer the reader an analysis of the methods of contemporary voter suppression, including the deliberate fostering of the myth of voter fraud that justifies these techniques and also paves the way for the introduction of new administrative procedures that limit access to the ballot box.

We write these pages at an extraordinary moment in American electoral politics. After a fiercely fought primary campaign, only occasionally tainted by the racist allusions of the Southern Strategy, Barack Obama has become the presidential nominee of the Democratic Party. His campaign is tapping the perennial faith of African Americans in the emancipatory possibilities of the vote, and their turnout has been exceptionally high in the primaries. But of course, it is not just African Americans who see in this astonishing development the possibility of a new era in American politics. Turnout among the young has surged, their voting patterns reveal little racial bias, and there is jubilation in the air. Perhaps the obsession with race is receding, and this indeed is a new day in American electoral politics. We do hope so. But even as the Obama campaign rolls on, the states are moving to introduce photo identification requirements as well as new restrictions on voter registration efforts that hamstring nonpartisan groups and undermine the National Voter Registration Act. Obama speaks to cheering multiracial crowds, but the Supreme Court has approved a new law in Indiana requiring government-issued photo identification to vote, which even proponents have admitted would make it harder for poorer voters, who are more likely black and more likely Democrats, to cast their ballots. Other states are already poised to follow, and as many as ten states could pass similar laws before the upcoming presidential election.

An Obama victory could bury the Southern Strategy once and for all. But the logic of party competition that produces and reproduces electoral rules designed to make voting difficult remains in place. It will take a lot more than a presidential victory—*even of a black man*—to uproot it, because vote suppression is embedded in the electoral institutions of the United States. In the short run, we can expect partisan operatives and campaigns to continue to manipulate electoral rules to their advantage and to target marginalized groups in the opposition for vote suppression. In tight races, efforts to keep down the vote will continue: misinformation campaigns, inordinately long lines at the polls, sloppy and inaccurate registration records, the abuse of felon disenfranchisement laws, new voter ID rules that prevent eligible voters from casting regular ballots, party-run voter challenge campaigns, the use of provisional ballots that are then not counted, and so on. And through it all, we can expect lots of talk and lots of press about the dangers of voter fraud to make the restrictive features of the electoral system seem reasonable.

These tactics will be used even if race recedes as a distinguishing feature of American electoral politics. When elections are close, the logic of two-party competition presses toward voter demobilization, and as long as other marginalized groups like immigrants or the poor are with us, their votes, too, will be ripe for targeted vote suppression campaigns. In the long run, we need to make the entire electoral process, from registration to the counting of ballots, simple and transparent. We need a system of election administration that encourages and facilitates the most basic right in a democracy, the right to vote.

1

THE PARTY LOGIC OF
VOTER DEMOBILIZATION

The two parties have combined against us to nullify our power by a "gentleman's agreement" of non-recognition, no matter how we vote. . . . May God write us down as asses if ever again we are found putting our trust in either the Republican or the Democratic Parties.

—W.E.B. Du Bois, 1922[1]

This book argues that American political parties compete as much by demobilizing voters as by mobilizing them, and that it is black Americans who are usually singled out as the targets of demobilization. "Keeping the black vote down" has been an important Republican strategy in recent campaigns, as we will show in this book. But vote suppression is not simply a facet of recent shenanigans by party operatives. Keeping the vote down is a long-standing feature of American campaign politics. Since this assertion flies in the face of the usual view that parties do the work of democracy by mobilizing voters, we have much to explain.

Two preoccupations run through American history. One has to do with the expansion of democracy, and especially the idea that ordinary people should have the right to vote. The other has to do with race, and specifically the subordination of blacks in most areas of social life. The politics generated by struggles over the right to vote, and the politics generated by racial policies and practices, each explain much of American history, including contemporary history. But these preoccupations have always been in tension. For one thing, to extend the right to vote to black Americans is to grant them standing and respect, which clashes with their subordination in other

spheres.[2] For another, when black Americans have the vote, they inevitably try to use their voting power to put a halt to the policies that
ensure their subordination.

This tension or contradiction has recurrently been evident in the
century and a half since emancipation. African Americans have repeatedly mobilized to realize what for them was the apocalyptic
promise of the franchise, and what they hoped the franchise would
mean. In the midst of Reconstruction, with "Negroes all crazy on
politics,"[3] a northern observer in Alabama reported on the 1868 election: "In defiance of fatigue, hardship, hunger and threats of employ-
ers, blacks had come en masse to the polls. Not one in fifty wore an
'unpatched garment,' few possessed a pair of shoes, yet for hours they
stood on line in a 'pitiless storm.' Why? 'The hunger to have the same
chances as the white men they feel and comprehend. . . . That is what
brings them here.' "[4] Nearly one hundred years later, Fannie Lou
Hamer told the story of her beating and jailing at the hands of the
police as she returned to Mississippi with other civil rights workers
from South Carolina, where they had gone to attend a voter registration training workshop. With a bloody eye from the assault still visible, Mrs. Hamer explained how she was ordered to lie facedown and
beaten with a blackjack by a black prisoner whom the police had
ordered to the attack, and how a second prisoner was forced to sit
on her legs as she fought back so that she could be beaten some
more. She told this story—on national television[5]—to the Credentials Committee of the Democratic Party at its 1964 presidential
nominating convention, where Mrs. Hamer was part of an alternate
slate of delegates from Mississippi who had come to the convention
in Atlantic City to challenge the party's seating of Mississippi's regular all-white delegation. Fannie Lou Hamer had been hunted by vig-
ilantes who shot into the homes of her friends while looking for her;
had lost her employment as a sharecropper for attending a mass
meeting about voting; and had suffered permanent kidney damage
and other physical disabilities from police beatings for her voter registration work with the Student Nonviolent Coordinating Committee. She endured these ordeals, she told the Credentials Committee,
"on account of we want to register, to become first-class citizens."[6]

Just as regularly as blacks have yearned for their rights, the major political parties have turned their backs on that hunger and exerted themselves to stifle the black vote. In the past, this has been done with organized violence, intimidation, and trickery, and also by introducing laws and rules governing the right to vote that have the practical effect of barring blacks from the polls.

However, in the post–civil rights era, the strategies that reconcile the contradiction between the deeply felt passion for voting rights and the social practices of racial subordination are typically not so overt. Rather, vote suppression is often accomplished by legal and administrative subterfuge, with justifications that proclaim the rules and practices to be essential to safeguarding American democracy. Although hidden in the deadening bureaucracy of election administration, these strategies of vote suppression are enormously important. They limit the right to vote not only for blacks, but for many other Americans as well.

We quickly note that the franchise is only one element in electoral representative democracies, and constriction of that right is only one way that democratic arrangements can be distorted. The history of the manipulation of the franchise and of the struggles that sometimes resulted is paralleled by a history of manipulation that results from formulas for representation that make some votes count more, often much more, than others. The skewing of representation was indeed written into the American Constitution itself in the provisions that enlarged the representation in the Congress of the southern slavocracy, including the infamous three-fifths rule, as well as with the allocation of Senate seats without regard to population.

We live with the consequences of distorted representation, in both the Senate and the Electoral College.[7] Or think of the limits on democratic influence that result when crucial government decision makers, such as federal judges and the governors of the Federal Reserve, are not exposed to the electorate. Or consider the huge effects on democratic possibilities that result from the unfettered flow of money into campaign propaganda machines. Or the looming menace of privatized electronic voting. These are only some of the important flaws in American electoral-representative democracy.

Nevertheless, in this book we put all this to one side and focus on voting rights, the element in the panoply of electoral-representative arrangements that has always excited the passion of ordinary people. Or as the influential political scientist V.O. Key Jr. said a half century ago, "The electorate occupies, at least in the mystique of [democratic] orders, the position of the principal organ of governance."[8]

Americans take pride in being the world's leading democracy, and the main reason for the pride is the comparatively early and broad distribution of the right to vote. The franchise was extended to white working-class men much earlier than elsewhere. Indeed, even before the American Revolution, historians estimate, as many as half of white men had the franchise.[9] By contrast, after the passage of Britain's 1832 Reform Act, still only about one in five men possessed the vote in England and Wales.[10] In the aftermath of the American revolutionary war and the passion for radical democracy that it fueled, voting rights were expanded: property restrictions were replaced by taxpaying requirements, and then these also were gradually eliminated, along with poll taxes and religious and literacy requirements, and more and more state and local officials were required to stand for election. By the 1830s, most white men enjoyed the right to vote. Then, in the aftermath of the Civil War, African Americans were enfranchised by the Fifteenth Amendment to the Constitution. Women gained the right to vote after World War I, and eighteen- to twenty-year-olds were enfranchised as American involvement in the Vietnam War wound down. In legal principle, the right to vote, a foundational element in democratic arrangements, had become nearly universal.

But the proportion of the population that actually voted did not change nearly as much as the proportion legally enfranchised. The reason is that the expansion of formal enfranchisement has been paralleled by the erection of legal and administrative obstructions to the ballot box, as well as by party strategies of intimidation and harassment of unwanted voters, or simply by the apathy that results when parties fail to appeal to potential voters by naming their grievances and their aspirations. In other words, many features of American electoral politics demobilize voters instead of mobilizing them. The result is that rather than being the world's leading democracy, the United States ranks near the bottom when levels of turnout here are compared with turnout in other major democracies (see table 1).

Table 1
Voter Turnout in OECD Member Nations in the 1990s National Legislative Elections

	Number of Elections	Average Turnout
Italy	3	90.2
Iceland	2	88.3
Greece	3	84.7
Belgium	2	84.1
Czech Republic*	4	82.8
Australia	3	82.7
Sweden	3	82.6
Denmark	2	81.7
New Zealand	3	80.4
Austria	3	79.6
Turkey	2	79.4
Spain	2	79.0
Portugal	2	78.4
Slovak Republic	1	75.9
Norway	2	75.7
Netherlands	1	75.2
Germany	2	72.7
United Kingdom	2	72.4
Finland	2	71.5
Ireland	2	70.2
Korea	2	70.0
Hungary	3	64.1
France	2	60.6
Luxembourg	1	60.5

(continued)

Voter Turnout in OECD Member Nations
in the 1990s (*continued*)

	Number of Elections	Average Turnout
Canada	2	60.1
Japan	4	57.0
Mexico	3	56.3
United States Presidential	**2**	**51.2**
Poland	3	48.4
United States Congressional**	**4**	**44.9**
Switzerland	1	37.7

*Czech Republic includes elections in Czechoslovakia 1990 and 1992.
**Virtually unique among democracies, the United States attracts much higher turnout for presidential elections than for national legislative elections. Thus here we include the average for both presidential elections (1992, 1996) and for all federal elections (1992, 1994, 1996, 1998).
SOURCE: International Institute for Democracy and Electoral Assistance, www.idea.int/vt/survey/voter_turnout_pop1.cfm (accessed November 29, 2007).

Moreover, the active voting universe is skewed to overrepresent those who are better off and better educated. Ironically, the historical expansion and celebration of the legal right to vote may help to obscure the intricacies of electoral administration and campaign tactics that lead to the actual disenfranchisement of many voters.

George W. Bush recapitulated this great irony when he applauded the 2006 extension of the Voting Rights Act of 1965 because, he said, it gave the vote to many blacks who had hitherto been barred from the polls.[11] Rhetorically, Bush was sharing in the legitimating myth of democratic participation in America. But as we will show, the operatives in his campaigns of 2000 and 2004 exerted themselves to devise on-the-ground tactics that effectively blocked many people, and especially blacks, from the polls. As Joe Rich, who headed the Voting Section of the Justice Department during the tumultuous elections of 2000 and 2004, said, "The GOP agenda is to make it harder to vote. You purge voters. You don't register voters. . . . You pick the states where you go after Democrats."[12]

Systematic and enduring vote suppression is usually given little attention, either by academics or by pundits. This is at least partly because of a widely believed proposition that has acquired axiomatic status in discussions of American electoral politics. The consensus is that presumably, political parties competing for majorities necessarily work to mobilize new voters. The argument is celebratory. For decades scholars have argued that competitive parties make democracy work. So, for example, E.E. Schattschneider in his authoritative 1942 book *Party Government* argued, "Once party organization becomes active in the electorate, a vast field for extension and intensification of effort is opened up, the extension of the franchise to new social classes, for example. The natural history of the parties is a story of continuous expansion and intensification . . . to a larger and larger electorate."[13]

Or, more simply, "modern democracy is unthinkable save in terms of parties."[14] Legions of other scholars of American politics echo this view. Because the parties compete for voters, "they attempt to include as many groups as they possibly can," write Edward Greenberg and Benjamin Page.[15] Or as Robert Dahl says, parties "enable the many to pool their resources to offset the advantages of the few."[16] "The essential feature of electoral politics," according to Steven Rosenstone and John Mark Hansen, "is electoral mobilization."[17] The parties are thus given an iconic role in making democracy work.[18] The parties need voters, and because they do, they pay close heed to what voters want in choosing candidates and programmatic appeals, and then they deploy their resources to bring voters to the polls.[19]

To be sure, there is also a major qualification of this view, and once again, Schattschneider provides the authoritative opinion. Parties play their appointed role in mobilizing voters around issues and candidates and in bringing them to the polls because competition for electoral victory forces party leaders to be oriented to *potential* voters. However, if one party becomes overwhelmingly dominant, the logic that makes the parties agents of democracy collapses. Without the need for voters, the party becomes prey to the influence of elites. For Schattschneider, this is the significance of "the system of

1896," when the Republican Party became for a time overwhelmingly dominant in the North, the Democratic Party became dominant in the South, and national voter turnout declined precipitously. Without competition, there was little need for new voters, or indeed, for voters in general, or so the argument goes.[20]

In fact, the historical evidence shows that the argument that attributes the democratizing function of voter mobilization to competitive parties is sometimes right, but also often wrong. While party competition has on occasion led the parties to mobilize new voters, much of the time it has not, and it has certainly not led them to mobilize marginalized groups of nonvoters. Thus, after winning the 1964 election with the largest landslide in American history, 61 percent, Lyndon Baines Johnson simply shut down the Democratic National Committee's highly successful voter registration operation.[21] Within the framework of the party system, how do we understand the logic that drives voter mobilization some of the time, and voter demobilization much of the time?

Election contests can be won by bringing more voters to the polls or by deterring the voters who support the opposition from casting their ballots. In other words, by voter mobilization or by vote suppression. We propose that voter demobilization is often the more attractive strategy to campaign operatives because the consequences are more readily manageable. The politicians who are the main actors in the parties usually do not want new voters. Politicians seek the stability that makes electoral outcomes predictable and manageable, and manageable with limited effort. They are reluctant to undertake the mobilization of new voters, even when the "logic" of electoral competition suggests such a course. This is especially the case when the new voters are drawn from marginalized groups that risk antagonizing others in the party's electoral coalition.[22] Moreover, new voters are not reliable, nor are they reliably loyal to party, which makes it inefficient to pump resources into mobilizing them. So there is nothing inevitable in the logic of party competition that drives the parties to expand the electorate.

Instead, the formal rights extended to new groups often precipitate multiple strategies for suppressing registration and voting among these groups. These strategies of vote suppression range widely, from campaign appeals that ignore or disparage the material interests, the leaders, and the cultural dispositions of the new groups; to get-out-the-vote tactics that deliberately circumvent the neighborhoods and workplaces where they congregate; to the development of new rules and tactics to prevent their registration; to the voter intimidation, list purging, and caging strategies that we will describe in greater detail throughout this book. From the surreptitious campaigns of parties and candidates to shrink their opponent's vote, to the rules governing registration and voting that are the legacy of these efforts in the past, vote suppression to demobilize the electorate is a powerful tendency in American politics.

Not only does demobilization produce a smaller and more manageable electorate over time, making campaigns easier and cheaper, but demobilization strategies can be targeted at those potential opposition voters whose discordant cultural identities and contentious political demands make them easier to isolate. Indeed, even the leaders of the opposition party that would benefit from their votes may nevertheless tacitly allow vote suppression because of the opposition the marginal group provokes among other groups in their voter and interest-group coalitions. We suggest that this in part explains why African Americans have so often been the target of successful vote suppression stratagems since first winning the vote over a century ago. Their subordination within party coalitions, from the Republican Party in the late nineteenth century to the Democrats after the New Deal, made them vulnerable.

This more complex logic of voter mobilization and demobilization is evident in recurrent efforts at "getting out the vote" on the one hand, and vote suppression on the other. Thus, when campaigns to mobilize voters do occur, or when new groups enter the electorate for other reasons, the challenge they represent can be met with efforts at voter suppression. Similarly, efforts to suppress particular voter blocs can be countered by the efforts of political opponents, inside or outside the opposition party, to mobilize them. This leads to a level of electoral contestation that has to do not with what is usually discussed by pundits, such as the appeal of the candidates, their promises and programs, or the funds they can raise. Rather, this level of electoral contestation has to do with the scale and shape of the electoral universe within which the contest for office is played out. As Stanley Kelley Jr. and his colleagues point out in a classic statement on this subject, "electorates are much more the product of political forces than many have appreciated. . . . Within limits, they can be constructed to a size and composition deemed desirable by those in power."[23] In effect, not only do the voters pick the parties, but the parties pick the voters. Extraparty social movements are the usual source of an expanded electorate in American history, not parties that take the initiative to mobilize new voters on their own.

Another cautionary point has to do with the way we think about parties. Put simply, although American parties are often treated as unified and coherent organizations, they are not. Even when the simple logic of a particular campaign might push the parties toward voter mobilization, the more complex logic created by the decentralized American party organization usually does not. From the beginnings of mass parties in the Jacksonian era, American parties have been unwieldy alliances of state and local campaign organizations. Since parties exist to win elections for government office, and government in the United States is highly decentralized, political parties are better understood in the American reality as congeries of politicians whose actions are usually loosely coordinated, when they are coordinated at all.[24]

These politicians compete to win positions in a sprawling and fragmented government by winning majorities for themselves from among diverse voters in their districts and under diverse conditions. They only rarely compete nationally for party rule. Thus, after World War II, when blacks were becoming a voting bloc in the cities that threatened to disturb the ethnic working-class voter coalitions on which Democratic big-city mayors relied, the mayors fiercely resisted efforts by Democratic presidents to incorporate these voters. Instead, they struck a tacit alliance with Republicans in suppressing the black vote, with white Democrats sometimes shifting their votes en masse to support Republican contenders rather than give their votes to black Democrats. Most of the time politicians compete for their own victories in their own jurisdictions. To assume that a mobilizing logic based on national party goals drives the actions of these politicians is dubious, most of the time.

But not all of the time. There have been exceptional periods of political crisis, such as the Civil War and the Great Depression, or periods when party leadership has passed to exceptionally aggressive entrepreneurs backed by exceptional campaign resources, when a degree of party unification has been achieved. The reign of Mark Hanna during the campaign of 1896 is an example, as is the campaign led by Newt Gingrich in 1994 to gain party control of the House of Representatives, or the successful campaigns led by Karl Rove from 2000 to 2004. Gingrich was able to muscle congressional representatives into working for the election of the party's slate, and Rove was able to herd party representatives behind the presidential candidate.[25] But these moments of party unity are unusual. Disunity is also evident in the opposite direction. Presidential candidates are ordinarily reluctant to expend much political capital on the party's other candidates. So while American electoral campaigns are typically campaigns between Democrats and Republicans, it is a mistake to think of either side as a unitary actor.

When the electorate does expand, whether because new groups gain the legal franchise or because enfranchised nonvoters are motivated to flock to the polls, the momentum usually does not originate with the parties and party competition. To be sure, the occasional long-shot candidate may have nothing to lose by trying to mobilize new voters, but neither does the long shot ordinarily have the resources to mount effective voter mobilization drives. Sometimes the entry of large numbers of new voters into the electorate is the result of demographic shifts, as when the rising tide of European immigrants changed the complexion of the big cities at the end of the nineteenth century, or when the economically driven migration of blacks to the North in the mid-twentieth century brought them into states where they were allowed to vote, and the rising black freedom movement motivated them to vote.

The role of movements in the expansion of the franchise has not been given much attention, but it is important. Movements can generate political fractures that endanger existing party coalitions, prompting politicians to try to shore up their base by expanding voting rights to new groups. Movements use the drama of street action to raise issues that threaten to fragment an existing electoral coalition, as the abolitionists fragmented the pre–Civil War Whigs and Democrats,[26] setting off a chain of events that eventually led to emancipation and the formal enfranchisement of blacks. The civil rights movement of the mid-twentieth century forced conciliatory responses from a reluctant national Democratic leadership, precipitating the defection of the white South from Democratic ranks, and eventually Democratic support for voting rights legislation that would enfranchise southern blacks and help to at least partially restore the Democratic base.

Movements are also inspirational. They generate the hopes that bring formally enfranchised nonvoters to the polls even when the parties ignore them. From Reconstruction on, surges in black voter participation have been fueled by movements. In the pages that follow we will show that the civil rights movement not only forced the passage of legislation that enfranchised blacks in the South, but also that the continuing influence of the movement inspired successive black voter mobilizations in the big cities where blacks were concentrating. As a consequence, blacks gained the leadership of many of these cities and also became a major bloc in national politics.

In fact, surges in black electoral participation have been closely intertwined with the rise and fall of movements. The drama and disruptions of movement actions galvanize potential voters by thrusting contentious issues into the limelight, by raising the hopes of movement followers and the fears of their adversaries, and by generating the solidarities that make the movement's constituents a voter bloc that can be relied upon for electoral influence or a voter bloc to be feared for the same reason.

As for the parties, while the logic of electoral competition has on occasion led them to invest in the mobilization of new voters, it more often leads to strategies of voter demobilization, mainly in the form of campaigns to keep down the votes of the opposition. This helps explain the American anomaly of an expanding universe of legally enfranchised voters and a static universe of actual voters. Elections are, as Schattschneider put it, "a maneuver with numbers," and vote suppression changes the numbers.[27] It does this without any of the risks associated with mobilizing new voters, especially voters from marginalized populations. It also avoids the longer-term costs associated with sustaining the allegiance of voters from such potentially dissident groups. The legendary tactics of organized voter intimidation, of tossing out ballot boxes from targeted precincts, or of piling increasingly burdensome requirements on the process of registering and voting, all have their origin in the competitive logic of voter demobilization.

The selection of groups for vote suppression is not random. Richard McCormick thought it was the "socially discordant" voters who would be targeted.[28] Here, McCormick was referring to immigrant working-class groups in the late nineteenth century, but the term can be applied to any excluded or marginalized group. Martin Shefter similarly thinks politicians will resist competitive mobilization if party leaders have reason to fear the new groups will bring with them issues that politicians or parties do not want to address.[29] And where electoral rights and procedures are well established, it is safer to target marginalized or outcast groups for vote suppression techniques, simply because the broader electorate is unlikely to rally to protect them. No group fits the description of "discordant" more predictably than African Americans, and efforts to suppress black votes have been a recurrent feature of American political history.

The nineteenth century provides a series of dramatic tests both of the conventional view that party competition leads to voter mobilization, and of our amendment of that view to argue that the logic of party competition can also lead to voter suppression. Schattschneider's thesis gains its credibility from the mass parties that emerged earlier in the nineteenth century. These parties were often competitive, and voter turnout was high. Such evidence as we have, although much of it is anecdotal, and even folkloric, suggests that competing political parties did pull voters to the polls.[30]

But even antebellum parties competed by repelling voters, and

African Americans were a main target, as Christopher Malone shows in his study of black enfranchisement and disenfranchisement in the antebellum northern states of New York, Pennsylvania, Rhode Island, and Massachusetts.[31] During the decades after the Revolution, most northern states legislated a process of gradual emancipation of African Americans, who were only a small percentage of the population. Agriculture was declining, while manufacturing was gaining in importance, and as this change unfolded, immigration from Europe increased, vastly overwhelming the relatively small numbers of African Americans. Nevertheless, in the states where African Americans were enfranchised, they were occasionally decisive in elections. In New York City municipal elections, for example, enfranchised blacks were allied with the Federalist Party, and this alliance provided the grounds for fierce Jeffersonian Republican racist agitation among white immigrants. Malone reports that by 1809 this racial divide "had escalated into physical intimidation at voting places in New York City. . . . Republican inspectors at polling places began to question the free status of any black man wishing to cast his vote."[32] In ensuing years, Republicans followed up by introducing procedural restrictions—freedmen were required to bear a certificate testifying to their status, for example—on the black vote, and black turnout dropped. Finally, at the state constitutional convention of 1821, a $250 property qualification was introduced that applied only to black voters. A Federalist judge delivered a eulogy on the matter: "[T]hirty seven thousand of our free black citizens, and their posterity, for ever, shall be degraded by our constitution below the common rank of freeman."[33]

Party competition took the broadly similar form of racial targeting and suppression in Pennsylvania, no matter that it had been one of the more racially lenient and democratic colonies in the revolutionary era. Slavery was abolished in the state in 1780. Subsequently, the state became a kind of gateway to the North for freedmen, and the population of free blacks increased, even as the population of white immigrants was also increasing. Race conflict rose, inflamed not only by the growing presence of poor blacks but also by white working-class hostility to the well-to-do Quakers who were ardent abolitionists. By 1838, in the wake of riots by whites that destroyed black homes, and after an election in which a handful of black votes helped decide a closely contested race between the Democrats and the Whigs with whom blacks were allied, a state constitutional convention dominated by Democrats simply disenfranchised blacks.[34]

A second series of episodes of racial targeting and disenfranchisement occurred in the South in the wake of the post–Civil War period known as Reconstruction, and it had enormous consequences for the pattern of American political development. Immediately after the Civil War, Congress had acted forcefully with the Reconstruction Act of 1867 to enfranchise the freedmen, followed in 1870 by the passage of the Fifteenth Amendment, which prohibited federal or state governments from depriving any citizen of the vote on racial grounds. These measures were buttressed by the occupation of the South by federal troops to suppress white violence. But extraordinarily high levels of black voting during this period were not only the result of the protection afforded by federal law and federal troops, and of the pride gained from black participation in the Union army, but were also driven by a vast black voter mobilization movement. Under these conditions, writes Eric Foner, "the church, and indeed every other black political institution, became politicized."[35] Foner quotes a plantation manager: "You never saw a people more excited on the subject of politics than are the negroes of the south. They are perfectly wild."[36] Black men not only voted in extraordinarily high numbers but also succeeded in electing black representatives to national and state governments.

This dramatic development could not reasonably be ascribed to the dynamic of two-party competition. Indeed, it occurred at a time when the Democrats, weakened by their association with the Confederacy and by the disenfranchisement of many whites in the rebel states, were not competitive in the South.[37] More likely it was the result of the complex and convoluted events that began with the rise of the abolitionist movement and the widening sectional divisions they caused, leading to southern secession and culminating in a bloody civil war. Before the war, there was not much support in the North for emancipation, much less for the enfranchisement of African Americans. But the war itself had consequences. For one thing, Lincoln issued the Emancipation Proclamation in the hope of shoring up a straitened Union army by recruiting masses of black runaways. It worked: the slaves came, devastating the southern economy by their defections, and strengthening the Union army. And then, in the aftermath of the bloody war, black suffrage gained support in the victorious North from the fierce hatred of the South that a bloody war had caused.[38] But the widening sectional divisions that led to war had begun with the abolitionist movement, whose intransigent fight for legal emancipation broke apart the intersectional parties of the antebellum period. And it was abolitionists, now absorbed into the radical wing of the Republican Party, who took advantage of public anger in the North to push for the suffrage for the freedmen.

Thus, in 1867, two years after the surrender of the Confederacy, Congress required the southern states to hold constitutional conventions. Many whites who had supported the Confederacy were barred by the Fourteenth Amendment from the elections at which convention delegates were chosen, while the freedmen were allowed to register.[39] In other words, it was not party competition, but the interplay of movement and electoral politics, which led to the expansion of the black electorate. And movement politics mattered again immediately after the war as African Americans responded to the heady promises of emancipation (and land reform) with a "soldier-citizen" mobilization of activists known as the Union Leagues. By midsummer of 1867, says Richard M. Valelly, the national headquarters of the Union Leagues had organized two hundred thousand to three hundred thousand members, determined to realize the promises of Reconstruction and "the new birth of freedom."[40]

The freedmen enjoyed the franchise for a relatively brief, albeit remarkable, period. Leon Litwack captures the transformation:

[B]lack activists canvassed their respective counties and states, discussed with prospective voters the issues that should determine their selection of candidates, warned them that a failure to exercise their newly acquired rights might result in the forfeiture of those rights, and explained to them the mechanics of registration. . . . The *New Orleans Tribune* . . . chose to frame the issues so that few freedmen could afford to ignore them. "The vote is the means to reach the composition of juries, the dispensation of education, the organization of the militia and the police force, in such manner that the interests of all races be represented and protected."[41]

As newly enfranchised African Americans flocked to the polls, constituting a majority or near majority in many districts,[42] black candidates gained office, some at the federal and state levels,[43] but mainly at the local level, and mainly in the Deep South, where the black population was concentrated. And the impact on policy of the newly enfranchised and their representatives was large. State constitutions were rewritten and democratized, investment in education and educational integration increased, and the laws were modified to protect agricultural laborers. In some places, juries became biracial, and black sheriffs with integrated police forces took office.[44] Had these arrangements persisted, the development of the new South, which employed the entire apparatus of state and local governments to return blacks to a position of servitude, could not have unfolded. But of course they did not persist, because enfranchisement interfered with a broader effort by the southern planter class to erect a system of political, economic, and social coercion over blacks that would permit the reestablishment of a quasi-feudal labor system. This goal could not be reached as long as blacks exercised any influence in state or local government.[45]

During Reconstruction, national and state Republicans resisted efforts to strip blacks of the vote. But as memories of the Civil War faded, the influence of radical abolitionists on the Republican Party waned. In 1874, Alabama Democrats gained control of the state government after a campaign of violence in which whites shot blacks on their way to the polls in Mobile and in Barbour County, killing several, wounding many, and intimidating many more. The first legislature controlled by Democrats then acted to designate those forms of election fraud believed to be committed more by blacks than by whites as felony crimes (and forms of fraud more likely to be committed by whites could be overlooked by those who controlled the electoral apparatus), while also removing predominantly black neighborhoods from within the boundaries of Montgomery and Selma to ensure safe white majorities. Peyton McCrary and his colleagues report that in Mobile, Democrats pushed through at-large elections for the county school board, which had the effect of eliminating black representatives:

> Thereafter county commissioners and election officials . . . [o]ften refused to open the polling places at all, or kept them open for only a few hours, in overwhelmingly black precincts. They used wholesale election fraud to win congressional, legislative and gubernatorial races, regularly casting black votes intended for Republican or Populist candidates on behalf of their own conservative Democratic ticket, and justifying these tactics as a necessary evil to prevent a return to the "horrors" of Reconstruction.[46]

In 1876, the deal was struck which gave Republican Rutherford Hayes the presidency in a contested election, on condition that federal troops be withdrawn from the South. The effort by Southern Democrats to disenfranchise blacks escalated, and Republican efforts to compete weakened. In the election of 1882, for example, only eight independents (sympathetic to the Republicans) were elected to the House of Representatives from the South and eight Republicans, yielding the Republicans a slim overall House majority. Paul Frymer reports that African Americans constituted majorities in thirty-four districts, and constituted 45 percent of the population in another ten districts. In his judgment, the national Republicans simply gave up roughly thirty House seats and six Senate seats in the South in the 1880s because of reluctance to forcefully protect black voting rights in the face of white southern violence and northern racism. The logic of electoral competition that fueled the Democratic disenfranchisers was not matched by Republican efforts to compete by protecting their "discordant" black voters.[47]

By the end of the nineteenth century, African Americans had been virtually purged from the electorate of the southern states, at first by strategies of violent intimidation and trickery deployed by the recovering southern political establishment,[48] later by the introduction or reintroduction of a series of superficially color-blind requirements that circumvented the Fourteenth and Fifteenth amendments to the Constitution. These included poll taxes, literacy tests or an ability to "understand" the constitution or laws according to the judgment of election officials,[49] and a voter registration process that was in practice administered so as to ensure the disenfranchisement of blacks.[50] Voter registration arrangements were particularly important because of the discretion they ceded to the registrars. Sheldon Hackney quotes a letter written by Alabama governor William D. Jelks in 1902: "The Board of Appointment spent thirty days selecting these Registrars and in every instance we were assured positively that the appointees would carry out the spirit of the Constitution, which looks to the registration of all men not convicted of a crime, and only a few negroes."[51] Of course, the obstacles thus placed in the way of access to the ballot also disenfranchised most poor whites, whose ire seems to have been assuaged by some less-than-workable loopholes, as well as by their understanding that it was African Americans who were the target of the campaign.

Thus, an 1873 Georgia law allowed local registrars to close their books to new registrants except during planting and harvesting time, when black farmworkers were toiling in the fields and unable to travel to the country courthouse to register. Disenfranchisers in Alabama and North Carolina admired the results of Georgia's law and followed suit. Laws requiring voters to show their registration certificates before they were permitted to cast a ballot usually diminished black voting because registration closed long before an election, and it would not be uncommon for illiterate and impoverished migrant farmers to lose track of paperwork. Moreover, this rule made blacks doubly vulnerable to harassment and attack as they made their way to the polling place. There are numerous accounts of blacks traveling to the country seat and being set upon by white mobs and robbed of their registration papers. For example, in November 1876, the Republican governor of Louisiana wrote to Republican National Committee officials in New York:

> Dispatches from Ouachita and Morehouse Parishes, near the Arkansas line, and West Feliciana near the Mississippi line, report that these parishes are now patrolled by the White League, reinforced by armed bodies from Arkansas and Mississippi. Most of the Republican leaders have been driven away or murdered. Under the State law voters are entitled to vote at any poll in the parish in which they reside. The colored people generally are attempting to reach the parish seats of those parishes in order to vote under protection of the authorities. Numbers of them have been intercepted by the White League pickets, and their registration papers destroyed.[52]

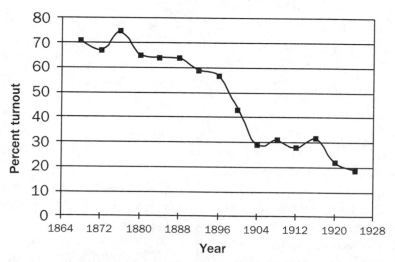

Figure 1
Turnout Decline in the South, 1868–1924

SOURCE: Walter Dean Burnham, "The Turnout Problem," in A. James Reichley, ed., *Elections American Style* (Washington, DC: Brookings Institution, 1987), 113.

The overall result in the South was massive disenfranchisement. Turnout in presidential elections in the South fell, from 57 percent in the election of 1896, to 43 percent in 1900, to 28 percent in 1912, to a nadir of 19 percent in 1924 (see figure 1).[53]

Blacks and most poor whites had lost their right to vote, and as they did the politics of the southern states became more racist and more conservative. And southern representatives in Congress brought that politics to the national government as well. This was the southern Democratic bloc that weakened, perhaps fatally, the welfare and labor initiatives of the New Deal. The story is of course well known. What we want to highlight here is that the resurgent southern Democratic Party and its elite planter and business allies did not gain ascendance in the South and in the nation's capital by recruiting new voters. Rather, their unchallenged domination in the South for almost a century was the result of suppressing the votes of formally enfranchised blacks.

The South pioneered the construction of the model of a new kind of polity that left formal voting rights intact but ensured that in practice poorer and less-educated people would not be able to exercise those rights. The northern states soon followed suit with a less well-known campaign of voter suppression, singling out not African Americans, whose numbers were few, but the masses of immigrant working people who were crowding into the industrializing cities.[54] The campaign occurred during roughly the same period that the southern disenfranchisement campaign was unfolding and took the form of identity checks requiring foreign-born citizens to show their naturalization papers at the time of registration and/or voting; longer waiting periods between naturalization and the granting of the right to vote; and, increasingly, literacy tests—all made effective by a system of voter registration that placed the burden of figuring out how and when to register on the voter, and required him to then reregister before each election.[55] And while the Chinese, Italian, and Eastern European immigrants who were the targets of the campaign were not African Americans, the rhetoric deployed against them, and the antipathies they provoked, made clear nevertheless that they were perceived to be of a different and a lesser race than true Americans. What was needed, it was said, was "a more intelligent ballot," [56] with intelligence measured by the ability to read and write English.

During the post–Civil War decades, and until the election of 1896, party competition in the North was relatively vigorous. Closely contested elections helped inspire Republicans and business-backed reform groups, who were strong in the state capitals, to target for disenfranchisement the immigrant constituencies of the machine political organizations that held sway in the big cities. With much public railing against corrupt boss-led political organizations and the disreputable foreign poor, efforts at disenfranchisement could take on the garb of a reform movement. The reformers invoked all of the problems associated with the contaminated big cities, their growing foreign populations, and the corrupt political machines that held sway over the cities. More often than not, the reformers were particularly obsessed with solutions that restricted access to the vote. In 1904, the muckraking journalist Lincoln Steffens investigated municipal corruption in six cities and found it everywhere tied to fraud at the polls. In Philadelphia, where the voting lists were compiled by the tax assessor, Steffens found, "The assessor pads the list with the names of dead dogs, children, and non-existent persons. One newspaper printed the picture of a dog, another that of a little four-year-old negro boy [whose names were] down on such a list." [57] Two years later, Philadelphia had a new personal registration law. It is probably to this era and the folklore about fraud and corruption—stories of stuffed ballot boxes, easy voter payoffs, ballots cast by long-dead voters, and the use of neighborhood bullies as "ballot police"—that the credibility of contemporary charges of voter fraud is owed. Of course there was plenty of election fraud, and almost surely votes were bought, sold, and fixed. But the buying, selling, and fixing of votes was not organized by the voters who faced the new restrictions, but by party operatives.

In any case, voter fraud was not the main problem motivating the campaign. By the 1880s there was evidence that party strategies of pervasive clientelism and ethno-cultural appeals were losing some of their grip on popular allegiance as a result of the economic instabilities generated by rapid but tumultuous post–Civil War economic growth. Unprecedented mass strikes and riots erupted in the cities with each economic downturn, in the 1870s, the 1880s, and the 1890s, along with recurrent third-party challenges. The grip of the big-city party organizations that cultivated the allegiance of the immigrant working classes with tribal and clientelist appeals appeared to be loosening. The resulting political instability was not the only problem that could be traced to malfunctioning machine politics. The reformers were preoccupied with the high costs in money and efficiency of a graft-based system of running the cities. Hence the two prongs of the reform effort. One prong was directed to weakening the largely Democratic machines. The other was a long-term effort to limit electoral participation among the machine's electoral base in the increasingly insurgent immigrant working class.

The methods used were borrowed in part from the southern campaign: the introduction of literacy tests, along with the reintroduction in some places of poll taxes, extended residency requirements (designed of course to target immigrants), and cumbersome and difficult personal periodic registration requirements, all of which were at first directed at the population of the biggest cities, where immigrants were concentrated, and then gradually expanded to smaller towns and to entire states.[58] Registration requirements were stricter in New York City, where immigrants were concentrated, for example, than in the rest of the state. Other states followed the same pattern, with special registration procedures for the cities and their immigrant populations.[59] Indeed, southerners encouraged the northern campaign. In Arkansas, for example, the *Pine Bluff Commercial* seemed to be speaking of the immigrants as blacks: "When a native born citizen of the United States thinks of the fearful fact that the offscouring of Europe, a people without homes, friends, or language; and in seventy-five percent of the cases lacking only a tail to complete the brute structure [could vote] . . . it makes one . . . proud of the boon of American citizenship."[60]

Simultaneously, the big-city political machines that might have subverted these requirements were gradually stripped of resources by means of a battery of anticorruption reforms, including nonpartisan government, civil service requirements, the spinning off of functions of city government to independent agencies, the introduction of the printed ballot, and the spread of elaborate personal periodic voter registration requirements, along with the reintroduction in some places of poll taxes and literacy tests.[61] Both the weakening of the machine and the new conditions on the right to vote were, of course, justified as preventing voter fraud, especially fraud among the immigrant masses, depicted as racially different and prone to fraud. These justifications were trumpeted not only by the reformers themselves but also by the political scientists who wrote about these developments later. Even the dramatic fall in turnout that resulted was ascribed in significant part to the elimination of fraudulent ballots, downplaying the fact that the new rules eliminated many legitimate ballots, too.[62]

Of course, administrative stratagems for disenfranchisement

Figure 2
National Turnout Decline, 1840–1924

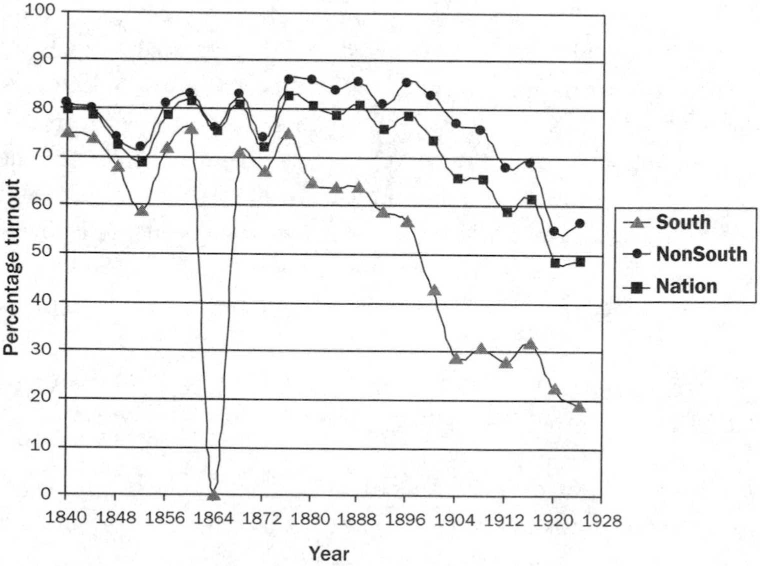

SOURCE: Burnham, "The Turnout Problem," 113.

worked, and voter turnout fell, from 86 percent in the non-South in 1896 to 57 percent in 1924 (see figure 2).[63] It fell especially among the less well-off, who were inevitably less able to circumvent the new procedural obstacles to the ballot. The universe of active American voters developed its distinctive contours. It was a smaller portion of the voting-age population than the voter universe in other affluent democracies, and it was sharply constricted among poorer and darker voters. Even the crisis of the Great Depression and the rise of the New Deal Democratic Party did not much change the apparatus of electoral administration, or the pattern of low and unrepresentative voter turnout that it produced.

The significance of these developments can hardly be overstated. They occurred on the eve of industrialization, and at the very time that many European working people were fighting for the right to vote. As they won that right, working-class political parties grew and eventually became the sponsors or defenders of the public policies that still to this day make European countries kinder and gentler places, where inequality is limited, far fewer families are poor, health care and child care are generally available to all, and most workers earn more for working less. Electoral politics does matter. But the benign effects of electoral politics depend on an inclusive electorate, which is what the American parties have prevented. We turn to the contemporary story.

2

RACE AND PARTY COMPETITION IN POST-WORLD WAR II AMERICA

Rassal Jacob, rassal
as you did in the days of old,
Gonna rassal all night
till broad day light
And ask God to bless my soul.

—traditional African American spiritual [1]

When the twentieth century began, most African Americans lived in the South, where they had been stripped of the right to vote. Those few who did vote remained Republican, in memory of the hopes generated by the Great Emancipator. But they were irrelevant in the elections of the southern one-party system. By midcentury, however, the struggle for the franchise had revived, and by the close of the 1960s, African Americans had finally won the century-long dream of the legal right to vote that had been denied them after Reconstruction. In the course of the struggles that led to this momentous achievement, the electoral coalitions of both major parties were transformed, and blacks came to figure hugely in American electoral politics.

Key to all of these developments was the Great Migration of blacks from the rural South to the cities of the South and North, a migration set in motion by the mechanization of southern agriculture and the hardship and displacement of tenant farmers and laborers that ensued (see figure 3). Migration was important in part because it gave some blacks the vote by virtue of their removal from the feudal plantations or subsistence farms of the South to urban centers. By the mid-1950s, over 2.5 million blacks had moved north,

Figure 3
Net Outmigration of Blacks from the South

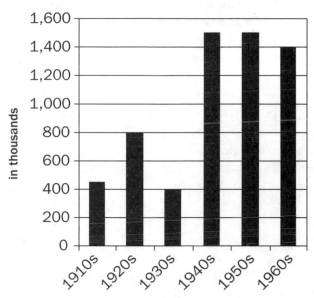

SOURCE: Bureau of the Census, *The Social and Economic Status of Negroes in the United States, 1970*, Current Population Reports, Series P-23, No. 38 (Washington, DC: 1971); Bureau of the Census, *The Social and Economic Status of the Black Population in the United States: An Historical View, 1790–1978* (Washington, DC: GPO, 1979).

principally to seven states that controlled 197 electoral votes. They constituted 5 percent of the vote in seventy-two congressional districts outside the South, and in forty-three of these districts, the incumbent member of Congress had won with less than 55 percent of the vote.[2] The electoral leverage thus gained helped to generate the expectations that fueled the rise of the civil rights movement. As Fred Morrow, an African American who served as White House counselor for special projects in the Eisenhower administration, advised Attorney General Herbert Brownell in 1955, northern blacks with family in the South expected a White House statement that "the Administration is aware and condemns with vigor any kind of racist activity in the United States."[3] The rise of a protest movement was also made possible by the very fact of migration, which, while it entailed terrible hardships, nevertheless meant that blacks were being gradually liberated from the system of plantation servitude, legal apartheid, and lynch mob terror that characterized the rural South. Migration also yielded blacks some of the political resources associated with wage labor and urban concentration. All of these developments contributed to the momentum of the civil rights movement. As the twentieth century drew to a close, it was clear that the movement in turn had transformed American politics.

The electoral context that framed these changes was formed during the New Deal. When the Great Depression struck, low levels of voter turnout had become the norm across the country. After the election of 1896, Democratic control of the outcome of southern elections from which blacks and many poor whites had been barred was unchallenged. Republicans reigned across most of the North, and their domination also yielded them control of national government, most of the time.[4] But economic catastrophe shook the Republican grip on the farmers and working-class voters of the North, a development that was already prefigured in the election of 1928, when the Democratic nomination of Al Smith, Catholic and "wet," caused a jump in turnout and in Democratic voting, especially in the big cities. In 1932, with entire industries idle and the banks on the verge of collapse, Franklin Delano Roosevelt swept into office with a Democratic Congress. And once in office, the Democrats launched the array of New Deal relief and public works initiatives that came to shape the allegiances of the urban working-class voters who undergirded the fabled New Deal coalition.

That coalition was peculiar, in two ways. First, it was a coalition between the relatively liberal North and its working-class constituents on the one hand, and the near-feudal one-party white South on the other hand. During the Depression, northern Democrats generally championed working-class demands for unionization and social protections. Southern Democrats were glad to receive federal agricultural subsidies, but they were wary of regulatory or relief programs that might undermine the caste-bound political and

economic system that had been created by resurgent southern Bour-
bons during the period known as Redemption.

The other way in which the coalition was peculiar is that it was
anchored in an apparatus of legal and procedural constrictions on
the vote that had been developed in the late nineteenth century in
both the South and the North, and neither the shock of the Great Depression nor New Deal programs undid these constrictions. As a result, however much voters were provoked by economic collapse and
the hardship it caused, electoral participation expanded only very
modestly. Turnout in the South rose to a mere 24 percent in 1932 and
then to 25 percent in 1936 from its low point of 19 percent in 1924.
Blacks and most poor whites continued to be excluded. Turnout rose
somewhat more in the North, from 57 percent in 1924 to 66 percent
in 1932, and then to 71 percent in 1936.[5] Still, considering the shock
of economic collapse, it was clear that the administrative obstacles to
voter participation of the late nineteenth century were still in place.

The Great Migration meant that growing numbers of African
Americans would move from the near-feudal South to the big cities,
and into the heart of the Democratic base in the North. While there
were procedural obstacles to the ballot in the North, these were by no
means as forbidding as in most of the South. In the cities, especially
the cities of the North, many blacks voted, and by 1936, their votes
were firmly in Democratic columns. But their numbers were still
small, and they were "discordant" voters besides. They did not get
much for their allegiance: some emergency relief during the early
years of the Depression, and the sympathy and support of Eleanor
Roosevelt. Then, in 1941, FDR, pressed by A. Philip Randolph's
threat of a march on Washington, established the Fair Employment
Practices Commission. And in 1944, the Supreme Court, influenced
by the New Deal, declared the white primary unconstitutional.[6] The
estimated number of blacks registered in the South grew from
151,000 to 595,000 as a result of this decision.[7]

These gestures notwithstanding, the southern wing of the party
prevailed in national policy. The agricultural and domestic occupa-
tions in which blacks were concentrated were exempted from New
Deal labor law and social security legislation, and the categorical

programs to provide cash assistance to some of the impoverished who were blind or disabled or orphaned were left to the states to administer.[8] Voting-rights legislation, indeed even antilynching legislation, was off the table. But as the movement of African Americans into the electoral strongholds of the northern wing of the party swelled, there were signs that national Democratic political leaders were not oblivious. The train of events began that first weakened the North-South Democratic coalition and then destroyed it.

The first strong evidence that the North-South Democratic partnership was in trouble occurred in the election of 1948, when Harry Truman, the incumbent Democratic president, was locked in a tight race with the Republican nominee, Thomas E. Dewey. We earlier argued that the logic of party competition sometimes leads political operatives to mobilize voters. In this instance, that logic was sharpened by the entry into the presidential race of a third party, the Progressive Party led by Henry Wallace, who was directing his appeals to labor and to blacks. Truman accepted the advice of Clark Clifford, his chief campaign strategist, to counter this challenge by taking action to "protect the rights of minority groups."[9] The South, Clifford thought, would always remain Democratic, and could be "safely ignored."[10]

Following the advice of his strategists, Truman called for a broad range of civil rights measures in an address to Congress on January 7, 1948, and shortly afterward forwarded a ten-point program to Congress proposing the outlawing of the poll tax, a permanent Fair Employment Practices Commission, and laws to make lynching a federal crime. At the Democratic nominating convention that year, liberals pushed through a strong civil rights plank, with the backing of northern machine leaders who cared less about a Truman victory than about solidifying the black vote behind their local, state, and congressional candidates. Southern leaders reacted immediately. The Mississippi delegation and part of the Alabama delegation walked out and convened with other southern politicians only two days later to form the States' Rights Party ticket, with Strom Thurmond of South Carolina as its presidential nominee. In the ensuing election, four southern states defected to the States' Rights revolt.[11]

Truman won nevertheless, and with the support of the northern black vote. The demise of the North-South New Deal coalition was foretold in these events.

But there was a great deal at stake in the preservation of the coalition, both for Democratic presidential contenders who relied on southern Electoral College votes for national victory and for the southern politicians whose longevity in Congress privileged them in committee appointments. Southern political leaders tried to cope with their dilemma by encouraging split-ticket voting for Republican presidential contenders and for Democratic congressional and state candidates. So the unraveling of the North-South coalition did not occur all at once. Meanwhile, Adlai Stevenson, the Democratic presidential nominee in 1952 and again in 1956, worried openly that the conflict over civil rights might drive the South out of the party, and conciliation of the South became the order of the day.[12] For example, in a speech before the 1952 convention, Stevenson declared, "I reject as contemptible the reckless assertions that the South is a prison in which half the people are prisoners and the other half are wardens."[13]

The Democratic presidential ticket lost four outer-South states in 1952 and again in 1956, when it also lost Louisiana. But by 1956, wobbling on civil rights was also costing the Democratic ticket urban black votes.[14] Stevenson won 73 percent of the black vote in 1952 but only 60 percent in 1956.[15] The effort to hold the peculiar North-South Democratic coalition together was in trouble. It was ultimately shattered by the rise of civil rights protests, first in the South and then in the cities of the North. Something like this had happened a century before, when the uncompromising demands and tactics of the abolitionists for the immediate emancipation of the slaves had driven deep fissures into the intersectional coalition of the Whigs, leading first to the rise of the Republican Party and the election of Abraham Lincoln, and then to southern secession, civil war, and Emancipation.

The story of the civil rights movement has been told many times, and does not need repeating here. We want only to highlight the close interplay of the movement with rising black voting levels. In fact, voter mobilization was already occurring among African Americans as a result of migration to the cities and the recognition by national politicians, albeit often muffled, of its potential importance. These were signs that the black vote might matter, and the hopes those signs generated help account for the rise of the movement. People ordinarily do not join together in defiant action if they think their cause is hopeless. The rise of the movement in turn had a large impact on the voter mobilization that was already occurring.

The movement's influence was direct, in the sense that it reawakened the long-standing faith of African Americans in the transformational power of the vote. That mesmerizing idea had gripped the freedmen in the Reconstruction period, when blacks formed thousands of voter leagues and risked bullets to exercise the franchise. Now, with the idea reawakened by the civil rights protests spreading across the South, and strengthened by the endorsement it had received first from the Truman civil rights planks and then again in 1960 by John F. Kennedy's adoption of the same planks, black voter participation in the South began to climb. And of course, the idea helped fuel the hard and dangerous work of organizing registration drives and freedom schools, preparing people to pass literacy tests and withstand the other challenges they would face if they tried to register to vote. Black voter registration increased from 4.5 percent in 1940, to 12.5 percent in 1947 after the white primary had been abolished, to 20.7 percent in 1952, to 29.1 percent in 1960, to 35.5 percent in 1965.[16] In at least four southern states, black voter registration increased more than 15 percentage points between 1960 and 1964 (see table 2). This meant that many voters were taking courage from the civil rights rhetoric of national politicians and from emerging civil rights activism to brave the social and administrative hurdles of the southern system.

The movement's influence was also indirect, because it changed the laws and procedures that governed access to the ballot for blacks. By the mid-1960s, in the wake of Kennedy's assassination, and with southern civil rights protests escalating and northern cities burning, the scales had tipped in the calculations of Democratic Party leaders. The allegiance of the "solid" white South was in any case continuing

Table 2

Percentage of Blacks Registered to Vote in Eleven Southern States

State	1956	1960	1964	1960–1964 Increase	1968	1964–1968 Increase
Alabama	11.0	13.7	23.0	+9.3	56.7	+33.7
Arkansas	36.0	37.7	54.4	+16.7	67.5	+13.1
Florida	32.0	39.0	63.7	+24.7	62.1	−1.6
Georgia	27.0	N/A	38.8	N/A	56.1	+17.3
Louisiana	31.0	30.9	32.0	+1.1	59.3	+27.3
Mississippi	5.0	6.1	6.7	+0.6	59.4	+52.7
North Carolina	24.0	38.2	46.8	+8.6	55.3	+8.5
South Carolina	27.0	N/A	38.8	N/A	50.8	+12.0
Tennessee	29.0	64.1	69.4	+5.3	72.8	+3.4
Texas	37.0	33.7	57.7	+24.0	83.1	+25.4
Virginia	19.0	23.0	45.7	+22.7	58.4	+12.7
SOUTH	24.9	29.1	43.1		62.0	

N/A = not available
SOURCE: Chandler Davidson and Bernard Grofman, eds., *Quiet Revolution in the South* (Princeton: Princeton University Press, 1994), 374; and United States Commission on Civil Rights, *Voting: 1961 Commission of Civil Rights Report* (Washington, DC: GPO, 1961), 252–307. Data for Tennessee and Texas for 1960 are incomplete; for Tennessee, percentage reflects data for 63 counties; for Texas, 213 counties. Calculations for columns four and six performed by authors.

to slip away. Just before the presidential election of 1964, as demonstrations and riots spread to the northern cities, a Democratic president led a Democratic congressional majority to pass the Civil Rights Act of 1964.

Lyndon Baines Johnson won the ensuing election, capturing 90 percent of the black vote and losing the Deep South by wide margins. In the cities of the northern states, black voters had returned to Democratic columns. And in the South, had it not been for black support, the Democrats would have lost four additional states (Arkansas, Florida, Tennessee, and Virginia).[17] Shortly afterward, Johnson threw

his weight behind the Voting Rights Act of 1965, after famously con-
fiding to his aide, Bill Moyers, that he was signing away the Democratic South. The act struck down literacy tests, reaffirmed the
abolition of the poll tax by the Twenty-fourth Amendment to the
Constitution passed a year earlier, and sent federal examiners to
monitor voter registration in southern counties.[18] With its passage,
black voter registration in the South soared, to over 60 percent.[19]

The stage was set for the emergence of blacks as an important
Democratic voter bloc and a focal point of national electoral campaign strategies during the past four decades. Party competition
took the form of Republican electoral campaigns that attacked the
Democrats by associating them with blacks, or more accurately, with
the political code words that came to be understood as referring to
blacks or to black demands. Harangues about crime, the invocation
of law and order, and incessant talk about welfare became standard
fare in Republican speeches, as did talk about the dangers of an over-
reaching federal government that suffocated "states' rights." By the
late 1960s, Republican politicians also began to rail against the Great
Society, the bevy of programs initiated by the Democrats that was
widely understood as a response to black protests in the cities. This
sort of campaigning was of necessity loud and public, and memori-
alized in tactics like the Willie Horton campaign ad that tarred Democratic presidential nominee Michael Dukakis, then governor of
Massachusetts, by associating him with a black felon who had committed a murder while on a prison furlough on Dukakis's watch.[20] All
this is widely known. Less familiar and less public were the multiple
Republican tactics intended to keep the black—and Democratic—
vote down.[21]

Beginning as early as 1954, Republican organizations around the
country experimented with "ballot-security" programs—a variety
of strategies putatively designed to combat fraud, but clearly providing the more important advantage of limiting voter participation in
heavily Democratic black communities. The Republican National
Committee inaugurated a nationwide ballot security program, "Operation Eagle Eye," in 1962, which recommended mail verification,
poll monitoring, and publicity as strategies to secure the vote.[22] By

the time Barry Goldwater ran for president in 1964, Operation Eagle Eye was in full swing. Across the country, Republican operatives sent out mailings to registered voters in minority communities, to identify a list of people whose voter registration they could challenge. Any mail returned as "undeliverable" was used to compile challenge lists on the assumption that the registration records were inaccurate or even fraudulent. (This practice is called "caging" and is discussed further in chapter 6.) In Chicago in 1964, for example, after a canvass, Republicans challenged 4,000 names in six heavily Democratic wards (this after the board of elections had done its own canvass and removed 139,000 names from the rolls). More than a quarter of the 4,000 names turned out to be those of legitimate voters.[23] Republican volunteers monitored the polls on election day, brandishing cameras and challenging voters, leading to numerous complaints and, in Miami, a circuit court injunction banning "illegal mass challenging without cause, conducted in such manner as to obstruct the orderly conduct of this election."[24]

Although not mentioned in the national Operation Eagle Eye training materials, other voter suppression tactics also cropped up where the campaign was active. Latinos in the Rio Grande valley of Texas received letters saying, "It probably would be wiser to simply stay at home and not go near the voting place on election day, rather than get arrested for interfering with the election judge." Threats of imprisonment and false information about the election were widely distributed, intimidating, confusing, and misleading voters. Democratic presidential candidate Hubert Humphrey dubbed the campaign "operation evil eye." John M. Bailey, chairman of the Democratic National Committee, sent out an angry press release charging that "under the guise of setting up an apparatus to protect the sanctity of the ballot, the Republicans are actually creating the machinery for a carefully organized campaign to intimidate voters and to frighten members of minority groups from casting their ballots on November 3rd."[25] Courts have found that the Republican ballot-security programs were aimed at suppressing minority voters, but the tactics have continued to this day, as we show in chapter 6.

While the national Democratic Party loudly criticized the Republican Party's voter suppression masked as ballot security, Democrats in local communities often used similar tactics where minority Democratic voters challenged white Democrats in power. When Operation PUSH registered black voters in Chicago in the 1970s, Mayor Richard M. Daley purged more voters than PUSH registered. Frank Watkins, who worked for Operation PUSH in the 1970s, said new voters who were not bankable Daley supporters were issued a "show cause" notice. "If you didn't go downtown and show proof of residence and ID within 10 days you were removed from the rolls."[26]

At the beginning of this era of racially based contestation, the presidential candidates of both parties had viewed the emerging choice between white southern support and the enlarging and politicized black vote with uncertainty. As a general and military hero, Eisenhower had campaigned in the South and done relatively well, drawing support from both staunch Dixiecrats and a growing white middle class, despite his relatively liberal attitudes on race.[27] The Republican strategy in the fifties, "Operation Dixie" it was called, seemed limited to efforts to avoid a position on the heated question of race in order to make the party competitive there. In 1957, Eisenhower had, after all (albeit with considerable reluctance), federalized the Arkansas National Guard and sent in paratroopers to face down white mobs protesting a court-ordered school-desegregation plan.[28]

In 1960, Richard Nixon's campaign strategists wavered as they weighed the potential gains from appeals to black voters against the gains that could be had by appealing to white southerners. In the election, both Kennedy and Nixon chose to make appeals to blacks, and both parties included civil rights planks in their program. But this did not stop the Kennedy campaign from simultaneously circulating materials in the white South highlighting Nixon's racial liberalism, including his membership in the NAACP.[29] And once elected, Kennedy became very cautious about civil rights issues. He appointed blacks to top positions in his administration but did not propose civil rights legislation, and named three southerners— "known racists" in the opinion of the civil rights leader James Farmer[30]—to the federal bench.

Meanwhile, the example of the civil rights movement was help-ing to inspire other movements, including the black protests for economic and civil rights in the cities, the anti–Vietnam War move-ment, and the environmentalist movement, as well as emancipatory movements among women, gays, and lesbians. The black freedom movements and their sister movements also provoked reactive "backlash" movements among groups who felt threatened by de-mands that threatened to topple traditional caste and family arrangements.

The black movement, in short, helped to give birth to the pop-ulist right. But it did not do that by itself. The animosities provoked by the movement were fanned to white heat by the politicians who saw opportunities in the electoral instabilities the movement had created. By the mid-1960s, Republican politicians were scrambling to develop an electoral strategy that would take advantage of the es-trangement of the white South from the Democratic Party. This be-came known as the Southern Strategy. Moreover, the hostilities that black demands—for desegregated schools or civilian control of the police, or for a fair share of municipal patronage, for example—were now generating among the white working class of the cities made it almost inevitable that the Southern Strategy would become a na-tional Republican strategy.

Barry Goldwater in 1964, and then in 1968 the third-party chal-lenger George Wallace, former governor of Alabama and an erst-while Democrat, led the way to a more racially aggressive Southern Strategy. Goldwater's 1964 campaign speeches asserted that civil rights laws were unconstitutional infringements on states' rights. He lost the election by a wide margin. However, the Republican ticket carried a swath of states across the Deep South, despite the fact that southerner Lyndon Baines Johnson led the Democratic ticket.

Then, in the election of 1968, and in the wake of rising turmoil in the big cities, the insurgent candidacy of George Wallace showed that the same race-based appeals that had worked to win over white Democratic voters in the South could be used to peel white working-class voters from Democratic columns in the northern base of the party. Wallace, says Dan Carter, knew that a substantial percentage of the American electorate despised the civil rights agitators and the anti-war demonstrators as symptoms of a fundamental decline in the traditional cultural compass of God, family, and country; a decline reflected in the rising crime rates, legalization of abortion, the rise in out-of-wedlock pregnancies, the increase in divorce rates, the Supreme Court's decision against school prayer, and the proliferation of "obscene" literature and films. And moving always beneath the surface was the fear that blacks were moving beyond their safely encapsulated ghettos into "our" streets, "our" schools, "our" neighborhoods.[31]

As the election of 1968 approached, Wallace formed the American Independent Party and managed to get on the ballot in all fifty states. His flamboyant racist appeals were as much a threat to the Republicans as to the Democrats, and polls showed his support growing, especially in the South, but increasingly in the North as well. To ward off the threat that the racial backlash vote would be divided, throwing the election to Democrat Hubert Humphrey, the Republican campaign team increasingly adopted more inflammatory racist rhetoric itself. And once in office, Nixon seems to have followed the advice of his young strategist Kevin Phillips, who called on the Republican Party to expand black voting rights in the South to accelerate the defection of white southerners to the Republicans.[32] Then, in the 1972 presidential race, Republican strategists pressured Wallace to run in the Democratic primary instead of mounting another third-party assault by threatening a grand jury indictment of his brother and some of his political supporters. In the fierce primary races that followed, Wallace's "savage attacks on anti-war demonstrators and busing and 'forced integration' " tore into Democratic support, helping to hand Nixon a landslide victory.[33]

Could the Democratic Party recover? If the principle that parties compete by mobilizing voters were correct, the party could have exerted itself to respond to the ongoing loss of support among white southerners, and the bleeding of white working-class voters from its northern base, by mobilizing new voters to make up for the defectors or by launching new appeals to stanch the bleeding of old voters. The potential voters were there, not only among blacks and other minorities but also among the legions of the worse-off of all colors who make up the nonvoting population. To be sure, it would be hard to reproduce the once-solid South. But the solid South had always extracted a high price for its allegiance. It had prevented the national Democratic Party from vigorously promoting the programs that might have cemented the loyalty of northern working-class voters even in the face of racist appeals, and southern representatives had joined with Republicans in Congress to defeat those programs the party did sponsor.

Obviously, the electoral upheavals of the 1960s were costly to the Democrats, at least in the short run. In principle, however, these very upheavals might in the longer run lay the basis for overcoming the crippling effects of the peculiar coalition. After all, shorn of its southern one-party leg iron, the Democratic Party might develop into something like an interracial working-class political party. That did not happen, of course, and for several reasons. First, the Democrats were not a unified party capable of acting to achieve shared party goals. The concessions that national Democratic leaders had made to the black freedom movement in civil rights and Great Society initiatives had succeeded in solidifying the black vote. But from the beginning, the presence of blacks, and the initiatives that responded to their movements, were often anathema to local Democratic leaders. Blacks were discordant voters, and their presence and their demands antagonized other blocs in Democratic coalitions. Moreover, once the riotous sixties were over, a more business-oriented national Democratic leadership also turned against both the Great Society programs and the people to whom they were oriented. So overall, the national Democrats remained passive, accepting black votes, but not vigorously reaching out to increase black turnout.[34] Meanwhile, fierce struggles broke out in the big cities as blacks made their bid for electoral power.

3

BLACK VOTING POWER IN THE CITIES

If there is anything positive in the spread of the ghetto, it is the potential political power base thus created, and to realize this potential is one of the most challenging and urgent tasks before the civil rights movement. If the movement can wrest leadership of the ghetto vote from the machines, it will have acquired an organized constituency such as other major groups in our society now have.

—Bayard Rustin, 1965 [1]

In the story of how blacks became a force in American politics, the contest for the cities was pivotal. We turn to this story, examining three historic African American mayoralty campaigns that illustrate the themes of our argument. By the mid-1960s, demographic shifts, the civil rights movement, and the Voting Rights Act produced a new black electorate eager to participate and increasingly impatient with the pace of change. The national Democrats, especially the presidential wing of the party, acquired an important stake in this development and often supported the mayoral aspirations of black reformers. Democratic presidents sought to build national electoral majorities and needed black votes. Their responsiveness only encouraged blacks to see more clearly the potential power of the vote and the possibilities it represented for local control. But, as discussed in chapter 1, American political parties are not unitary actors.

In the big cities, Democratic organizations had a problem with black power and especially with black demands for integration, better housing and schools, a share of municipal jobs, and curbs on police power. Their constituent groups among municipal workers, labor unions, and the social service bureaucracies were often staunchly against sharing jobs, resources, and power with blacks. Where developments at the national level fueled black electoral mobilization, local party organizations, notably the big-city machines and their white working-class voters, resisted it. When they could, local party organizations tried to ward off the black threat with vote suppression tactics, as in Richard Hatcher's historic mayoral campaign in Gary, Indiana, described below.

Big-city Democrats also adopted as their own the Republican Southern Strategy. Beginning with the earliest independent efforts of blacks to win the mayor's office, such as the 1967 candidacies of Hatcher in Gary and Carl Stokes in Cleveland, black electoral mobilization was countered by Democratic Party organizations, which launched campaigns against "open housing," crime, and later school busing. Similarly, when the Harold Washington campaign in Chicago threatened to defeat what remained of the storied Daley machine, it confronted both vote suppression and a party campaign intent on inflaming white resentment to raise white turnout.

The Great Migration had not only brought blacks to the North but also concentrated them in the big cities. Between 1950 and 1975, the urban black population nearly doubled, from 6.6 to 13.1 million. In cities with more than a million residents, blacks were 27.6 percent of the population by 1975. This concentration obviously did not occur for politically strategic reasons, but it had politically strategic consequences. On the national level, black numbers were rising in the cities that were crucial to carrying the big industrial states in presidential elections. This emerging northern black voting power helped give the protests of the civil rights movement in the South leverage with presidential contenders, and also led to the election of the representatives who eventually formed the Congressional Black Caucus.

The path "from protest to [electoral] politics," the title of a much-cited 1965 article by Bayard Rustin, gained increasing credibility among African American leaders, and the number running for and winning public office grew.[2] Between 1964 and 1974 the number of black public officials increased from 914 to 2,991.[3] By 1980 the number had risen to 4,912. These were predominantly local and minor

Table 3

Black Population, 1950, 1960, 1970 (in millions)

	1950	1960	1970
Total Black Population	15.0	18.9	22.7
Metropolitan Areas	8.8	12.8	16.8
Central Cities	6.6	9.9	13.1
Outside Central Cities	2.2	2.8	3.7
Outside Metro Areas	6.2	6.1	5.8
30 Cities With Largest			
Black Population	4.5	6.8	9.2
As a percentage	15	22	29

SOURCE: Bureau of the Census, *The Social and Economic Status of Negroes in the United States, 1970,* Current Population Reports, Series P-23, No. 38 (Washington, DC: GPO, 1979), table 6, table 11.

offices, of course, and in any case represented only 1 percent of the nearly 500,000 elected officials in the United States. Still, the rate of progress was rapid, and accounts for the heady enthusiasm with which blacks entered the electoral lists.

The prospect of elected office was especially compelling in the big cities, where blacks were now concentrated, and a good many observers began to talk of a new phase in ethnic political succession. Of course, there would be resistance to black succession, and the resistance would be made more intransigent because it was embedded in city bureaucracies and civil service regulations. But just as the Irish had succeeded the white Protestants who once controlled the cities, and in some places the Italians had succeeded the Irish, now it was the turn of African Americans.[4]

To be sure, ongoing changes in the cities cast a shadow on these hopes. Even as early as the 1960s, the industrial base that had provided employment for earlier waves of newcomers was shrinking, partly because investors were relocating in the low-wage South or overseas, and partly in reflection of new "lean-production" methods and the shift of American investment to service industries. These economic trends would accelerate in coming years, with the consequence that the black leaders who ascended to control of city govern-ments were confronted with dire revenue shortfalls combined with housing abandonment, unemployment, and poverty. Moreover, the trend of expanding federal aid to the cities was reversed with the as-cendance of a Republican national regime in 1968.[5] But while those worries might dim the prospect of municipal power, the historic sig-nificance of the possibility was more compelling.

The mobilization of blacks in the cities was influenced by the newly conciliatory policies of the federal government, particularly by the Great Society programs initiated by John F. Kennedy and ex-panded by Lyndon Baines Johnson, which tried to cement the alle-giance of growing numbers of black voters with a series of programs dealing with delinquency, or mental illness, or blighted neighbor-hoods, or by waging a "war on poverty." (At the outset, some of these programs even spurred voter registration efforts, outraging the reigning white Democratic big-city organizations.) Whatever was intended, the hopes thus generated helped to fuel the defiance of urban blacks. From 1963 to 1968, demonstrations escalated across the country, and so did urban riots.

The first major black electoral bids for municipal executive power occurred in 1967, with mayoralty contests in Gary, Indiana, and Cleveland, Ohio. Richard Hatcher's run for mayor followed a course that would be repeated across the North, as he took on both his own Democratic Party and the Republicans, whose prospects for municipal power in what had been a one-party Democratic fief-dom were considerably brightened by the race war tearing apart the Democrats.

Gary was founded in 1906 by the U.S. Steel Corporation as the home for its largest new manufacturing facility. By the 1960s, it was a middle-sized city of 180,000, and Richard Hatcher rapidly became one of the most prominent black leaders in the country, the symbol of a new, more practical stage in the development of black politics. Hatcher grew up twenty-five miles from Gary, the thirteenth of four-teen children born to a Pullman factory worker, and the grandson of a Georgia sharecropper. He worked his way through school, graduat-ing with a degree in political science and economics from Indiana

University, and later with honors in criminal law from Valparaiso University. Hatcher's stubbornness and forthrightness, and his squeaky-clean living habits (he did not drink or smoke, and regularly attended church) endeared him to the black community. Elected to the city council in 1963, he had been an outspoken young leader of local struggles in education, policing, hiring practices, housing, and in fact all of the local conflicts that were associated with the black freedom movement in the North. Hatcher fought tirelessly for the black community and showed little interest in the material benefits of the job for himself. This, too, earned him wide support and trust among blacks, and fashioned for Hatcher an image as one of a totally "new breed" of black politicians.[6] In 1966, after continued migrations from the South to jobs in the steel mills transformed Gary into a black-majority city, local civil rights activists presented Hatcher with a petition signed by five thousand people urging him to run for mayor.[7] He accepted the challenge.

In 1967, Gary was a sharply racially segregated and divided city. Between 1950 and the mid-1960s, the black population had climbed from 38,000 to more than 85,000, sending "many thousands of Serbs, Croats, Poles, Italians and white Southerners . . . fleeing to the suburbs."[8] In the May 5, 1964, Indiana preference primary, George Wallace won every white precinct in Gary, as well as the Lake County vote.[9] Ironically, Hatcher was helped in winning the Democratic primary by the entrance into the race of a Wallace supporter named Bernard Konrady, who drew voters away from the incumbent, Democrat A. Martin Katz.

As an underdog candidate about to take on not only the Democratic Party organization but also its black "submachine," Hatcher knew he had to build an alternative campaign organization that paralleled the machine's operation at the district, precinct, and block level. To win, Hatcher and his advisers would have to create the excitement that would generate an outpouring of support from the black community. He set about attracting a talented, energetic, multiracial campaign of young political "amateurs" and reformers who researched urban problems, wrote position papers, coordinated transportation and "lit" drops, and organized dinners and drawings and potluck fund-raisers. Most important, Hatcher and his advisers set up a large and coordinated street operation that put at least ten people on each block in black neighborhoods who were willing to go door-to-door and use whatever gimmicks it might take to promote their candidate and convince people to vote for him.[10]

Victory in the primary would require at least 75 percent of the black vote and a huge black turnout, and the street operation concentrated first on voter registration.[11] At this time, to register in Indiana, a citizen needed to be twenty-one, a resident of the state for at least one year, and a resident of his or her precinct for at least three months. Registration services were provided primarily at the Lake County Board of Elections in Crown Point, about fifteen miles from Gary, or at a handful of more centrally located registration stations within the corporate borders of the fifty-seven-square-mile city. A massive voter registration drive to first identify eligible unregistered blacks, then convince them that their votes mattered, and finally help transport them to registration offices where they could complete applications would be the key to turning on and turning out Hatcher's base in the black community.

Hatcher volunteers combed the registration records and hit the pavement. They canvassed every nook and cranny of the black community, spending hours trawling for unregistered black citizens by hanging out at pool halls, bars, supermarkets, department stores, movie houses, and churches. They developed a persuasive rap to encourage elderly blacks embarrassed by the fact that they had never voted before that the time was now, offering them support and a ride to the registrar's office. They delivered thousands of handbills with information about the free transportation available to register to vote. In the end, their efforts paid off. William Nelson and Philip Meranto report that between November 1966 and May 1967, 2,200 blacks registered to vote.

These efforts were met with a campaign of official obstruction, delay, and denial on the part of the Democratic Party machine, which controlled the county election board and appointed most of its workers. For example, county clerk and Lake County Democratic Party boss John Krupa denied the Hatcher campaign permission to launch a roving caravan to register blacks at their homes or jobs or on the street, ruling that the registration laws prohibited county committeemen from registering voters outside their precincts. When the Hatcher campaign asked for more deputized registrars to work in black neighborhoods, Krupa refused. Election officials delayed setting up registration boards, usually organized well in advance of an election, until just one month before the primary. Then, their hours of operation were curtailed to discourage black registration. "In Crown Point," report Nelson and Meranto,

> a slow-down procedure was instituted to discourage voters from remaining long enough to complete the registration process. . . . At the grass-roots level, precinct committeemen intimidated welfare mothers with threats of having child support payments cut off if they registered to vote for Hatcher. Anyone having Hatcher literature in his home was subject to receive [sic] an ominous warning from his committeemen.[12]

Even whites who supported Hatcher were not spared the machine's campaign of harassment and intimidation:

> Scurrilous leaflets were circulated through the white community, which identified leading whites in the Hatcher campaign and labeled them communists. These whites were generally harassed with threatening phone calls, damage to their homes and other public property, hate mail, and so forth. Their children were also taunted by other children at school who often repeated remarks they had heard expressed by their parents. Similarly, students distributing literature for Hatcher in white areas were severely beaten on several occasions. The Hatcher headquarters in Miller [a white neighborhood] was the target of frequent vandalism with windows being damaged by bricks and gun shots.[13]

During the primary campaign itself, efforts were made to physically intimidate Hatcher and his supporters. According to Ed Greer, who later served as Hatcher's director of program coordination, "[d]eath threats were common, and many beatings occurred."[14] The

Hatcher organization formed self-defense squads and relied on armed groups to force open polling places in black neighborhoods on election day. In fact, the Hatcher campaign organized what might be called today an "election-protection" operation of as many as two thousand volunteers, including a large contingent of trained poll watchers, mechanics able to repair the voting machines, and a watchful lawyers' organization prepared to bring legal action in the event that the Democratic Party machine attempted to steal the election.[15] Hatcher was able to get his voting machine mechanics approved by the county as official election mechanics. The volunteers surveyed precincts in black neighborhoods the night before the election and identified likely problem hot spots. On the morning of election day, without prompting, Hatcher's mechanics visited those hot spots to check on the operations and make emergency repairs. Despite the preemption, campaign headquarters was inundated with phone calls from angry black voters who reported arriving at their precinct polling places as early as 6 A.M., only to wait on line for hours because their machines were "out of order."

To ease voters' fears, Hatcher campaign workers spread rumors that the FBI would be observing the election. They rented big black cars, dressed in dark suits and wore hats pulled down over their eyes, and drove from precinct to precinct, jotting down notes on legal pads to create the impression that the federal government was watching. Poll workers observed every polling-place transaction and ritual, reporting any irregularities to roving campaign vehicles and lawyers, a local radio station, and the *Gary Post-Tribune*. They recorded the final vote tallies on each and every machine in the black precincts and reported them back to headquarters, so sure were they that the party bosses would try to stuff the ballot box.

Their confidence in Democratic Party corruption was reaffirmed when Hatcher's campaign got a tip from a man who claimed to have taught the opposition how to steal votes. He told Hatcher's advisers that there were two basic ways this might be done. Either an election inspector would drive to city hall and exchange tally sheets with someone stationed inside the city hall garage before he took the sheets up to the tally room, or he might ride the elevator to the fourth floor, meet his connection, exchange the sheets, and ride back down to the second-floor tally room, where he would turn in the phony results. Hatcher stationed volunteers at every possible point along the trail from the precinct to the city hall tally room and followed the election inspector until he deposited the final tally sheets with election officials. The surveillance and security efforts paid off. Even though the Hatcher campaign believed some votes had been stolen from their candidate, Hatcher pulled off a narrow victory, winning 39 percent of the vote in the three-way race. Black turnout was a record high, with an estimated 61 percent of eligible blacks participating in the primary election. In fact, although there were more registered whites than blacks, blacks outpolled whites by more than three thousand votes.

Once Hatcher won the primary, the notoriously corrupt Lake County Democratic machine tried to cut a deal with him.[16] Party leaders offered Hatcher $100,000 for the general election campaign in return for naming the chief of police, corporation counsel, and controller. Hatcher wanted and needed their money, but in what would become a hallmark of his governing style, he refused to make a deal with the local party organization.[17] Moreover, he was running on an anticorruption platform and promised Gary voters that as mayor he would crack down on crime, gambling, prostitution, and public officials who condoned vice. Unaccustomed to black insubordination, the machine went to war, endorsing Hatcher's Republican opponent and plotting his defeat with the help of local election officials including the secretary of the Lake County Election Board, John Krupa, who also served as the local Democratic Party boss (in addition, Krupa was the county clerk and secretary of the board of canvassers). Krupa denied that the Democratic organization's endorsement of the Republican candidate, Joseph B. Radigan, was motivated by racism. Instead, he said it was because Hatcher was not the "right kind" of Negro, adding that he would "groom" one for mayor after Hatcher was defeated. He accused Hatcher of supporting "black power" and left-wing disloyalty by opposing the war in Vietnam.[18]

Hatcher claimed the Democratic Party usually spent about $500,000 on a mayoral campaign.[19] Once he refused their deal for control over high-ranking city jobs, he was left to raise money on his own (he also claimed that he refused $70,000 from organized crime). Desperate for funds, Hatcher did something that was unheard of at the time, especially for a local candidate from a midsize midwestern city. He placed a full-page ad in the *New York Times*: "For God's sake," it pleaded above a photograph of a white cop beating a black demonstrator, "let's get ourselves together."

> We're at war, you know. With ourselves. And with the family down the street that comes from a different country. We're at war with anyone who has a different shade of skin than ours. We're at war with anyone who looks different. Or talks different. Or goes to a different church than we do. . . . It seems all too apparent, at this point, that we really do hate each other. It shows, fellow Americans. And it's a national disgrace. The enemy, in case you haven't noticed lately, is ourselves! For God's sake, let's get ourselves together. . . . Richard Hatcher is running for his life. And yours. And the life of every American saddened and sickened by the mounting violence in this country. Richard Hatcher is running to become the first Negro mayor of a major metropolitan city—Gary, Indiana. Hatcher's crusade: Peace and unity among all men—black and white. (And every shade in between!) Richard Hatcher is battling bigotry and ignorance. And he desperately needs your help. . . . Will 5 or 10 dollars hurt you? Indifference sure will! Give a little. Send what you can.[20]

The cost of the ad reduced Hatcher's campaign treasury to $15, but the strategy paid off.[21] Campaign contributions poured in from all over the world and ranged in size from $1,000 to 50¢ donated by a poor family in Brooklyn who wrote that they wished "they could do more."[22] The ad catapulted Hatcher's crusade onto the national political scene. The rift between Hatcher and the local Democratic Party organization suddenly took on more troubling dimensions for national Democrats and put enormous pressure on national leaders to settle those differences. Key figures in the Johnson wing of the party came to the aid of the young, unknown politician from Gary.

In September 1967, Vice President Hubert Humphrey was the fea-
tured speaker at a Washington fund-raiser for Hatcher.[23] Aides to the
more liberal Senator Robert Kennedy saw the *Times* ad and quickly
organized a fund-raiser for Hatcher in New York City. Reflecting the
politics of the liberal wing of the party, Kennedy told the assembled
guests that Hatcher's was a "worthy cause." He recalled how as attorney general he had investigated Gary's former mayor and district
attorney for corruption, sending them and other public officials to
jail, and pledged his support to Hatcher.[24] Through these sorts of efforts, Hatcher was able to raise over $100,000 and received offers of
free advertising space and radio/television time as his story went
national.[25]

If Hatcher had been a white Democrat, of course, his victory in
the general election would have been guaranteed. But the county
organization was not taking assertiveness on the part of blacks ly-
ing down. Between the primary and general elections, Hatcher discovered yet another plot by the Lake County machine to commit
massive election fraud in order to thwart his bid for office. Two out-
of-town reporters covering the race for *Life* magazine learned of the
plot and convinced a white precinct committeewoman who was in
on it to go to Hatcher with what she knew. She revealed that the
machine in collusion with the Republicans was in the process of
loading the voter lists with phony names that would then be used to
stuff the ballot box with upwards of twenty thousand "ghost" votes
against Hatcher. Later, the committeewoman recalled that this was
too much for Hatcher to believe. "When I told him they were going
to steal 15,000 to 20,000 votes, he kept saying 'That's fantastic, that's
fantastic.' "[26]

Hatcher was despondent as more evidence of fraud came to light.
Eyewitnesses told Hatcher that election officials were tampering
with absentee ballots. When applicants requested absentee ballots,
election officials were instructing them to remove Hatcher's name
and vote for his opponent. They asked applicants to leave their ballots unsealed before returning them to the county courthouse.
Hatcher pleaded with the Justice Department to intervene under
its new authority granted by the Civil Rights Act of 1964 and the Vot-

ing Rights Act of 1965, and to investigate what he believed was ongoing gross fraud and discrimination in the city's voter registration
operation.

In an October 26, 1967, telegram to the president and U.S. attorney general, Hatcher contended that the two party organizations
through their control of the county registration and election boards
were conspiring to help the Democratic Party machine steal the election, and that their failure to protect black voting rights would result
in a race riot for which federal officials would be held responsible.
This was not hyperbole on Hatcher's part. Electrifying momentum
for change and elevated expectations were rapidly building behind
Hatcher's candidacy, and it was not hard to imagine the anger that
would erupt at the revelations of a stolen election. Hatcher alleged
the convoluted plot involved several different scams. First, the registration records of five thousand to six thousand qualified black
voters were being illegally purged, while four thousand voter registrations of "ghost voters" from white precincts had been illegally
added to the rolls after the closing date for registration.[27] At a press
conference following ten days of meetings with FBI agents who later
provided evidence in court supporting his charges, Hatcher claimed
a group of 250 people planned to float from precinct to precinct in
white areas and vote multiple times under the phony names. "If they
are allowed to get away with this scheme," he said, "in my opinion I
stand little hope of winning this election. I will be 20,000 votes behind at the start of the voting."[28]

The scam to purge black voters was itself remarkably devious.
Some months before it was uncovered, a journalist named Hilbert
Bradley had become interested in why Hatcher had not run as well as
expected in certain black precincts during the primary. Bradley discovered that the Lake County machine routinely stuffed ballot boxes
by padding the registration rolls with phony names registered from
phony addresses in black neighborhoods, then voting those names
for its own candidates. Normally, inflated votes for Democrats in
black precincts would not have been noticed, since blacks routinely
gave the vast majority of their votes to the party's candidates. Economic prosperity among Gary's unionized white working class had

devalued what the machine could offer white voters. They had become homeowners and adherents of a low-tax, anticorruption, good-government ideology. The less-prosperous black community was more in need of the machine's patronage and influence. According to Charles Levine and Clifford Kaufman, "by the mid-1960s, the only faction of its coalition that the machine could count on for consistent disciplined voting support was the city's black voters." [29] Black politicians in Gary, as in many cities of the urban industrial Northeast and Midwest, were politically incorporated through their subordination to white machine control. In exchange for the crumbs of the patronage system, black politicians consistently delivered an overwhelming majority of the black vote to the machine. Padding the voter rolls with fake machine voters would go unnoticed.

In Gary, Hatcher's insurgent candidacy exposed the machine's vote inflation scam during the primary. Bradley spent months gathering information showing the fraud that reduced Hatcher's margins in precincts where he should have been a big winner. He wrote a piece about it for *Info* magazine, titled "Election Fraud—Gary Style." He appealed to the board of elections for a hearing on his allegations of fraud but was turned down. Then four months after the *Info* article ran, the board members changed their minds and invited Bradley to testify. It's not clear why the board had a sudden change of heart and became concerned about voter fraud. If the Republicans and Democrats were colluding to defeat Hatcher, could it have been to plant in the public's mind the potential for black voter fraud in order to justify the illegitimate cleansing of registration rolls they had planned for later? After Bradley's appearance on October 25, 1967, the board announced it was launching a full-scale investigation of voting irregularities in black precincts.

Republican campaigners for Hatcher's opponent, Joseph Radigan, then moved into action. They quickly organized a canvass of black neighborhoods in search of more evidence in support of Bradley's claims. The next day, October 26, Robert H. Rooda, a Republican city councilman and Lake County Registration Board member, presented the board of elections with a list of 5,268 names representing what the Republicans claimed were "ghost voters."

The total number of names on the list was similar to what Bradley alleged, but instead of identifying phony registrations, the Republicans listed thousands of qualified black voters living at legitimate addresses.

Democratic Party boss Krupa said he had no choice but to purge the rolls of the names presented to the board by the Republicans, a direct violation of Indiana's registration law, which restricted voter roll purges to the January following a presidential election. Krupa and his cronies had to move fast. The week before the mayoral election, Krupa challenged more than 5,000 black voters on the Republicans' list, sending out letters of notification that their voter registration would be canceled unless they could prove their eligibility. In order to reinstate their eligibility, challenged voters had to provide personal information and data, return the board's letter by registered mail, and then appear before the county election board in Crown Point within a matter of days. Failure to respond to the notice would result in automatic cancellation of the recipient's voter registration. Of course, there was almost no time to respond to the letter and appear before the county board even if a voter wanted to—the election was scheduled for November 7. Together the regular Democrats and Republicans were colluding in a classic voter "caging" operation to suppress black votes. Hatcher later recalled,

> They sent everybody and his uncle those letters. Some people had been living at the same address for 12 or 13 years and owned their own homes. . . . Many of them said they were not going to send this letter back because they would have to send it by registered mail which involved money. If they sent it, then they would have to come out to [the county seat] and appear before the election board. So when they did this we knew we had lost.[30]

Determined to prevent an independent black reformer from ascending to the mayor's office, the Lake County Democrats bucked the state and national Democratic parties and endorsed the Republican candidate for mayor. They then attempted to "cage" legitimate, properly registered black Democrats under the pretense of a rigged mailing in order to justify purging their registration records and suppressing their votes.

The same day Krupa announced his plans to purge the voter rolls, Hatcher sent his telegram to the president and the attorney general. Their response was not forthcoming. After several days and many efforts to contact the Justice Department by telephone, the campaign was told it was on its own.[31] A reluctant Hatcher agreed to pursue his case in the federal courts. He hired W. Robert Ming, an African American considered one of the best constitutional lawyers in the Midwest, to put together his case. Ming filed a complaint in U.S. district court charging a conspiracy of actions against black voters in violation of the Fourteenth and Fifteenth amendments and federal civil rights statutes. The complaint requested the convening of a three-judge panel to hear arguments and render a decision, and was brought on behalf of the candidate and all registered Democrats who had participated in the primary, including those whom John Krupa had threatened to purge from the rolls. It named twenty-seven people including Krupa and Richard Rooda and asked the court to do whatever was necessary to ensure a free and fair election in Gary. If this request was not possible to grant, the complaint asked for a permanent injunction to postpone the election. District Judge George N. Beamer scheduled a hearing for Monday, November 6, one day before the election. Krupa denied Hatcher's charges to the press and defended his attempt to purge the rolls of illegal voters. "There is ample proof of ghost voting," he said. As Lake County Democratic boss, he presumably would have known.[32]

Meanwhile, a new development boded well for Hatcher. The Justice Department suddenly reversed its position and announced it was filing a companion lawsuit in support of Hatcher's, alleging that Lake County election officials were inflating the number of registered whites while illegally diminishing the number of legally registered blacks. Unbeknownst to just about everyone, the FBI had been investigating voting irregularities in Gary for nearly six months. In fact, after Hatcher sent his telegram, behind the scenes, "there was as much dramatic action as the assembling of a cast for the shooting of 'Ben Hur,' " reported Ethel L. Payne of the *Chicago Defender*.[33] Louis

Martin, the deputy chairman of the Democratic National Committee, was dispatched to Gary by President Johnson on a fact-finding
mission. Attorney General Ramsey Clark and his aides "arrived at
the White House with bulging briefcases."[34] J. Edgar Hoover was on
the phone with both of Indiana's senators, Vance Hartke and Birch
Bayh, as well as state Democratic Party officials, perhaps because the
organized-crime syndicate in Gary had let it be known that it would
not allow a black reform candidate to be the next mayor.

The FBI's investigation involved twenty agents who reviewed
nine thousand voter registration records and turned up 1,099 fictitious names registered in predominantly white precincts.[35] Twenty-
two lawyers from the Civil Rights Division of the Justice Department
supplemented the FBI investigation as soon as the Hatcher suit had
been filed. One person interviewed at the time by Nelson and
Meranto said that the evidence documenting the fraud collected by
the federal government in just a matter of days was astounding. "I've
never seen such a collection of data, such a compilation of material,
which required fantastic physical effort and expertise. I would hate to
have the federal government come after me the way it came in that
case. It was just an absolutely incredible display of logistical ability."[36]

The hearing room in the Hammond Federal Courthouse was
jammed on the morning of November 6. Over the objection of the
defendants, the two suits were consolidated, and witnesses were then
called to testify. A number of government witnesses with personal
knowledge of residents and properties located at various addresses
reviewed the names of voters allegedly illegally registered to vote.
These names were added in predominantly white neighborhoods.
All witnesses denied such persons lived at the addresses. A Gary FBI
agent testified that over a thousand fictitious registrations in white
neighborhoods had been added to the rolls since Hatcher defeated
Katz in the primary; a canvass of fifty-seven predominantly black
precincts by the FBI had turned up no fictitious names in the poll
books. One of the voters on Krupa's purge list, John L. Howard, testified that he had voted in every Gary election since he first registered
to vote in 1936. He was turned away from the board of registration
when he appeared to protest the letter challenging his eligibility.[37]

The most dramatic testimony came from the Democratic precinct committeewoman, Marion Tokarski, who had turned against
the machine to expose the fraud. Tokarski testified that she personally added 51 fictitious names to the rolls in her precinct and failed to
remove another 107 names of people she knew had died or moved
away. She claimed she had been acting under the direction of another
Democratic committeewoman, Helen Repya, a matron in the Gary
Police Department; Tokarski herself had worked as a police clerk.
When she asked who would come to the polls to vote the fraudulent
names, Tokarski was told by a Democratic Party voting official that
"iron workers would vote for the men and prostitutes would vote for
the women because they are the only ones who had guts." [38] Ironically, noted the *Chicago Tribune*, "charges of vote stealing by the
Democratic organization were designed not to guarantee victory for
the Democratic candidate, Hatcher, but for the Republican candidate, Radigan." [39]

Hatcher's was the first federal voting rights case invoking violations of the 1964 Civil Rights Act and 1965 Voting Rights Act
brought by the Justice Department in the North. After closing arguments, the panel of judges recessed and then quickly returned a
unanimous decision in favor of the plaintiffs. The court denied
Hatcher's petition to postpone the election, instead issuing a preliminary injunction against actions by the defendants that would impair
the execution of a free and fair election. The 1,099 fictitious ghost
voters were barred from participating in the election unless they
could prove their eligibility, and election officials were ordered to restore the 5,268 voter registrations on Krupa's purge list. [40] Written
records on the challenge of any voter were to be maintained for later
inspection by Justice Department officials. The court retained jurisdiction in the case until after the election and ordered U.S. marshals
to post the court order and the names of the alleged fraudulent voters at all polling places. [41]

In the general election that followed, most Democratic precinct
captains and the county Democratic organization supported the
Republican candidate, as did about 87 percent of Gary's white Democratic voters. Hatcher's campaign organization drew on its experi-

ence in the primary, sending out hundreds of volunteer poll watchers, roving lawyers, and get-out-the-vote recruiters to expand and
protect Hatcher's vote. Their ranks were swollen by a huge contingent of college students, many with family connections to the city,
who traveled from around the country to Gary to work on election
day. Black union workers from the packinghouses of Chicago joined
the effort, along with Chicago-based black elected officials like state
senator Richard Newhouse and state representative Harold Washington. Overall, the Hatcher campaign put more than three thousand volunteers and paid campaign staff into the field on election
day and generated a massive turnout in the black community. Meanwhile, five thousand National Guardsmen in their armored personnel carriers called out by the mayor and governor on fears of a
possible race riot mustered outside the city limits.[42]

By noon, more than 60 percent of the black electorate and 50 percent of the white electorate had voted. As we have become accus-
tomed to expect, record high turnout collided with breakdowns in
election administration. Despite the court order and the retention of
jurisdiction by the federal court to deal with any election fraud, the
Hatcher campaign received hundreds of calls from supporters disenfranchised by bureaucratic mix-ups, flawed registration records, and
deliberate vote suppression. Chuck Ware, head of the Hatcher campaign's election-security unit, told the press that by 7:15 in the morning, "[s]ome 46 machines were reported jammed in Negro voting
areas. Flagrant abuses were being committed in many precincts."[43]

Radigan and Hatcher ran neck and neck throughout the day. By
7 p.m., when the polls closed, both declared victory. By 10 p.m. Radigan had pulled ahead by 4,900 votes, but as votes from the black
precincts continued to pour in, the jubilation in the Radigan camp
subsided. An hour later, with just three precincts left to report,
Hatcher was leading by over 2,000 votes. He was put over the top by
his own precinct, which gave him 1,003 votes to just 14 for Radigan.
Hatcher went on to win the election by 1,865 votes out of 77,759
cast.[44] His organization had pulled 76 percent of all eligible black voters to the polls, compared to 72 percent turnout of the white electorate. While both whites and blacks voted as blocs, Hatcher won in

part because he earned more of the white vote (14 percent) than Radigan won of the black vote (4 percent). Importantly, blacks made their choice over the opposition of local Democratic Party leaders, delivering 96 percent of their votes to the young reformer.

Richard Hatcher went on to govern the city for twenty years, although these were twenty years during which his many initiatives for the economic empowerment of black residents, supported by Great Society programs and eastern foundations, were nevertheless foiled by the ongoing hollowing out of the city caused by white flight and business disinvestment.[45]

The Carl Stokes victory in Cleveland occurred the same year as Hatcher's successful race. Stokes was already a pioneer in Cleveland electoral politics. He ran unsuccessfully for the Ohio House of Representatives in 1960, and ran again two years later when his victory made him the first black Democrat to serve in the Ohio legislature. Then, in early 1965, Stokes was recruited to run for mayor by grassroots community activists.

As in Gary, the black population in Cleveland had swelled rapidly in the 1950s. This bode well for a black mayoral candidacy, but even more important, blacks, who were 34 percent of the population in 1965, were 40 percent of the electorate due to a large voter registration drive conducted by the Democratic Party for the 1964 presidential race. That drive added 14,626 new black voters to the rolls at a rate that exceeded comparable trends for whites. Moreover, and unlike in Gary, the Democratic Party machine in Cleveland did not have an iron grip on the city's politics. Cleveland had a tradition of maverick mayors that made an independent candidacy by a black reformer like Stokes appealing. Before Stokes declared his intent to run, it was clear there would be three whites on the ballot in the general election (the incumbent Democratic mayor, a Republican, and another independent). The white vote would split. With unified black support, the right black candidate could win.

Stokes decided to run. But without the support of his party, he had to create a campaign organization from the bottom up. The ten black city councilmen in Cleveland decided to play it safe and stuck

with the party's candidate, the incumbent mayor, Ralph Locher, forcing Stokes to rely on inexperienced volunteers to duplicate the
party's ward organizations. This was another campaign fueled by
grassroots enthusiasm. According to Nelson and Meranto, "What the
Stokes campaign organization lacked in terms of rational structure
and coordination was supplanted, however, by the raw zeal, enthusiasm, and inventiveness of the workers. . . . The campaign took on a
'crusade-like quality.' "[46]

Stokes ran on a good-government platform and the conviction that he was the candidate best qualified to reverse the deterioration of Cleveland. With its ragtag, freewheeling band of neophyte
political supporters, Stokes's was an improbable campaign. None of
the other candidates took him seriously until the end, when the momentum building in the black community suddenly could no longer
be ignored. "Consequently," write Nelson and Meranto, "each of
them [the white candidates] employed a late campaign technique
aimed at defeating Stokes. All of them conducted a whispering campaign among white voters that a vote for the other two white candidates was a wasted vote and would result in electing 'that Nigger
mayor.' "[47]

The tactic worked and favored Locher, who, in addition to being
backed by the Democratic organization, enjoyed broad institutional
support among the city's editorial boards, the labor unions, and the
downtown business establishment, and appeared to many whites to
be the best hope against Stokes. Locher defeated Stokes by a slim
margin of just 2,458 votes. Stokes's supporters quickly studied the
patterns of precinct returns and discovered that some precincts had
100 percent turnout of all registered voters and not one vote for
Stokes. On election night, two ballot bags (most precincts used paper
ballots) from two black precincts disappeared and were never accounted for.[48] If turnout patterns in the uncounted black precincts
had been consistent with those in other black precincts, it is possible
that Stokes got more votes than Locher.[49] His campaign advisers suspected fraud on the part of white registrars and asked for a recount
(which later reduced Locher's margin by about 300 votes).

Though he hadn't won, the race had been a victory of sorts for

Stokes. His candidacy was an eye-opening trial run producing record high voting levels among blacks. This took many political professionals, black and white, by complete surprise. Even without the apparatus of the Democratic Party organization pulling out the vote, black turnout increased a whopping 15 percentage points over the previous mayor's contest just two years before, from 57 to 72 percent. Moreover, Stokes's near win was a moral victory that changed many minds about how far a dynamic black reform candidate could go. In defeat, Stokes continued to fire up black community support. At the end of the race, the Stokes campaign organization was $4,000 in debt, and money needed to be raised to finance the recount. Nelson and Meranto report this account from an individual on Stokes's finance committee:

> The recount in 1965 was an experience that I'll never live through again, and I don't think anybody else ever will because it was as exciting as anything that happened. People just started to bring money in from all over. Bars would put up big containers—in fact, these containers were all through the neighborhoods, in the bars, stores, barber shops, everywhere. . . . People were walking up and down the streets collecting nickels and dimes and bringing it all into the office.[50]

Enough money poured in to not only finance the recount but also retire the campaign's debt.

By the time Carl Stokes ran for mayor again two years later, Cleveland had joined the ranks of other major cities experiencing racial strife and violence. Conditions for many black Clevelanders were harsh. Overcrowded and substandard housing, segregated inferior schools, unemployment, and police brutality and misconduct topped the list of grievances. To highlight the desperate conditions of black life in northern ghettos, in 1966 the U.S. Commission on Civil Rights initiated a series of field investigations in a number of large cities, kicking it off with a six-day televised hearing in Cleveland.[51] Three months later, in the middle of a heat wave, the white owner of a bar near the Hough ghetto advertised, "No Water for Niggers."[52]

Two patrons of the bar claimed they had been called "niggers" by the bartender, and an angry crowd began gathering on the street, where the bar owner and another white man confronted them with guns drawn.[53] The police quickly descended on the scene, pushing and shoving ensued, and someone set off a cherry bomb or fired a shot, and then all hell broke loose. "The crowd threw bottles and bricks, began to break store windows, and sniper shots rang through the air. For a full week massive civil disorder—burning, looting, vandalism, sniping, police shooting, and National Guard occupation—raged in Cleveland's black ghetto."[54]

The Hough riots were a turning point in Cleveland. Years of pent-up resentment and frustration with deteriorating conditions were unleashed in a fury that at one point during the four-day riot set over two hundred buildings ablaze. Conditions for blacks were not "gradually improving" as white leaders insisted; in fact, the evidence shows they were deteriorating, as they were in many other northern ghettos. Between 1960 and 1965, black poverty in Cleveland increased as black median income dropped from $4,732 to $3,966. Thirty-eight thousand blacks in Cleveland were on welfare (Aid to Families with Dependent Children [AFDC]), including a fifth of all blacks in the Hough ghetto, at a benefit rate pegged to below poverty (73¢ a day after rent) by Ohio law. Black unemployment hovered around 15 percent for those living in these poverty areas, with 58 percent of young males jobless or earning below poverty-level wages. African Americans faced racial discrimination across a host of job sectors; for example, there were only 13 blacks employed in the building trades in Cleveland, an industry that employed 11,500 workers; in 1966, there were only 43 blacks among the 1,350 apprentice trainees in federally sponsored programs.[55]

Violence seemed out of control even before the riots. The Ku Klux Klan and other white racist groups held summer programs in the city. White gangs routinely beat up black youths, and residents on the edge of Hough—black and white alike—took turns keeping armed guard on the rooftops. A cultural center surrounded by the black ghetto had its own police force, while suburban communities passed new antiriot laws and invested in antiriot police equipment.

Virtually all of the businesses in Hough were owned by whites, and absentee white landlords owned many of the homes. Official white indifference toward black suffering and the repressive role of local institutions like the police, the school system, and the welfare agencies pushed black anger to the boiling point.

The local business community also played a role. In the mid-1960s, Cleveland was the home to more Fortune 500 corporations than any other city but New York and Chicago.[56] Its business establishment had a vested interest in improving downtown real estate values and had created the Cleveland Development Foundation (CDF) to front its efforts in guiding the city's federal urban-renewal program. According to veteran Cleveland-based journalist Roldo Bartimole, the CDF was funded with millions of dollars from some eighty corporations and the Cleveland Foundation to eliminate "slum and blight." But the real mission for the corporate leaders on the CDF board was not housing for the poor; it was to make land available for industrial and commercial use and to keep property values in the downtown high.[57] The Locher administration was proving to be an inept manager of urban-renewal funds, clearing land and pushing and crowding the black poor into increasingly deteriorating ghettos, but then stalling the rebuilding process. In the eleven years since the start of urban renewal, Cleveland had failed to complete a single one of its eleven projects, leaving the city stuck with more land under renewal than any other city in the nation. The delays led to the complete decay of the cleared areas, setting off a chain reaction of collapsed investment. Tax revenues dropped, causing the credit rating agencies to downgrade the city, which, in turn, increased interest rates on improvement bonds. After Robert Weaver, Lyndon Johnson's secretary of housing and urban development, canceled some $33 million in federal urban-renewal funds in the pipeline because of local mismanagement, business leaders had had enough. They wanted Locher gone.[58]

Stokes ran his winning race in 1967 as a Democrat. Some important lessons had been learned in his first bid for the mayoralty. First and foremost was the potential power of the black vote and the importance of getting everyone registered and mobilized. An exciting and inspiring candidate could wake up a sleeping giant. Stokes himself later reflected on the meaning of the 1965 race:

> We had taken on an incumbent who had the support of the two newspapers, the local Democratic Party, organized labor and his twelve thousand city employees and we had come within one percent of beating him. As far as I was concerned, we had beaten not only Locher but the whole traditional establishment of political power, [and] in two years we would take it for good.[59]

While the issues raised by the Hatcher and Stokes campaigns were similar[60]—schools, housing, jobs, police brutality—the Stokes race in 1967 cast light on another dynamic that underlay many of the black mayoralty races. The urban riots of the 1960s were prompting powerful elites, including national Democratic politicians, the Ford Foundation, and major business leaders, to work to incorporate blacks in regular local electoral politics. Stokes's campaign also showed once again that black incorporation would be fiercely resisted by the entrenched local Democratic organization.

During the preceding summer, there was a massive voter mobilization as national civil rights organizations came to Cleveland to help organize a voter registration drive. Ohio law required the automatic purging from the registration rolls of any voter who did not vote over a two-year interval. That meant that despite high voter turnout for Stokes in 1965, nearly 30 percent of black registrations had been dropped by the board of elections by the time of the 1967 mayoral race.[61] The board of elections made available to the Locher campaign a list of all purged voters; when Stokes workers asked for the same information they encountered considerable difficulty obtaining it. Moreover, the Stokes campaign was unable to persuade the board to stay open longer hours or hold more "in-ward" registration days in black neighborhoods. The board scheduled only one such day, which meant that any voter who couldn't reregister (or register for the first time) during that day had to take time off from work to travel to board headquarters in downtown Cleveland in order to get on the rolls. Voters who moved within city limits could send a

change-of-address card in through the mail, but the Stokes campaign found that its supporters often never received back a confirmation or any information at all about the location of their polling
place.[62]

The Congress of Racial Equality (CORE) was the lead group
among the outside organizations participating in the registration
drive, its efforts funded by a $175,000 "Target City" grant from the
Ford Foundation.[63] CORE, like the Student Nonviolent Coordinating Committee, was moving away from integrationist politics. Its
more traditional civil rights leadership was replaced in 1966 by
younger advocates of black power. For these reasons, Ford's grant to
CORE was instantly controversial. But Ford also gave $127,000 to a
businessmen's group headed by Jack Reavis, a Jones-Day law partner
and Cleveland civic leader, and $200,000 to the Greater Cleveland
Associated Foundation, a subsidiary of the Cleveland Foundation.
Reavis's group, in turn, gave money to the Reverend Martin Luther
King Jr. to support his work in the black community in Cleveland,
where he turned as his campaign in Chicago faltered. Ford also supported the Southern Christian Leadership Conference directly, with
a grant of $230,000.

Black registration activity and enthusiasm gave Stokes good reason to fear a big white countermobilization. Behind the scenes he actually tried to keep national civil rights groups away from Cleveland
to let things settle down. The Democratic Party's newsletter railed
about the dangers of a Stokes victory: "DICTATORSHIP IN CLEVELAND:
. . . DO YOU WANT MLK [Martin Luther King] AND HIS DISCIPLES
RUNNING YOUR CITY?"[64] Not surprisingly, primary turnout was high,
almost equaling turnout in the general election of 1965. Stokes won
the Democratic nomination by a comfortable margin of 18,700
votes, and the black community celebrated.

To powerful elites, both in Cleveland and nationally, the election
of a big-city black mayor must have seemed necessary after the summer riots of the mid-1960s. Cleveland had been particularly tumultuous, with intermittent rioting since 1961. Stokes was increasingly
looked to by the white establishment as a capable leader, and the one

best able to keep the calm. Business support continued to shift from Locher to Stokes, as did the support from another white power base in local politics, the editorial boards of both of Cleveland's major newspapers, the *Cleveland Plain Dealer* and the *Cleveland Press.* Cleveland businessmen organized a commission that issued a series of reports condemning the conduct of city government, and the press followed up with daily front-page editorials decrying the city administration's performance on a range of issues.[65]

Meanwhile, national elites were also taking sides. At the annual meeting of the Urban League in 1966, McGeorge Bundy, the president of the Ford Foundation, told his audience of well-dressed black and white liberals that if blacks burned cities, "[t]he white man's companies will have to take the losses."[66] Under Bundy's energetic leadership, Ford had made race relations its top priority, and Bundy doubled the amount of money on race-related programs dispensed by the National Affairs Division to nearly $40 million annually by 1968. As riots erupted in Newark, Ford announced its $175,000 grant to Cleveland's CORE office. Journalist Tamar Jacoby writes,

> Bundy explained at a press conference that his board had considered the grant "with particular care." . . . The foundation had chosen Cleveland because it had been particularly hard hit by riots the past summer; Ford's theory was that CORE might channel the ghetto's grievances in a more constructive way, averting further violence in the streets.[67]

The Ford Foundation matched its initial grant to CORE with another $300,000 in 1968.

Cleveland's local Democratic Party, despite the defections of the local business elite, continued to resist the racial succession in political leadership under way. Stokes had broken Democratic Party ranks before over state redistricting that discriminated against black voters in 1964, siding with the Republican governor in order to increase black representation in Cuyahoga County. He also resisted a congressional redistricting plan that nullified the possibility of black congressional representation. The plan had been promoted by the chairman of the county Democratic Party. In the general election that followed Stokes's primary victory, sixteen white Democratic council members refused to endorse him, and so did several black Democratic political leaders. Stokes's opponent in the general election, Seth Taft, a moderate Republican from the Taft family political dynasty who had fired campaign workers for making flagrant racial appeals to whites, nevertheless allowed an inflammatory letter to be sent out on his behalf to 45,000 white ethnic voters. The letter urged support for Taft in order to "protect our way of life and to protect Cleveland. . . . Taft and Taft alone," the letter implored, "can give Cleveland back to the law-abiding citizenry."[68] Urged on, the vast majority of white Democratic voters shifted to the Republican candidate, as they had in Hatcher's race, "many pulling the Republican lever for the first time in their life."[69] Nevertheless, high black turnout gave Stokes the election by just 1,679 votes.[70] A year after he became mayor, Stokes took the lead in a lawsuit against the redistricting plan that reached the U.S. Supreme Court and resulted in the creation of the predominantly black Twenty-first Congressional District. Louis Stokes, Carl's brother, later became the first black congressional representative from the district,[71] and went on to serve for fourteen terms.[72]

The last, telling chapter of the story of the Stokes challenge was played out in the Congress, in "four days of boisterous hearings" on the Tax Reform Act of 1969 before the House Ways and Means Committee.[73] The bill included restrictions on the use of foundation money for voter registration. Clearly, the Ford Foundation's role in the Stokes campaign was very much on the minds of congressional Democrats allied with local Democratic organizations.[74] After the committee voted to approve the bill, Roy Wilkins, the executive director of the NAACP, expressed his concern in a letter to the *New York Times*. Wilkins charged, "Regardless of the language, the proposals before the Congress in the so-called tax reform bill to bar the use of foundation funds for voter registration are principally anti-black." After pointing out how foundation grants had funded voter registration drives that added eight hundred thousand more black voters before the 1968 election, he continued:

Now the Congress proposes to crush the rising participation of Negro voters in the election process under the guise of regulating the foundations. . . . At one stroke prejudice against the Negro franchise, foundations and anyone who endangers the existing political *status quo* by enlarging the number of voters, is satisfied. The record does not mention race, No, sir! It is one of tax reform, of adjusting inequities.[75]

The new legislation governing tax-exempt foundations would make it more difficult for foundations to fund voter registration drives in the future. Now foundations were required to certify that the voter registration activities they funded were not targeted to a particular place or campaign but extended over five or more states; the activities had to be nonpartisan; and no voter registration campaign could receive more than 25 percent of its funding from one tax-exempt organization.[76] All these provisions seem to have been designed to avoid a repeat of the Cleveland success, in which Ford had played a major role.

The succeeding years saw a string of black big-city electoral victories, as African American candidates scoring huge majorities among black voters took over the mayoralty in Newark in 1970, with the election of Kenneth Gibson; in Los Angeles in 1973, with the election of Tom Bradley, and in Detroit with the election of Coleman Young the same year; in Atlanta in 1974, with the election of Maynard Jackson, and in Washington, D.C., the same year with the election of Walter Washington; in Oakland in 1977, with the election of Lionel Wilson; in New Orleans in 1978, with the election of Ernest Morial; in Birmingham in 1979, with the election of Richard Arrington; and in Charlotte, North Carolina, in 1983, with the election of Harvey Gantt. African Americans would go on to ascend to the mayoralty in Baltimore, Denver, Dallas, Philadelphia, Minneapolis, Seattle, and many middle-sized cities as well. As in Gary and Cleveland, the mobilization of black voters could overcome the voter suppression embedded in electoral administration, as well as the stratagems of incumbent politicians.

• • •

Perhaps the most dramatic—and important—of these races was the remarkable 1983 movement to elect Harold Washington as Chicago's first black mayor, which political scientist Paul Kleppner called "a political revolution."[77] The road from Hatcher and Stokes to Washington certainly was not smooth. As the numbers of black elected officials mounted, especially at the state and local levels, seismic shifts were reordering national policy priorities and realigning party coalitions. A lot had happened since the heady days of enthusiasm for black electoral power in the 1960s.

For one, the Republican Party had come to national power in 1968 and, except for the interruption of Watergate, remained dominant in presidential politics. The Southern Strategy was in command. National Democrats floundered. Despite or maybe because of the steady black electoral gains at the state and local levels, the national party began moving away from blacks and the national initiatives with which they were associated. As the Republican electoral strategy to encode the Democrats' once expansive domestic agenda as a form of racial favoritism continued, Democrats lost enthusiasm for integration, urban social programs, affirmative action, and other concessions to blacks.

For a while, local electoral success continued to fuel hopes of blacks that their conditions could be improved through their inclusion in the political system. But as the 1970s came to a close, a decade in which blacks were ignored by both national parties despite multiple crises of rising unemployment, city services, oil shocks, stagflation, labor unrest, and strained public budgets, black enthusiasm for electoral politics ebbed.

The backlash in reaction to black gains seemed to peak with the election of Ronald Reagan in 1980, and as it did, it provoked a revival of black electoral activism, with consequences for the Democrats that are perhaps only now working themselves out.

Harold Washington's 1983 victory in the Chicago mayor's race was an expression of the revived faith in the possibility of black electoral success through movement activism. It made the black poor a force in Chicago, helped launch the national mobilization around the candidacy of Jesse Jackson in 1984, and also was an inspiration for the voter registration campaign discussed in the next chapter. Participation in the campaign to elect Harold Washington was extraordinary by anyone's measure, with black registration rates exceeding white rates by as much as 10 percentage points, and nearly three out of every four black Chicagoans of voting age turning out in the April 1983 election.[78] Studs Terkel called Washington's election "the most astonishing municipal campaign in American history."[79] The unprecedented and broad electoral activity of the black community in Chicago was a long time coming. Martin Luther King's effort in 1965 to bring the southern civil rights movement to Chicago and other ghettos of the North, and to turn the movement to the issues of the urban black poor, sputtered and failed, at least in the view of some of its organizers.[80] The city's long-serving mayor, Richard J. Daley, continued to manage black discontent as he always had, blocking fuller black empowerment through limited incorporation of black elites and patronage.[81]

There were both national and local spurs to the political mobilization behind Washington that began in 1982. Reagan's readiness to use racist appeals to win white votes was signaled by his decision, against the advice of some of his aides, to kick off his bid for the presidency before a nearly all-white crowd at the Neshoba County Fair in Philadelphia, Mississippi—the very place where three young civil rights workers, Andrew Goodman, James Chaney, and Michael Schwerner, had been murdered just sixteen years before. His domestic policies of budget cutbacks and high deficits pushed black unemployment to near Depression-era levels, cut off opportunities for public-sector employment, and slashed social programs for the poor. Political scientist Steven P. Erie observed about this period, "In Chicago, welfare-state contraction . . . fueled the black revolt."[82]

National black political leaders quickly recognized the significance of the Washington contest. Members of the Congressional Black Caucus (CBC) like Harold Ford, Ron Dellums, and Shirley Chisholm pressed a reluctant national Democratic Party to support Washington. John Conyers brought his leading organizers to Chicago, spent three weeks there assisting Washington's campaign, and helped with election day operations during both the primary and general elections. Other caucus members raised money for Washington—at least a quarter of the $3 million Washington spent in the general election was raised from national sources with CBC members serving as conduits for the funds. In this way, Washington's campaign "was 'nationalized,' with troubling implications for much of the national Democratic Party leadership."[83]

The local spur to Harold Washington's election was a growing recognition among Chicago blacks of the limits of "plantation-style" machine politics. Scholars have described black political participation in Chicago from the emergence of the party machine in the 1930s until Washington's victory as characterized by patron-client relationships.[84] Black leaders were chosen by the party bosses, rewarded with patronage, and expected to maintain black electoral support for machine candidates.[85] Richard J. Daley's first election in 1955 accomplished a political consolidation of the vote in the city's black wards, with blacks giving an unprecedented 72 percent of their votes to the new boss. "[U]nder Daley," writes William Grimshaw, "the black wards became so firmly Democratic they began serving as the machine's principal electoral stronghold, displacing the poor white ethnic wards that had fulfilled the role since the machine's inception in 1931."[86]

The Daley machine incorporated blacks in ways that institutionalized their subordination. Daley boasted about what "the organization" did for blacks, with appointments to the Chicago Housing Authority (CHA), school boards, and city jobs. His principal lieutenant in the black wards and the most powerful black politician during Daley's heyday (until his death in 1970) was William Dawson, who had been elected to Congress in 1942. "Where else," Dawson asked, "but in the Democratic organization could a black man, whose ancestors were slaves, rise so high?"[87] But while Dawson and Daley's other black ward heelers did well, the mass of Chicago's blacks got little from the machine. Daley had long supported white interests over his black constituents, and signaled his support through both his rhetoric and his policy agenda. In 1963, for example, he refused even to acknowledge the possibility of black misery on his watch, announcing in a speech before the NAACP that "there are no ghettos in Chicago."[88] Nevertheless, facing a tough reelection fight that year, Daley received overwhelming support from "captive" black voters. He won his largest plurality in the black Third Ward, and, according to Grimshaw, "the black wards very likely saved Mayor Daley from defeat."[89]

Black loyalty to the Daley machine began to waver with the turbulence of the 1960s and the growing articulation of black identity and demands. The turmoil of the 1960s also heightened the racial divide between blacks demanding better treatment and white ethnics who steadfastly resisted any change in the racial order. Before that time, the machine formula for victory involved running competitive races in white areas to split the vote and drain off support for machine challengers, while piling up huge majorities in the black wards. As late as 1967, Daley was confident enough of his grip on power and his ability to accommodate black demands that he publicly praised the election of Richard Hatcher and Carl Stokes as great victories for the Democratic Party and for the nation.[90] By the early 1970s, however, his formula no longer worked. Increasingly less satisfied with their second-class citizenship status and frustrated with the failure of electoral politics to change their conditions, many blacks either dropped out of the electorate or began voting against machine candidates.[91] Black machine leaders were losing control of black voters, especially following the police raid on the headquarters of the Black Panther Party in 1969 that resulted in the brutal murder of Panther leaders Fred Hampton and Mark Clark.

To blacks in Chicago and elsewhere, the unprovoked violence of the Panther raid symbolized the daily violence many associated with the human warehouses that were the Robert Taylor Homes, or the crime-ridden streets of the black ghettos, or what had become some of the worst overcrowded schools in urban America. The Daley organization adapted, shifting from working to sustain majorities in the black wards to consolidating support in white ethnic areas, where it fanned racial animosities to mobilize white voters. It developed Chicago's own version of the Southern Strategy. In 1971, for the first time in Daley's long career, a machine candidate won with wider margins in the white ethnic wards than in the black wards.[92]

Just four years later, however, the first effort to run an independent black Democrat against the machine attracted practically no support. In fact, most blacks again didn't bother to vote, and Daley won a majority among those who did. The election was instructive; it showed that the white vote could be consolidated by pushing troublesome, disruptive blacks even further to the margins of the machine's electoral coalition. As black voters withdrew, they also diminished the ability of black committeemen to deliver votes to the machine, and a cycle of demobilization and declining influence ensued. The growing disorganization of the black vote caused the traditional relationships between black machine lieutenants and the organization to corrode: "Whites in power," observed a respected campaign strategist at the time, "can basically write off the black vote. They don't need it, they don't want it. In fact, they snicker about black committeemen not being able to deliver the vote from their wards.[93]

Thus, by 1975, blacks were increasingly isolated politically in Chicago—as elected officials, party workers, and voters. The demobilization of black voters was matched by the mobilization of whites, as defecting blacks were replaced in the machine coalition by a new solidarity and involvement of once divided white ethnic groups. The Daley machine now relied first and foremost on high mobilization and cohesive support from the white ethnic areas it had once sought to split. Then, after twenty-one years in power, Daley died in office and another effort to run a black independent against the machine was launched.

The candidate was Harold Washington, a state legislator who had gotten his start in politics when he took over his father's responsibilities as a Daley machine precinct captain for the Third Ward. Washington was not a typical precinct captain. He was an air force veteran with a Northwestern law degree. His pride often got the best of him and he made trouble by confronting whites who insulted him. He was valuable to the machine because he delivered the vote, but he also organized an independent base of support among the young

Table 4

Percentage of Voting-Age Population Supporting Daley, 1963–1975

	1963 General	1967 General	1971 General	1975 Primary
Black Wards*	37.5	36.6	30.0	16.3
Dawson Five**	38.6	36.0	29.8	19.1
South Side	27.4	31.4	27.2	14.7
West Side	47.6	38.8	35.1	17.6
White Ethnic	28.0	39.2	43.2	30.6
Northwest Side	24.0	34.0	39.0	24.1
South Side	31.7	44.3	47.3	37.3
Total for Daley Citywide	29.8	37.6	35.1	22.1
Total Turnout Citywide	**53.5**	**51.5**	**50.1**	**38.3**

* Black-majority wards: 1963 and 1967, N=9; 1971, N=15; 1975, N=19
** "Dawson Five" refers to the 2nd, 3rd, 4th, 5th, and 6th wards, controlled by William Dawson.
SOURCE: Adapted from Paul Kleppner, *Chicago Divided: The Making of a Black Mayor* (Dekalb, IL: Northern Illinois University, 1985), 75.

people he recruited for the Third Ward's Young Democrats, and earlier in his career he expressed his restlessness with his city job by sometimes failing to show up for it. Ralph Metcalfe, whom Daley had been grooming as a counterforce to keep William Dawson in line, was Washington's immediate boss in the organization. Washington's actions began to make trouble for Metcalfe, so he arranged for Washington to move downstate to Springfield to replace a retiring state representative.[94]

As a precinct captain, Washington had been uncomfortable collecting IOUs from poor people and enforcing loyalty, and in the legislature, the "idiot cards" distributed by party bosses instructing their representatives how to vote only insulted his intelligence. As Washington's stock with the Chicago machine began to slide, his reputation as a tough and innovative legislator grew. He was the principal author of a number of important pieces of legislation that curtailed business exploitation in the black community; made January 15 a holiday in Illinois in honor of Dr. Martin Luther King Jr.; improved the ability of black-owned businesses to compete for state contracts; and in the face of a state fiscal crisis, saved Provident Hospital, an historic black institution in Chicago.[95] But despite both Washington's former connections to the Daley machine and his growing reputation as a progressive maverick in the state legislature, his 1977 candidacy garnered only 11 percent of the citywide vote.

Black voter defections from the machine continued and accelerated in the late 1970s. More than any other ethnic group in Chicago, blacks began giving a larger and larger share of their votes to antimachine candidates. As political scientist Michael Preston notes, "Black voters were becoming increasingly more unloyal [sic], unpredictable, uncontrollable, and undeliverable. They were now more aware than ever that blacks had the power to defeat unresponsive candidates."[96]

By the summer of 1981, black civic leaders, ministers, and community organizers had decided the time was ripe to set aside their differences and try to change politics in Chicago at the ballot box. Meetings, conferences, and campaigns "to raise the level of awareness of black people about electoral politics" intensified over the next year, and by early 1982, independent political groups had organized a broad coalition to challenge machine domination of the Democratic mayoral nomination process.[97]

The welfare state was at the heart of the black voter mobilization campaign in Chicago and indeed throughout the nation, as we will show in the next chapter.[98] Between 1981 and 1982, the federal government, and then the Illinois state legislature and the Chicago City Council, all cut back social programs for the poor, aged, and disabled. In August 1981, Congress reduced food stamp, housing, and welfare benefits; the following month, the state legislature, partly in response to the federal cutbacks, reduced general assistance payments and tightened Medicaid eligibility rules for children and seniors; and then in March, the Chicago City Council failed to fund emergency shelters and reduced funding to food pantries.[99]

Black activists saw the cutbacks as creating the basis for an appeal to new voters by raising the issues that mattered most. To do this, restrictions on access to voter registration needed to be overcome, and a campaign unfolded to do that. State law gave the Chicago Board of Election Commissioners complete discretion over voter registration. The board required registrants to apply in person at its office during normal business hours or, through a program of "special registration" begun in 1973, at sites it designated in local communities. For example, the board operated a registration program at certain public libraries. But many community residents were unaware of these and other opportunities to register off-site. Only board staff were permitted to serve as registrars, an arrangement that obviously impeded voter registration efforts by community-based organizations.

An interracial coalition of sixteen civil rights, welfare rights, and community groups called People Organized for Welfare and Employment Rights (POWER) formed to coordinate the drive. One of the first things POWER did was enter into negotiations and then litigation to force the state and the Board of Election Commissioners to use its discretion to establish voter registration programs at thirty-five Chicago offices of the Illinois Department of Public Aid and the Illinois Department of Labor. Organizers believed that the best places to register constituencies supportive of a campaign against welfare cuts were the unemployment and public aid offices. State officials responded by forbidding voter registration in the waiting rooms of either welfare or unemployment offices, claiming it might "disrupt business at the offices . . . or lead applicants and recipients to believe that registration was a condition to receiving benefits." [100] POWER sued in federal court, not once but twice, to gain access. [101] In its first registration campaign, in August and September 1982, POWER helped register more than 42,000 people, or over 10,000 people waiting on welfare and unemployment lines each week. The initiative contributed to the most successful special registration effort in the city's history. [102]

A second major registration drive was undertaken by Renault Robinson and Edward Gardner, a leading black businessman and the president of Soft Sheen Products Inc., a black-owned hair care products company. Robinson and Gardner drew on traditional leadership groups in the business community, church congregations, the Chicago Urban League, and Operation PUSH to form an umbrella organization, VOTE (Voice of the Ethnic) Community, to coordinate the drive. Where POWER sent volunteers to welfare and unemployment lines to recruit voters and tied registration to movement activism, VOTE Community focused its message on a call to flood the board with new applications on October 5, 1982, the closing date for voter registration. On closing day the board conducted a special registration program at the city's more than three thousand local polling places. VOTE Community used the date as a call to action, encouraging prospective black voters to "Come Alive, October Five—Register to Vote!"

Minority neighborhoods with the lowest levels of registered voters were saturated with posters and printed material, and Soft Sheen's marketing staff developed media spots to target younger African Americans, spending about $200,000 to run ads featuring rap music and celebrities on major black radio stations. The campaign was a success: at least 135,000 registered to vote during the last day of precinct registration before the November 2, 1982, election. Two and a half months later, another 120,000 signed up on the last day before the mayoral primary, with most of the new registrants coming from the north Lake Shore area and the black wards.[103] New registrants swelled by about 50 percent over any previous mayoral primary.

Kleppner has shown that until the 1980s, black registration and turnout rates in Chicago lagged behind white rates. Then, between 1979 and the November general election in 1982, black registration increased by over 127,000, bringing the total number of black registrants to over 647,000 before the 1982 general election. Analysts also credit the drives, which targeted low-income blacks, for changing the composition of the black electorate. Before the drives got under way, one in five registered blacks in the city reported an annual income of less than $7,500; after the drives the ratio had changed to one in three.[104] According to a February 1982 exit poll, gains in black registration were concentrated among those under the age of thirty-five and those with the lowest levels of income (below $7,500 a year). In

Table 5

Black Registration and Turnout in Chicago, 1975–1983

	Registration		Turnout	
	White	Black	White	Black
Primary 1975	81.1	70.9	48.5	34.1
Primary 1977	84.5	77.9	44.8	27.4
Primary 1979	77.4	69.4	48.9	34.5
General 1982	78.3	86.7	54.0	55.8
Primary 1983	82.2	87.2	64.6	64.2
General 1983	83.2	89.1	67.2	73.0

SOURCE: Adapted from Kleppner, *Chicago Divided*, 149. Registration and turn-out rates are reported as percentages of the voting-age population, and are derived by weighting estimates for each group in eight subareas of the city.

contrast, white registration lagged between 1979 and 1982, showing a net gain of only 1,656. The prospect of a black mayoral candidate, however, did spur a white countermobilization, and white registration increased between November 1982 and April 1983 by 52,000 (see table 5).[105]

The potential for electoral change by social movement activism was evident in the surprise outcome of the 1982 Illinois gubernatorial race. Incumbent Republican governor Jim Thompson was challenged by Democrat Adlai Stevenson III.[106] Thompson was predicted to win by over a million votes. He did win, but by less than 1 percent or fewer than 5,000 votes statewide, due in part to the solid turnout in favor of Stevenson among African Americans in Chicago. Three-quarters of Stevenson's 467,000-vote plurality over Thompson in the Democratic-controlled city was accounted for by the cohesive black vote. In the black wards where African Americans made up at least 90 percent of the population, Stevenson garnered 85 to 90 percent of the vote.[107] Postelection analysts missed the full significance of black bloc voting and attributed the rejection of Thompson to simply a reaction to Reaganism. This was only half the answer. Chicago ward bosses didn't understand the change that was afoot either, wrongly assuming that the large black voter turnout was evidence of loyalty to the machine.[108] Local movement activists understood better what was going on. Said Lu Palmer, "black people were practicing up for February 22nd,"[109] the date of the impending mayoral primary. The strength and size of the black vote in Chicago underscored the viability of a black candidacy in the 1983 mayor's race.

Harold Washington was drafted by the movement and its neighborhood supporters in a deliberate effort to flout machine practices.[110] "Slating" or nominating candidates had always been the sole province of the machine, and a principal means by which the party maintained control of the electoral process. As one admirer put it, "political slatemaking in Chicago is a throwback to the days when politics required guts, nerve, and wit instead of media advisers and computers."[111] Ward committeemen gathered, usually in the basement of a big hotel, to hammer out the party's endorsements. Over the years, black committeemen may have had some influence, but their choices had to pass muster with the white ward bosses who controlled the machine. The movement to draft a black mayoral candidate was a rebellion against the time-worn practice by which blacks had their leaders chosen for them by white machine bosses. Moreover, as Twiley Barker notes, "these 'cleansing' actions for self-determination illustrated the growing vulnerability of the Democratic machine in the black community."[112]

Washington, however, was reluctant to enter the race. He upped the ante and said he would not run unless fifty thousand more voters were added to the rolls. The movement to draft a candidate had to become a movement to register voters. By September 1982, the original fifty thousand goal had been reached, but Washington still wasn't satisfied and told his supporters he wanted more. His concerns reflected his experience in the 1977 primary, when only 27 percent of age-eligible blacks voted and Washington came in a dismal third. While he probably had made up his mind to run for mayor before the November 1982 general election, Washington waited until he was sure that there would be two white candidates in the race. When Richard M. Daley, the "Boss's" son, stepped forward to run against incumbent mayor Jane Byrne, Washington announced his candidacy.

Once the race was joined, Byrne treated Daley as her main competitor. The Cook County Democratic organization was split between the two, so Byrne, following the advice of some of her campaign consultants, who helped make the 1983 mayor's race the most expensive in Chicago's history, blitzed the media with a slick ad campaign that immediately put Daley on the defensive. The wheel turned in the final days of the campaign, however, when the two major daily newspapers endorsed Daley, spurring him to the attack. Byrne complained she was being picked on because she was a woman. "But it was the race issue," writes Paul Green, "and the fear of a Washington victory that energized Byrne's campaign in the final days." [113] As Washington surged in the polls, Byrne ally Cook County Democratic Party chair Ed Vrdolyak told supporters at a rally on the Northwest Side that "a vote for Daley is a vote for Washington," and that the campaign had become "a racial thing. . . . I'm calling on you to save your city, to save your precinct," he implored; "we're fighting to keep the city the way it is." [114] On the weekend before the election, thousands of voters received phone calls urging them not to throw their votes away on Daley, but to support Byrne "as the best hope of keeping Washington out of City Hall." [115]

Washington's campaign was a stinging rebuke to the machine's business as usual, and it isolated black ward bosses who refused to see the writing on the wall. As Abdul Alkalimat and Doug Gills describe it, in the black neighborhoods,

> Working people held hands with the unemployed and the impoverished across racial lines. The church support was reminiscent of the energy of the 1960s, a period when the politically "dead" rose up. And there were many Lazarus-like winos and street people in the campaign who put on ties, picked up notebooks, pens, and pencils—not merely to vote, but to advocate that others do so also. Women's groups united under the Women's Network in Support of Harold Washington, where

middle-class highbrows joined hands with welfare recipients. Youth joined together with senior citizens who had passed on the baton of active struggle to those younger. The elderly, many of whom had been trapped in their high-rises for years in fear, walked in defiance (of the gangs) to "punch 9" and await the unfolding of their wildest dreams—a Black mayor in their lifetimes.[116]

Not surprisingly, eighteen black state legislators and nine black aldermen loyal to the machine opposed Washington. Yet, with little money and poor organization, he managed to eke out a stunning upset victory that shocked political observers, pundits, and a good many of the white citizens of Chicago.

Byrne's electoral strategy of raising the specter of a black victory to win her battle with Daley was a gross miscalculation. In the closing days of the campaign, Byrne's machine allies worked overtime, "cranking out scare letters and brochures" that were dropped into the white Northwest and Southwest Side wards.[117] One leaflet from the "Concerned Citizens of the Neighborhood" claimed Washington would break up white communities, and to prevent that, voters should "Vote No. 10" (Byrne's ballot line); in certain neighborhoods machine precinct captains distributed photographs of Jesse Jackson, claiming he would be the real mayor if Washington were to be elected. A letter circulated to thousands of predominantly white homes on the Northwest Side from former Republican governor Richard Ogilvie endorsing Byrne made the rounds. "Although you and I are loyal Republicans," wrote Ogilvie, "I am asking you personally to join me in voting in the Democratic primary to re-elect Jane Byrne as mayor of Chicago."[118] In the "race neutral" language of race-baiting elites, Ogilvie warned that the contest had now narrowed to a choice between Byrne and Washington. He needn't have said more.

Byrne hadn't worried about maintaining support among lower-income blacks, whose loyalty to the machine had been proven before. She also had seemed to want to lure into the race a black candidate who she hoped would prevent dissatisfied blacks from voting for Daley.[119] Her enemy was the young Daley, who she believed was out to destroy her for assuming his family's mantle.[120] Her preoccupation caused her to give less attention to Harold Washington and the tsunami of energized black voters coming at her until the last days of the campaign. By that time, it was too late. Washington defeated Byrne and Daley in the Democratic primary by winning 36 percent of the total vote in the three-way race. He received fully 85 percent of the black vote, and because few whites or Latinos voted for him, blacks made up 92 percent of his citywide total. One post-election analysis later found that Washington could have won the election without a single white vote.[121] An exit poll showed that 56 percent of blacks who said they voted for Washington also said they had registered to vote in the last year, underscoring the importance of the registration drives. The split in the white vote made his victory possible, but so did the expansion of the black vote brought about by the assertive political mobilization of the black community. As Kleppner notes, "Developing this sense of solidarity, of racial pride, and channeling it into electoral politics was the accomplishment of the primary campaign and the major reason for Washington's victory."[122]

As the Democratic Party's nominee, Harold Washington fully expected the local party's support and a general election victory. A Republican hadn't come close to winning a mayoral election in half a century. "Normally," write Alkalimat and Gills, in Chicago, "a Republican candidate for mayor must be 'accosted at gun point' and forced to run."[123] Washington was so confident of victory in the April general election, he immediately began to assemble his transition team. But there were early warning signs of what was to come. Late on election night, Jane Byrne addressed her supporters. Listeners expected a concession speech but they got instead instructions to go to bed and wait for the results in the morning. Washington was worried. "Lord," he was heard to grumble. "Those barracudas are going to steal us blind."[124]

By 2 A.M. it was over and it was Washington's turn to speak. In the early-morning hours of his primary victory, he addressed a deliriously happy crowd of some thirty thousand supporters waiting for him at the McCormick Inn. They weren't patient, because they knew that history was being made; they stomped their feet and chanted, "We want Harold! We want Harold!" exploding in pandemonium when Washington finally appeared and told them, "You want Harold? Well, you got him!" In a conciliatory tone directed especially at whites who had not voted for him, he "proudly and humbly" accepted the Democratic Party's nomination for mayor. "Our concern," he said, "is to build. Our concern is to heal. Our concern is to bring together. . . . I want to reach out my hand in friendship to every living soul in this city." [125] But, as Kleppner writes, "while Washington was delivering his message of unity and conciliation, strange things were going on in the precincts." [126] Within days, whites began flocking to Washington's Republican rival, an obscure former state legislator named Bernard Epton.

Epton had barely run a primary campaign. All but $1,000 of the $41,000 he raised came from his family or his own funds, and his daughter served as his campaign manager. Epton owed his fourteen years in the state legislature to the state's cumulative voting/multi-member districting rules for state legislative representation. He was such a nonentity that even after becoming the Republican Party's mayoral standard-bearer, he sat at the back of the room in the dark during a Reagan visit to Chicago because neither Reagan nor anyone else knew who he was. Epton had complained bitterly throughout the primary campaign that the well-connected Republican Donald Rumsfeld, who lived just north of Chicago, refused to return his calls. And yet, two days after the primary, a meeting between the two was hastily arranged, followed by hundreds of thousands of dollars for Epton from the national Republican Party. [127] So many people suddenly wanted to volunteer for Epton that his small staff had trouble keeping track of them, and the campaign was forced to open more than ten times as many satellite offices across the city than had been planned.

Within days of the primary, Committeeman Ed Kelly of the North Side Forty-seventh Ward was out trying to organize other Democratic Party committeemen for Epton. Vito Marzullo of the Twenty-fifth Ward, an old-line machine politician who referred to his Mexican American opponents as "wetbacks," was an early defector, as was Aloysius Majerczyk of the Southwest Side Twelfth Ward, a policeman who explained his decision to back Epton as based not on race, but on the need for "law and order." Party boss Ed Vrdolyak hailed from a racially conservative white ethnic enclave on the East Side that had been the scene of rioting and marches when Martin Luther King came to Chicago. He'd first won election as a ward committeeman in 1968 by suing the city to stop a busing plan in his neighborhood. Going against the party's nominee was nothing new; he'd supported Richard Nixon in 1972 over George McGovern. Now, however, he gritted his teeth and gave a hollow endorsement to Washington—but his precinct captains were already openly organizing and raising money for Epton.

"The question isn't Epton," explained one Democratic Party insider. "Everyone's for Epton. The question is whether it helps or hurts Epton for [white committeemen] to come out and openly say so." [128] It was a full month before the machine organization reluctantly endorsed Washington. By that time, several more Democratic alderman had thrown their weight behind Epton, saying that they were doing it for their constituents who were "afraid of scattered-site housing" and "concerned about the stability" of the neighborhood. When chairman Vrdolyak called an endorsement meeting of the Cook County Democratic Central Committee on March 24, ten committeemen stayed home and another twelve sent representatives. Vrdolyak, seeking to spare them the embarrassment of failing to show, was forced to call an unprecedented voice vote to endorse the man who had won the Democratic primary. [129] Ultimately, only six of fifty Democratic Party ward committeemen would support Washington, eight openly opposed him, and the rest, like the chairman, quietly aided the Epton campaign without ever formally endorsing him. Vrdolyak even surreptitiously funneled money into a rump organization in the Twenty-sixth Ward that was originally created by an aide, Tony Rocque, to help Jane Byrne in the primary, but was now working for Epton. [130] This is not the way a party is supposed to behave.

The machine's treachery was laced with the racism of white resentment that exploded in the neighborhoods over the seven weeks of the campaign. But there was more behind what its leaders did and why they did it than that. Washington ran as a reform candidate. He campaigned on a pledge to end the party's control over city government patronage. Later, he pledged to issue an executive order to dismantle the patronage system. "It's got to end," he said of the old way of doing business in Chicago. "It's costly. It's wasteful. It's a shutout mechanism that keeps people out of government rather than bringing them in."[131] This did not endear him to the men maneuvering for positions of power and control in the wake of Daley's demise. Washington, with his history of prior support for the organization—as late as 1975, he'd supported Daley's reelection over Richard Newhouse, a black challenger for the nomination—thought, nevertheless, that the party would lick its wounds and get behind his candidacy. He would talk to party officials and ask for their support, but, he told reporters, "There will be no deals made relative to that accommodation."[132]

To the machine stalwarts, Epton had appeal. With an unknown Republican in office, they, and not he, would rule. Unlike Washington, Epton had no support in the city council and no real constituency in the neighborhoods. Without the machine he could not govern. "I think people should realize that this isn't really a battle between Washington and Epton," one Democratic state legislator told the press. "It's a battle between Washington and Eddie Vrdolyak. Epton would be just a figurehead if elected."[133]

The defection of the aldermen and the slow and halfhearted endorsement of Washington by the machine organization sent a very public message that it was not only legitimate but even proper to abandon the party's nominee. Epton wasted no time urging white Chicagoans to support his bid. With the euphoric afterglow of Washington's primary victory still lingering over the city's black wards, Epton's handlers ignored the problem of his anonymity and instead mounted a bold assault on Washington's moral fiber. The goal was to make Washington the center of the fight, and to discredit him using hardball tactics like media revelation and character assassination, playing heavily on ugly stereotypes of racial inferiority and criminality. Epton's white supporters, most of them lifelong Democrats, only urged him on, attending his rallies in droves, cheering him wherever he went.

One of the ugliest scenes from the campaign occurred when Walter Mondale flew to Chicago to campaign on Washington's behalf. The two had been invited to attend services at St. Pascal's Roman Catholic Church on the far Northwest Side (Epton, too, had been invited but declined to attend). It was Palm Sunday. When they arrived they were greeted with the words "NIGGER DIE" freshly spray painted across the church doors. An angry white mob of about two hundred people, "faces red hot with hate," blocked their entry and chanted for Epton, hurling racial epithets at Washington.[134] Epton had made Harold Washington's race the issue, and his supporters only fed the growing hysteria in the white community at the thought that a black man might be their next mayor.

To hammer home his message, Epton's media consultants designed a campaign slogan that summed it all up: "Epton for Mayor— Before It's Too Late!" Ambiguous double meanings allowed people to read race while the messenger could claim the message was only about impending fiscal doom facing the city. This was Epton taking the high road, while his supporters were taking the low road in the wards, distributing more racist literature and appeals to "stop the nigger."[135] One leaflet said that if Washington were to be elected, elevators would be removed from city hall because *they* prefer swinging from cables. Another, simulating a job application for employment in a Harold Washington administration, listed the following questions: "Check machine you can operate: Crow Bar? Pinball? Straight Razor? Auto: Financed? Stolen? If financed, repossession date?" One notorious handbill contained a drawing of an imaginary insignia for the Chicago Police Department under Washington's rule. It was labeled "Chicongo Pol-lease;" at the center of the insignia were a pair of lips, a slice of watermelon, a can of beer, and a slab of ribs. The handbill suggested that Washington planned to hire comedian Richard Pryor as police chief.[136] Fears in the white community about a black mayor running the police department ran deep. Jane Byrne's police chief, Richard Brzeczek, only encouraged these damaging racial fantasies when he declared, "I won't work a day for that man.

Under Harold Washington I guarantee that it [the department] will be a circus. Law enforcement will suffer. The general level of competence will go down."[137] For his part, Epton said he deplored the racist flyers and buttons, the signs and T-shirts proclaiming "Vote White, Vote Right." After all, with so many supporters, he couldn't be held responsible for all of his volunteers.[138]

News accounts described the Washington campaign as highly disorganized and riven by internal dissension. Washington stumbled as the barrage of personal assaults on his race and character continued to build distrust among white Lake Shore liberals and inflame cruder forms of racist reaction in white ethnic neighborhoods. A handbill appeared claiming that the *Chicago Tribune* was sitting on a story that proved Washington was a child molester. A leaflet later tied to the rump organization in the Twenty-sixth Ward funded by Vrdolyak and peddled by his aides to the media urged people to call the *Tribune* and demand the story be published. Instead, after much hand-wringing, the paper published a story about the leaflet and about how they had not been able to corroborate the rumor about Washington.[139]

Washington fought back hard and in fighting back probably shifted enough votes his way in the white Lake Shore wards in the closing days of the campaign to seal his victory. Grabbing the Vrdolyak-sponsored flyer, he told a stunned audience at one Lake Shore campaign event:

> This particular piece of literature happens to describe me as a child molester. Here I am running a campaign in which little children all over my community are ecstatic . . . telling their mothers to vote for me. . . . Why am I the victim of this scurrilous, incessant low life kind of attack? Well, I've had enough. . . . I say to you, Mr. Epton: Do you want this job so badly. . . . Are you so singularly minded that you would try to destroy character? . . . If these are the kinds of dogs of racism and scurrilousness you are going to unleash, I say to you, Mr. Epton, I will fight you day and night.[140]

When it was all over, Washington's pollster told the press that at that moment, Washington "snatched victory from the jaws of defeat." [141] Just five days before, with the Lake Shore wards hemorrhaging white supporters, Washington was on his way to becoming the first Democrat to lose a mayoral election since 1927. Now, on the attack, and with many white liberals becoming disgusted with the blatant racism of the Epton/Vrdolyak campaign, Washington held on.

On election day, well over a million Chicagoans packed their polling sites. Gary Rivlin reports that "long lines had already formed before the polls opened in black precincts around the city. An election judge at one south side precinct called the Board of Elections in mid-afternoon to ask if they should close their doors: every registered voter had already cast a ballot." [142] At 73 percent, black turnout exceeded white turnout by 5.8 percentage points. Latinos, who had not supported Washington in the primary, and whose turnout overall remained low, massively shifted into his column in the general election, voting for Washington by just under three to one. Whites, on the other hand, gave Washington only 12 percent of their votes (Kleppner estimates this totaled about 78,518 votes), though support among white liberals in the Lake Shore wards was twice the size of Washington's white citywide level. Turnout in the white ethnic wards of the Northwest and South sides was higher than the citywide white average and more cohesively targeted in support of Epton.

Washington won Chicago's closest mayoral election since 1919 by just 48,250 votes out of 1.29 million cast. Although Epton carried six more wards than Washington, and turnout was high in the white ethnic wards of the Northwest and South sides, Epton's supporters could not overcome record turnout in the black wards and unified African American support for Washington. Indeed, in ten of the black wards among the twenty-two wards Washington won, he received 99 percent of the vote, and no demographic subgroup among African Americans gave Washington less than 95 percent of their votes. Epton's Southern Strategy–style campaign contributed to his own undoing. His race-baiting made it quite easy for hundreds of thousands of white ethnic Democrats to vote for a Jewish Republican.[143] But it had another effect: Epton's Southern Strategy helped undecided blacks make up their minds. And as Kleppner points out, "blacks woke up, turned out, and voted cohesively for Harold Washington. Their behavior was not a tribute to the activity of precinct captains or campaign volunteers. . . . their behavior was a sign of a political enthusiasm that swept through the black community, producing strong feelings of support for Washington among an incredible 84.3 percent of the black voters on election day."[144]

After Washington's victory, blacks would go on to win leadership of still more cities. Still, as with earlier urban victories, the promise of black power that fueled electoral enthusiasm was undermined by ongoing economic and demographic shifts. The big cities where blacks were concentrated struggled with the repercussions of the shifts of population and investment to the suburbs and the Sunbelt, shifts which not only reduced the resources of city governments and their ability to cope with the needs of their poorer populations but also weakened them in national politics. For a while, the cities had stayed afloat with the help of increasing federal aid. But after the ascendance of law-and-order politics and the Republican capture of the White House, federal programs for the big cities shrank, and federal dollars were redirected to Republican districts.

Moreover, Washington's campaign and the electoral awakening of Chicago's black community widened cracks in the fraying New Deal Democratic coalition. The voter mobilization in Chicago was followed quickly by the campaign of Jesse Jackson and his inspirational Rainbow Coalition in the Democratic presidential primaries of 1984 and 1988. To the liberal wing of the Democratic Party, Washington's victory and the subsequent rise of Jesse Jackson showed blacks stirring to the strength of their numbers. To the extent that black electoral organizing stayed inside the Democratic Party, some in the party were willing to reap the benefit. "Washington's victory has sent a tremendous signal to blacks in the country that participation can make a difference," said Ann Miller, political director of the Democratic National Committee. "It will have more of an impact on voting than any informational campaign or promotional gimmick could ever have."[145]

But it was not so simple. In the wake of rising conflict, urban riots, and an increasingly assertive black urban constituency, national Democratic leaders were conflicted. Opposition was building among groups in the Democratic coalition. Kleppner writes, "[T]he political strategists of both parties re-estimated the value of mobilizing black voters at the cost of antagonizing large numbers of whites. Under conditions of strong racial polarization, the black vote ceased to be a political asset."[146] In sum, Washington's stunning victory in Chicago spotlighted the new urban black vote and the possibilities it offered for reinvigorating the Democratic Party as a party of liberals, progressive elements of the labor movement, and blacks. The possibility cheered some Democrats. But it left more-conservative party stalwarts anxiously wondering where the party was going. The continuation of black political mobilization was to depend more on activist groups outside the party, who took inspiration from the Washington victory to launch a national campaign to transform American politics by registering millions of new voters, especially poor and minority voters. In the course of the effort, they found themselves entangled in the obstructions of the American voter registration system and the partisan politicians who defended it. In the end, reforming the system became their goal.

4

PARTY RESISTANCE TO NATIONAL
VOTER REGISTRATION REFORM

Numerous studies have concluded that . . . low levels of voter participation [in the United States], which are at the bottom in comparison with the world's other major democratic nations, are the result, in part, of the country's needlessly complex state-by-state system which places the burden of registration on the voter. The studies also conclude that burdensome registration procedures have a disproportionate impact on minorities and the poor. . . . Universal voter registration . . . is an idea whose time has come and will continue to be a civil rights priority.

—Laughlin McDonald, 1989[1]

The next phase in the struggle for black voting rights culminated in what appeared to be a victory, a national reform of voter registration procedures. However, after the jubilation subsided, the victory was badly tarnished, as key provisions in the law were not implemented, even while other provisions were actually used to justify new efforts at suppressing black votes.

The black electoral mobilization after 1960 had been remarkable, both in the numbers of voters mobilized and in the solidity of their voting patterns. Contrary to the received wisdom, this was not mainly the result of the mobilization efforts of either of the major political parties. Rather, it was the civil rights movement and its aftershocks in the big cities that had inspired and galvanized black voters. And once blacks became an electoral bloc, that fact became important in molding the campaign strategies of both parties, leading to new efforts at voter suppression. To appreciate this development, we have to pay attention to the rules and practices of voter

registration, which became the focus of the movement for black voting rights in the 1980s.

The American system of voter registration is usually taken for
granted, almost as if it were a feature of the natural environment.
After all, except in the small towns of yore, where everyone knew
everyone, how can an election proceed without a method for certifying who is eligible to vote in an election district? And in fact, election
officials do need such a method. The traditional American way has
been to require voters to establish their eligibility by registering with
election officials well before an election. Those officials produce lists
of eligible voters who are then allowed to cast a ballot on election day.

Certifying the eligibility of voters is reasonable. However, the
American system of doing this through a personal and periodic
rather than universal and permanent registration system is not so
reasonable. It requires an unjustifiable extra effort by voters, for one
thing. For another, administrative requirements are inherently sus-
ceptible to political manipulation, and the voter registration process
is a prime example. Voter registration sites can be made difficult to
access, available only during working hours or at distant locations, or
staffed by persons hostile to some prospective voters and not to others. The historical record is littered with such examples of how voter
registration can be and has been easily made into an instrument of
vote suppression, as our account of the difficulties encountered by
the 1984 effort to reform registration will show.

Moreover, the history of American voter registration makes clear
that the proponents of such requirements typically were trying
specifically to make voting more difficult for certain groups. When
Pennsylvania ratified its very first registration law in 1836, which applied only to the city of Philadelphia, supporters claimed it was
needed to prevent what they alleged were "gross election frauds" pre-
vailing in the city. Opponents assailed the measure as a partisan
move aimed at reducing the Philadelphia vote, and especially the
votes of workingmen. (This was the case even though this early law,
which required the city assessors to compile a list of qualified voters,
was far more accommodating to voters than the laws that followed

elsewhere. Later, laws placed the burden of figuring out how and where to register on the voter.) At the Pennsylvania constitutional convention the following year, the law was attacked in just those terms. A Mr. Porter complained:

> When the assessors went around, the laboring men were neces-sarily . . . absent from their homes, engaged in providing subsis-tence for themselves and their families. . . . When the election came on these men appeared to vote, and were spurned from the ballot boxes. . . . But how was it with the rich man? The gold and silver door plate with the name was enough, and there was no danger that the assessor would overlook that.[2]

During the late nineteenth century, Democrats in the South passed registration laws that implemented the poll taxes, literacy tests, and grandfather clauses designed to suppress the votes of blacks and many poor whites.[3] These vote suppression devices were administered through the voter registration system. Indeed, the reg-istration process itself became another barrier to the exercise of the vote. And in the North, Republicans in control of state capitals fol-lowed much the same method, passing registration laws first aimed at the big cities, where the immigrant working class was concen-trated, and then gradually expanding these laws to cover towns and rural areas.

As late as the 1960s, southern registrars conducted often unau-thorized oral exams and improperly asked blacks questions they couldn't answer in order to prevent them from qualifying to vote. For example, in 1956, U.S. attorney general Herbert Brownell testified before the Senate Committee on the Judiciary that his department had received affidavits from blacks claiming registrars "demanded that the Negro citizens answer such questions as 'What is due process of law?' 'How many bubbles are there in a bar of soap?' etc. Those submitting affidavits included college graduates, teachers and busi-nessmen yet none of them, according to the Registrar, could meet the voting requirements."[4] Georgia's Registration Act of 1958 provided for a new test for registration applicants unable to read or write. Illiterates were required to correctly answer twenty of thirty questions, among them items most Americans would find difficult to answer. For example, Georgia's new test asked applicants to identify the qualifications of a representative to the General Assembly, to provide a description of the amendment process of the U.S. Constitution, and to discuss how the writ of habeas corpus may be suspended. No correct answers were provided in the law.[5] In Mississippi, any applicant who made a mistake or error in filling out a registration form could be disqualified, as in Georgia and throughout the South, subject to the judgment of local registrars. Whites received assistance in filling out the forms, while blacks were disqualified for signing their names on the wrong line. It was the localism and intransigent racial discrimination of southern registrars that caused the U.S. Civil Rights Commission to conclude in its review of litigation under the 1957 Civil Rights Act that "some direct procedure for temporary Federal registration for Federal elections is required if these [black] citizens are not to be denied their right to register and vote in forthcoming national elections."[6]

The passage of the Voting Rights Act in 1965 (and the Twenty-fourth Amendment in 1964) limited some of the more racially discriminatory aspects of the personal voter registration system, but it left much of the encumbering administrative process intact. It was this surviving system of accumulated rules and procedures limiting access to the vote that came into focus for voting rights advocates and for both political parties during the period between 1983 and 1993.

For the Republicans, the growth of the black Democratic vote created two obvious strategic opportunities. As national campaigns since 1964 had shown, Democrats could be tarred by associating them with blacks and black demands. This, after all, was the Southern Strategy, which made the Republican Party competitive in the South, and which also played well among northern working-class voters. And what would seem at first glance a downside to the strategy—that blacks would respond with a spike in turnout for the Democrats—would only strengthen the Republican appeals to whites on the basis of race, as Kevin Phillips had so cynically advised.[7] The other strategic option was to lower Democratic totals by targeting blacks for vote suppression, as was done in the elections of 2000 and 2004, as we will show in chapters 5 and 6.

Ronald Reagan's election in 1980 was a triumph for the Southern Strategy. His campaign rallied racial conservatives, and once in office, he "put hundreds of school desegregation cases on hold, tried to weaken the Voting Rights Act, supported tax breaks for segregated schools, and molded the Civil Rights Commission, always before a bastion of racial liberalism, into an open opponent of it." In return, he won the second-lowest percentage of black votes of any Republican presidential candidate for which we have voting statistics.[8]

The emergence of the black voter bloc had more troubling strategic implications for the Democrats. Of course, Democrats were the beneficiaries of the new black votes, which could be important in national presidential elections. But the new voters posed other problems for the party. For one, they were anathema to other blocs in the voter coalitions that the party relied upon, as evident in the conflicts that had raged over black succession in big-city politics. For another, their growing presence facilitated the Republicans' use of racist appeals to win erstwhile Democratic votes. Finally, blacks were ardent supporters of New Deal and Great Society programs, and these domestic policies were exactly the policies that the "centrist" Democrats in the national party who soon came together under the Democratic Leadership Council wanted to contain.

In 1983 and 1984, a multiracial coalition on the left mobilized a huge drive to register nonvoters to oust Reagan from office. The religious right and other conservatives mobilized to counter that effort by registering more potential Republican voters. The media coverage of the election focused on the Herculean efforts under way to reverse low voter turnout in the United States.

The activists who led the campaigns were inspired by the results of the 1982 midterm elections, and particularly by the increase in registration and voting among blacks and the unemployed.[9] Although the Republicans gained one seat in the Senate, in the House, the Democrats gained twenty-seven seats and the Republicans lost twenty-four. Party majorities did not change in the Congress—the Republicans ruled the Senate, and the Democrats held the House— but the pattern of gains and losses revealed popular opposition to Reagan's policies. The president's popularity, which had peaked at 67 percent in April 1981, dropped to 43 percent by the 1982 election, which meant that more Americans disapproved of Reagan's perfor- mance in office (47 percent) than approved. Reagan's ratings were particularly low among African Americans and the poor, and his ap- proval-to-disapproval ratio in March of his second year was lower than that of all four of his predecessors—Carter, Nixon, Kennedy, and Eisenhower.[10] In January, after the midterm election, Reagan's job-approval numbers continued to plummet, reaching their lowest point during his tenure, with 35 percent approving and 56 percent disapproving (9 percent expressed no opinion).[11]

Conditions seemed ripe for political change, and a strategy emerged: if all those hurt by the Reagan administration's economic and domestic policies could be mobilized to register and vote their interests at the polls in November 1984, the Reagan Revolution could be rolled back. One brochure asked, "What if they gave an election and all of the poor, minorities and women came? That would save the social programs. It would create jobs, and promote equality. It might even bring peace."[12]

The 1984 presidential election saw an unprecedented surge of voter registration campaigns. In the summer of 1983, building on the inspiration of Harold Washington's campaign in Chicago, Jesse Jackson set out to register 2 million new voters in the South, using the slogan "Hands that once picked cotton can now pick the presi- dent."[13] Operation Big Vote, a project of the National Coalition on Black Voter Participation, organized sixty local voter registration and education drives in twenty-five states and the District of Colum- bia, using the slogan "Two Million More in 1984."

Project Vote, founded in 1982, developed a strategy to register more poor people and more rapidly. As POWER would do in Chi- cago, it sent volunteers to the long lines of people waiting to receive surplus government food and to waiting rooms at welfare agencies.

During an experiment in New Jersey, they learned that nearly forty thousand people passed through the state's largest food stamp distribution sites in the first week of every month.[14] Registering voters at such sites was far more efficient than going door to door in poor neighborhoods or standing on a street corner—waiting lines provided both a captive audience and a concentrated population of low-income people. Word spread, and many groups soon adopted the Project Vote model.

Frances Fox Piven and Richard Cloward thought Project Vote's strategy was promising but limited by its reliance on armies of volunteers to patrol the surplus-food lines. The logical solution seemed to be to get the staff of social service agencies, public and private, to register their clients to vote. Piven and Cloward created an organization called the Human Service Employees Registration and Voter Education (Human SERVE) Fund, and its field staff worked in the thirteen most populous states to encourage public and private agencies to offer registration. Human SERVE later estimated that 1,500 voluntary agencies had offered voter registration. In the public sector, six governors ordered voter registration to be conducted in at least one state agency, and twenty-one county executives or mayors authorized voter registration activities in some or all of the agencies under their control.[15]

To cap off the yearlong efforts, Human SERVE and the U.S. Public Interest Research Group (U.S. PIRG) jointly coordinated "Millions More, October 4," a large national one-day mobilization (reminiscent of "Come Alive, October Five" in Chicago) to register voters before the November 1984 election. The one-day mobilization had more than eighty national sponsors, including organizations representing seniors, youth, people of color, women, and the poor, as well as social service organizations, environmental groups, and other progressive organizations.

At the outset, the campaigners thought their hardest task would be to find enough volunteer registrars, or to recruit enough sympathetic social agency personnel to the effort. They saw registration as only a bureaucratic procedure that had to be mastered. Because they hadn't recognized that the system of rules and practices governing registration was deeply political, the crystallization in rules and practices of a history of voter suppression, they didn't yet know what they were getting into.

The left's effort to mobilize minorities and the poor was not welcomed by either political party. The drives obviously endangered the Republican Party. Polls taken in 1983 and 1984 showed that the unregistered were predominantly Democrats: 47 percent of the unregistered voters described themselves as Democrats, 34 percent as Republicans, and 19 percent as independents.[16] But, as we have already shown, massive registration of the poor and minorities also threatened elements in the Democratic Party.

Accordingly, even as the party publicly welcomed the prospect of new voters, it contributed little to the effort. At the party's national convention, Jesse Jackson tried to make the case for mobilizing new voters. He argued that "the key to a Democratic victory in 1984 is the enfranchisement of the progressive wing of the Democratic Party. They are the ones who have been devastated by Reaganomics and, therefore, it is in their self-interest to vote in record numbers to oust their oppressor."[17] But the Democratic Party itself did very little registration. Neither did it give much support to the ongoing registration drives. Although it pledged $5 million to voter registration efforts early in 1984, and Walter Mondale personally promised to raise another $1 million, neither the party nor Mondale followed through.[18] Some Democrats were concerned that reaching out to nonvoters in the way Jackson and the progressive wing suggested would hurt the party's chances of winning back moderate Democrats who had voted for Reagan. Jackson at one point accused the party of paying "lip service" to voter registration while outsider organizations that represented disenfranchised groups—the poor, people of color, and women—actually did the mobilization work.

The Republican Party took the threat of millions more poor and black voters seriously. Conservative groups redoubled their voter registration efforts to counteract the potential gains by the left. The Moral Majority, Christian Voice, and the Religious Roundtable, three national fundamentalist networks of clergy and lay activists, had mobilized conservative pastors in 1980 to register their congregations to vote. The Moral Majority claimed to have registered between 4 million and 8 million voters, although other observers considered 2 million a better estimate.[19]

James Kilpatrick, a conservative political columnist, warned that the GOP had to counter the various efforts on the left: "If the Republicans fail to mount a massive effort to register likely new Republican voters, the Republicans will take a drubbing in 1984."[20] The following month, the Reagan-Bush campaign announced a Republican voter registration drive. Since they were "prospecting for Republican nuggets in a field where conventional wisdom says Democrats have the most to mine,"[21] Republicans used a technologically sophisticated—and expensive—method of identifying unregistered prospective Republican voters. Typically, the state Republican Party hired a direct-mail marketing company, which matched a computer tape of registered voters with a tape of households with telephones to create a list of households with unregistered persons. They were called and asked if they supported the president, and if so, whether they would like to register. If the answers were yes, a party volunteer was sent to the individual's home with voter registration forms. In Buffalo, the first 540 calls yielded 65 new registrants; in New Jersey, the first 4,000 calls yielded 480 registrants. The yield was low and the cost high; it is estimated that state Republican parties spent as much as $14 a registrant using this method.[22]

The left voter registration drives faced not only countermobilization from the right, but the daily obstruction of their efforts by state and local election officials and the administrative apparatuses over which they presided. Project Vote volunteers were often barred from registering voters in unemployment offices, welfare offices, and food-distribution centers. An organizer canvassing a welfare waiting room in Cincinnati in September 1984 was arrested and strip-searched.[23] Republicans were especially indignant about registration at welfare agencies. George Strake, chairman of the Texas Republican Party, complained when Democratic governor Mark White instituted voter registration in the welfare agency: "They are using taxpayers' money to register predominantly Democrats. There are not a lot of Republicans in the welfare lines."[24] Project Vote successfully sued the states of Ohio, Indiana, Illinois, Missouri, and Pennsylvania—all then led by Republican governors—when its volunteers were barred from the waiting rooms of unemployment and welfare offices.[25]

State and local officials of both parties regularly obstructed the drive. In heavily Democratic New York City, the Democratic head of the board of elections complained to the *New York Times*, "This registration drive has gone to too much fanaticism. I'd like everybody to be registered. But not with hysteria."[26] Democratic mayor Ed Koch prevented the city's comptroller, also a Democrat, from including with city paychecks a reminder to city employees that they should register to vote, in an apparent tiff over who would get political credit.[27] In Boston, another heavily Democratic city, organizations wishing to register voters had to request approval of the dates, times, and locations of their efforts so that the board of elections could deliver materials to them at the beginning of the day and pick them up at the end of the day. Robin Leeds, who worked for Human SERVE in Boston, told of engaging in protracted negotiations to set up a satellite registration site at Dudley Station, a subway stop at the hub of predominantly black Roxbury. Although the group finally obtained approval, the board of elections sabotaged the effort by showing up late with materials and leaving before the evening rush hour.[28] Clearly, intraparty competition was at work. Mel King, a prominent African American activist, had run for mayor in 1983, inspiring an increase in black turnout, and Operation Big Vote was working to register more black voters in 1984. Registering voters in Roxbury was a challenge to white elected Democrats.

Human SERVE's efforts to get public and voluntary social agencies to offer voter registration were also often frustrated. Thinking that Democratic governors newly elected in the have-not surge of 1982 might be sympathetic to registration reform, Human SERVE organized local coalitions to press Governors Tony Anaya of New Mexico, Richard Celeste of Ohio, Mario Cuomo of New York, and Mark White of Texas to issue executive orders requiring intake workers in welfare and unemployment offices to offer registration to their clients. In some places, mayors and county executives did the same.

The executive orders attracted a flurry of press attention and Republican opposition. In New York and Ohio, state Republican parties immediately sued to stop the governors' orders. In New York, they were only partly successful when a judge ruled that registration forms could be made available at agencies, but that the agency staff should not ask people if they'd like to register or assist them in filling out the forms. The Reagan administration also stepped in. On September 27, 1984, Donald Devine, director of the Office of Personnel Management (OPM), threatened Governors Celeste, Cuomo, and White with a cutoff of federal grants-in-aid, on the ground that the Hatch Act would be violated if human-service workers registered citizens in the course of their regular duties.[29] The targeted governors called press conferences to announce their determination to push forward with registration. But when press attention turned elsewhere, the governors did little to implement their own orders.

After the 1984 election, the activists assessed their efforts. Operation Big Vote asked the conveners of its local coalitions to evaluate their registration campaigns. Most respondents reported that their efforts were hampered by administrative obstacles—for example, by clerks who wouldn't provide enough forms, or by limitations on acceptable sites for voter registration, or on who was permitted to offer registration.[30]

Resistance was clearest in the twenty-three states where anyone wishing to register others had to be deputized by local election officials. The officials used this power to limit the registration activities of voluntary groups, often favoring some groups over others. In Michigan, Massachusetts, and Connecticut, all led by Democratic governors, Human SERVE found it nearly impossible to get volunteers deputized. Michigan, for example, required those who wanted to do registration to be separately deputized and trained in each county where they would be working. This made the deputization process so onerous that social agencies weren't usually willing to commit staff time to completing the procedures. In any case, the process gave local officials the discretion to refuse to deputize. Applicants from Planned Parenthood in particular were frequently rejected.[31] Such obstacles led to a flurry of lawsuits against states. The Human SERVE Fund, the NAACP Legal Defense and Education Fund (LDF), the American Civil Liberties Union (ACLU), and the Association of Community Organizations for Reform Now (ACORN) sued the Democratic governors of Arkansas, Connecticut, Georgia, and Michigan and the Republican governors of Missouri and New Hampshire "to ensure the uniform application of state law permitting the deputization of volunteer registrars."[32] These governors included Bill Clinton, who later as president would sign the National Voter Registration Act (NVRA), and Kit Bond, who vigorously opposes voter registration reform today as a U.S. senator. They also sued Louisiana, where the appointment of volunteer registrars was simply prohibited by law.[33] The remedies won generally resulted in a modest increase in deputies, which Jo-Anne Chasnow, who worked for Human SERVE, termed "incremental," when "we wanted to blow the lid off it."[34] The lawsuits also delayed and distracted from the registration and mobilization effort.

Despite the obstacles, the 1984 election posted the first increase in voter registration in years. Overall, it was small—registration increased just 1.4 percentage points, and turnout by only 0.7 points. But among population groups targeted by the drives, census data showed registration and turnout were up considerably. Black registration climbed more than 6 percentage points, and black turnout went from 50.5 to 55.8 percent—the biggest increase since 1964. The gap between white and black registration rates narrowed to 3.3 points—again, the biggest change since 1964. Among Hispanics, registration was up 3.8 points, and turnout 2.7 points.[35]

Most groups tried to keep a tally of the numbers they had registered. A committee of foundations that had funded some of the drives concluded that the groups "collectively registered an unduplicated count of approximately 2 to 2.5 million new voters."[36] Since that count did not include every organization that had done voter registration, nor could it include people who may have been inspired by hearing of the voter mobilization campaign to register on their own, this was likely an underestimate.[37] Whatever the tally, those who hoped that registering new voters would translate into Reagan's defeat were disappointed. Reagan won reelection with 58.8 percent of the vote.

Although the drives did not change the outcome of the election, by exposing activists to the maddening labyrinths of the country's voter registration system and the obstructions of state and local officials, they inspired the push for national voter registration reform that eventually resulted in the passage of the NVRA. The direct experience of so many activists in the 1984 campaign proved to them the necessity of reforming the system, as Piven and Cloward wrote in 1985:

> The political arithmetic is simple: a reservoir of 20 million un-registered people above the median income level can be drawn on for years to cancel out those who may be registered from the 40 million below the median. The future of the registration drive is shaping up to be a treadmill, with the left having to run faster and faster to stay in the same place. Institutional reform is the obvious alternative.[38]

Voter registration reform proposals had been made before, and they had always died in the Congress. In the early 1970s, Senator Gale McGee (D-WY) had championed postcard registration, and in the first year of his presidency, Jimmy Carter had supported an election day registration bill.[39] The most vocal opposition came from Republicans and election officials, but Democrats were divided on the issue. When Senator McGee's first postcard-registration bill came to the floor of the Senate in March 1972, 81 percent of the northern Democrats voted in support of the bill, but only 17 percent of the southern Democrats did. Richard Moe, who spearheaded the Carter administration's voter registration reform effort, remembers that big-city Democratic leaders opposed voter registration reform, in particular those from Philadelphia and Chicago: "They wanted to know who was going to vote."[40] Tip O'Neill, the Boston congressman who was then Speaker of the House, was quoted in the *New York Times* saying he didn't know why Carter had made the bill a priority.[41]

There was some reason to expect things would be easier in the 1980s. For one, there were fewer southern Democrats in the Congress overall—the Democrats held 92 percent of the southern seats in 1960, but only 61 percent in 1992. In any case, southern Democratic members of Congress had become more liberal. As African Americans entered the electorate in greater numbers, southern Democrats had to court them in election campaigns.

On Capitol Hill, the postelection shuffling of committee assignments in 1984 and 1986 brought several advocates of voter registration reform to positions of power.[42] Registration-reform advocate Al Swift (D-WA) was made chair of a new elections subcommittee in the House. Wendell Ford, who had as governor of Kentucky from 1971 to 1974 tackled the corruption of Kentucky's voter rolls by ordering a complete reregistration of all citizens, became chair of the Senate Committee on Rules and Administration.

The 1986 election had also made Senator Alan Cranston (D-CA), the Senate majority whip, a convert to voter registration reform. Cranston had faced a very difficult race when the Republican Party targeted his seat to save the Republicans' Senate majority. "He [Cranston] was considered too old, too liberal, and very likely to run out of his amazing luck. But . . . Cranston . . . bucked his state's Republican trend and vanquished his toughest challenger ever by 116,622 votes."[43] Although overall turnout sank to an all-time low of 59 percent of registered voters, turnout was higher in Los Angeles County and San Francisco, where Cranston had a lot of support, than in many counties his opponent expected to win. Cranston believed voter registration had made the difference in his election, and during and after the election he raised millions for California-based and national voter registration organizations.

After the election Human SERVE started trying to build momentum for national legislative reform. The U.S. Public Interest Research Group, formed in 1983 as a national association of the twenty-four preexisting state PIRGs,[44] was ready to join in, and together they began by supporting efforts already under way in Congress by John Conyers, who had long championed voting rights legislation. During the summer before the 1984 election, he had introduced one bill "to provide for voter registration for Federal elections on all regular business days and at the polls on Election Day," and another bill to permit postcard registration. Similar bills had been debated in Congress in the 1970s but had been defeated. Gene Karpinski of U.S. PIRG and Human SERVE director Linda Davidoff persuaded forty organizations to sign a letter supporting Conyers's bills.[45] They also began to talk to other key players on Capitol Hill.

Human SERVE and U.S. PIRG needed allies to achieve reform if they were to overcome the opposition that had defeated voter registration reform efforts in the 1970s. There were some obvious candidates, including the established civil rights organizations, the voting rights organizations formed to support the Voting Rights Act, and the groups that had participated in the 1984 registration drives. The League of Women Voters Education Fund held a conference in July 1985 to evaluate the 1984 voter registration campaign, to which they invited the NAACP, the National Coalition on Black Voter Participation, the Southwest Voter Registration and Education Project, the Women's Vote Project, and ACORN, among others. Human SERVE used the opportunity to urge conference participants to jointly issue "a ringing endorsement of registration reform," and a coalition to support national legislation began to take shape.[46] At a conference in September, a consensus was reached on supporting four types of registration reform: national standards and enforcement, election day registration, mail registration, and agency-based registration.

National Standards. The very idea of pursuing national legislation implied the importance of national standards for voter registration and a national capacity to enforce those standards. Perhaps more than anything else, the campaign had revealed that the state and local agencies responsible for registration were governed by myriad distinct rules, and that whatever those rules, they also often made arbitrary decisions from which there was no easy recourse.

Election Day Registration. The Voting Rights Act and ensuing court decisions had reduced the closing date—the date in advance of the election by which a voter had to register—to a nationwide maximum of thirty days. Election day registration carried this to its logical conclusion, allowing people to register on the day of the election.

The reason was obvious, as Althea Simmons, director of the NAACP's Washington bureau, explained: "Many people do not get excited about an election until it is imminent. Under present law, in most states, it is too late to translate that excitement into action. Also, it is more convenient to vote if you only have to go to the courthouse or the place of registration/voting one time."[47]

In 1985, only Minnesota, Wisconsin, Oregon, and Maine used election day registration, and North Dakota did not require voters to register. The number of states offering an election day registration option had not changed since 1977, when President Carter had briefly tried to convince Congress to pass an election day registration bill. That bill had garnered little support from either party—Democratic majority leader Tip O'Neill had refused to bring it up to a vote in Congress. Nevertheless, civil rights groups were strongly committed to including election day registration in the bill.

Mail Registration. Mail registration was by far the most common reform enacted by the states to improve participation. By 1985, twenty-three states allowed voters to fill out a voter registration form and return it by mail. This simple reform meant that people did not have to appear at an elections board office during working hours, and it also ended the deputization process that had caused so much difficulty in the 1984 elections. Anyone could obtain voter registration forms and encourage other people to register. Mail registration would thus be useful to voter registration drives. But in the absence of such drives, it probably would not increase registration numbers.

Agency-Based Registration. Human SERVE was the primary advocate of requiring government-funded social agencies that served the public to offer voter registration to their clients, and it was primarily focused on agencies that served the poor. The group had learned from its efforts in the campaign that how registration was offered mattered a great deal. If stacks of mail-in registration cards were simply made available at an agency, they would eventually get moved to an underused area and be forgotten. If, alternatively, the question "Would you like to register to vote?" was included on the agency's application form or as a routine part of the intake interview, many more people would be registered.[48] There was a precedent for this reform. Michigan, under the leadership of its first black secretary of state, Richard Austin, instituted voter registration in motor vehicle agencies in 1975, and by 1985, nine states had followed suit with some kind of voter registration in driver's license agencies. But although driver's license registration seemed politically easier, some of the groups worried that this reform by itself would merely reproduce the class and racial barriers of the existing voter universe.

Through experience, by colliding head-on with the historical accumulation of rules governing access to the vote, voter registration activists had learned what was wrong with the system. Their proposals to ease barriers—with national standards and oversight, election day registration, a federal mail-in form that created an avenue to bypass obstacles put in their way by election administration bureaucracies, and with agency-based registration that affirmatively registered the poor as they came into contact with social service providers— were developed out of real-world experience in confronting history, tradition, and intransigent and obstructionist local election officials, and in assisting low-income people with registration. Though virtually forgotten today, *these* were the core components of the initial reform effort that became, eight years later, the National Voter Registration Act. The NVRA's signature feature, which gives it its nickname ("Motor Voter"), registration through driver's license bureaus, was not on the advocates' agenda. In the effort to actually push a bill through Congress, the original vision of an accessible registration system was negotiated and compromised. Afterward, even this compromised vision of a seamless voter registration process was weakened, as elements of the original reform plan that remained simply were not implemented.

The coalition began what would be a years-long campaign by discussing their dream bill with Senator Cranston and Congressman Conyers. Out of these conversations, the two elected officials introduced the Universal Voter Registration Act of 1987, which would require every state to offer registration by mail, at the polling place on the day of election, and at government agencies and government-funded private agencies that served the public directly. Later, Congressman Al Swift and Senator Wendell Ford took leading roles, both as chairs of the relevant committees and supporters of voter registration reform.

From the start, proponents anticipated objections about the possibility of voter fraud if registration were liberalized. To deal with these objections, the bill required more stringent proofs of identity for same-day registration than for advance registration, and segregated the votes of same-day registrants so their eligibility could be verified. In another attempt to head off complaints about fraud, the bill required states to establish a program for confirming the valid registration of voters, primarily by getting information on deaths and criminal convictions from the appropriate agencies, and change-of-address notices from the U.S. Postal Service. It also required that no voter would be removed from the rolls unless the voter had died, moved, been convicted of a crime or institutionalized, or requested that his or her name be removed.

The removal of names from the voter registration lists was a touchy subject. Although the ostensible purpose was to remove ineligible voters from the rolls, at least thirty-seven states simply purged anyone who had not voted in a number of years.[49] It was estimated that the nonvoting purge reduced turnout by 2 million.[50] Voter registration advocates were very concerned that purging, whether done for nonvoting or for other reasons, was often done with discriminatory intent, and discriminatory effects. Since at least 1958, when, anticipating the "voter caging" schemes employed later, Republicans in Phoenix, Arizona, sent nonforwardable postcards to eighteen thousand Democrats and then organized poll watchers to challenge their registration if they showed up to vote, Republican ballot-integrity programs have been charged with suppressing the black and Hispanic vote.[51] More recently, the Republican National Committee sponsored a "ballot-security" program in a 1986 Senate race in Louisiana in which "they challenged the registration of 31,000 voters in Democratic-leaning, minority precincts. A State court ordered a halt to the program prior to the election."[52] Although Cranston and Conyers had crafted language that required that the purged names be kept on the list as "challenged" voters for four years, and also outlawed the nonvoting purge, it would be the first federal legislation *re-quiring* states to purge their lists, and that made voting rights advocates justifiably nervous.

The Universal Voter Registration Act also included penalties for fraudulent registration or interference with another person's voting rights. This was a part of a strategy to counter the accusations that voter registration reform would lead to increased election fraud, allowing the advocates of the bill to "*lead* with the assertion that the sponsors of the Universal Voter Registration Act are acting to *reduce* election fraud by the enforcement sections of the bill." [53]

Nevertheless, fraud was one of the chief complaints raised against the bill from the earliest hearings on the bill in the spring of 1988. Opposition came mostly from the Republican side of the aisle. Senators Mitch McConnell (R-KY) and Ted Stevens (R-AL) led the fight against the bill, arguing that it would increase fraud, a claim they never substantiated. Stevens wanted to remove mail registration, which he asserted was the most fraud-prone method of voter registration. [54] Tamara Somerville, an aide to Mitch McConnell, viewed the fight in starkly partisan terms—perhaps because McConnell was in "the [reelection] fight of his life" back home in Kentucky, and Wendell Ford was supporting his opponent. [55] She saw the bill as part of a larger Democratic plan to protect Democratic incumbents, and said that McConnell's major concern was voter fraud, which had been widespread in Senator McConnell's home state of Kentucky. "I've got a pile of clips; they're still busting people down there for vote fraud." [56] Most cases of election fraud in Kentucky, however, have involved voter intimidation, ballot box stuffing, and vote buying, not fraudulent registration. [57]

Opponents also argued that the cost would be a burden on the states. Ernest Hawkins, the registrar of voters of Sacramento County, California, estimated that the Universal Voter Registration Act would add $65 million nationally to the cost of each federal election, costs borne by the various states and localities. [58] More broadly, some objected to the bill as an unnecessary encroachment on the rights of the states to conduct elections.

Election day registration in particular drew critical comments at the earliest congressional hearings on the bill. At that time, only four states had election day registration. Even election administrators from states with liberal registration laws feared being overwhelmed on the day of an election, with unknown consequences for fraud and delayed election returns. Swift thought that opposition to election day registration was strong, widespread, and, he felt, not without reason.[59] Believing the bill as then written didn't have a prayer of passage, Swift set out to draft his own bill, which he circulated in September 1988.

The bill reversed the advocates' priorities; election day registration had been eliminated, and registration at motor vehicle agencies had become the centerpiece of the legislation, earning it the nickname "Motor Voter." Swift's bill required that the voter registration application be part of the driver's license application, and prohibited requiring any duplicate information on the voter registration form. The bill also required states to offer mail registration and to designate appropriate state, federal, and private offices as voter registration agencies, although registration was not required to be part of the application in those agencies, as it was in motor vehicle bureaus. Regarding purges, Swift's bill allowed, but did not require, states to have a list-cleaning program, including a nonvoting purge.

Swift knew he would need at least some Republican support to pass the bill. Ranking minority member Bill Thomas (R-CA) told Swift he would support the bill—and get minority whip Newt Gingrich's support—if it included a provision requiring states to periodically confirm voters' eligibility by mail.[60] Gingrich, eying polls that showed the young unregistered leaning Republican, hoped to build a new Republican majority on a base of young Republican voters. Swift said the civil rights groups "had a paranoia about purging, but for good reason," given the history of Republican misuse of list-cleaning procedures.[61] Swift had the Democratic National Committee review Thomas's proposed address-verification provision and was satisfied that it was not discriminatory. Since list cleaning was the key to the bipartisan support he needed, Swift became an ardent supporter of it.

Swift won the support of the House leadership and crucial Republicans, but the elimination of election day registration, the addition of the first federal requirement that states purge their lists, and the privileging of registration in motor vehicle bureaus over other government agencies made it less likely, the advocates felt, that the bill would change the race and class skew in participation. The advocates' coalition was deeply divided along racial lines over whether "important issues were being lost in the rush to get some kind of bill." [62]

Most important was the issue of purging. Prohibiting a nonvoting purge, which almost three-quarters of the states used, was a victory. But Swift and Thomas insisted that the bill include a requirement that states have some kind of procedure for removing the names of ineligible voters from their lists, and on this the coalition was divided. The NAACP Legal Defense Fund (LDF), the NAACP, and the Citizens Education Fund strongly opposed including any purge in the bill. The League of Women Voters, Human SERVE, the ACLU, and People for the American Way saw the mail purge as a necessary compromise to get a bill passed, and wanted to focus on designing the least damaging purge.

The divisions caused by the insistence on purging nearly doomed registration reform altogether. To many in the civil rights community, institutionalizing potentially discriminatory purges and endangering the Voting Rights Act constituted too high a price to pay for a bill they weren't sure would increase black registration. Those who were most opposed stopped coming to coalition meetings. Human SERVE, the League of Women Voters, and others continued to work to get the best possible bill through Congress. When the bill passed the House in February 1990 and was headed for a vote in the Senate, the LDF released a memo criticizing the bill, and Senate action stalled as many senators were wary of supporting a bill on which civil rights organizations were divided.

Seeing the chances of winning reform slipping away, the advocates convened a summit, where they agreed on what amendments would be necessary for the coalition to support the bill: provisions that would prevent selective purging; agency registration in other agencies besides motor vehicle agencies, particularly agencies serving the poor and disabled; a guarantee that nothing in the bill would undermine the Voting Rights Act; and a provision allowing an individual or organization to sue for violations of the law.[63] Having agreed anew on their priorities, the coalition was ready for the final push.

The new bill passed both houses in 1992 but was vetoed by President George H. W. Bush, who in his veto statement invoked the familiar canard of "fraud" always thrown at efforts to ease voter registration, adding that in his view, the bill "imposes an unnecessary and costly federal regime on the states."[64] Coming in the midst of the 1992 presidential campaign, the veto received a great deal of attention. Independent presidential candidate Ross Perot made a forceful statement criticizing Bush's veto, saying, "The only reason to veto this bill is to try to keep people away from the polls this fall."[65]

Human SERVE and Rock the Vote won Clinton's commitment to support the bill in an MTV press conference just before the California primary, and later got Al Gore's commitment to make it part of the one hundred days' agenda. Thus Clinton's victory became a victory for the Motor Voter bill.

The National Voter Registration Act, as signed by Clinton on May 20, 1993, was not the reform proposal originally conceived by the advocates. It did not include election day registration, although it did result in two states adopting election day registration to avoid complying with the law.

The advocates fought hard to include registration in public assistance, unemployment, and disabilities agencies, calculating that these agencies served those least likely to be visiting motor vehicle agencies. Senate Republicans removed agencies serving the poor and disabled from the bill. California Republican Bill Thomas said, "All of us are interested in extending the right to vote to all. But at unemployment and welfare offices only? . . . If you want to pick a party affiliation of these people, take a guess. You won't pick ours."[66] Ultimately, the bill signed by President Clinton included public assistance and disabilities agencies, but not unemployment offices.

Those who register at welfare offices don't benefit from the seamless registration process used in the motor vehicle agencies. The NVRA created a two-tiered system, requiring voter registration applications to be part of the driver's license application but not the applications for other state or federal programs, mandating only that voter registration forms be made available and collected at certain agencies. The failure to mandate that the option to register to vote appear on social service agency applications forms has allowed many of those agencies to subvert the law's intent that their clients be given the opportunity to register when they fill out forms. Registration has been much more effectively implemented in motor vehicle agencies than elsewhere.

The biggest compromise involved accepting a requirement that states periodically purge their rolls. The NVRA requires states to "conduct a general program that makes a reasonable effort to remove the names of ineligible voters" from the rolls. While Swift, Ford, Conyers, and the advocates did as much as they could to prevent discriminatory use of the purge, and while they included provisions that allowed voters mistakenly identified as ineligible to correct the record at the polls, the large number of voters purged since NVRA raises concerns about the process. And still, list cleaning did not lessen Republican opposition, as only 11 percent of House Republicans voted for final passage.

Resistance to the Motor Voter bill did not stop when it became law. A week after its signing, an opinion piece appearing in the *Washington Times* began, "Future historians exploring the ashes of American democracy will mark May 20, 1993, as the date that shattered the nation's civic sense. On that day President Clinton signed into law the illegal alien voter registration act of 1993, otherwise known as H.R.2, the 'Motor-Voter Bill.' "[67] The obsession of the far right with how the NVRA is bringing down civilization by exposing American elections to rampant voter fraud has abated little since.

In Congress, Mitch McConnell, long an opponent of the NVRA, immediately introduced an amendment to the Better Nutrition and Health for Children Act, to "remove the burden WIC clinics will face after January 1, 1995, of registering WIC recipients to vote," which would, McConnell worried, "impair the ability of local WIC clinics to meet the needs of needy pregnant women, infants, and children."[68] Once Republicans took the majority of the House in 1995, Bob Stump (R-AZ) introduced a bill to repeal the NVRA, criticizing it as a "$200 million unfunded Federal mandate."[69] He introduced the same bill in every Congress until his death in 2003. In every Congress since 1995, other bills have been introduced to repeal the NVRA or limit its reach. Some bills would simply repeal the entire NVRA. Others would repeal the mail-registration provisions, or introduce requirements of proof of citizenship or photo identification, or make state implementation voluntary, or permit the removal of names from the registration rolls for failure to vote in two federal elections.

By August 31, 1994, four months before the January 1995 deadline for implementing the NVRA, all but sixteen states had either passed implementing legislation or been declared exempt. (States that did not require registration, or permitted registration on election day, were exempt, including Minnesota, North Dakota, Wisconsin, and Wyoming). Three states, Arkansas, Vermont, and Virginia, had con-stitutional conflicts with the bill and had been given extra time. Out-right resistance came primarily from states led by Republican governors; of the eleven states the voting rights advocates identified as "resistant"—California, Idaho, Illinois, Indiana, Kansas, Michigan, Mississippi, New Hampshire, New Jersey, Pennsylvania, and South Carolina—all but Indiana were led by Republicans.[70] Idaho and New Hampshire retroactively enacted election day registration as a way of avoiding compliance. Advocates were suspicious of this tactic, as were attorneys at the Department of Justice. Neither state had a particularly progressive history of voter registration. Idaho, for example, purges voters' names for nonvoting after four years. In the 1996 election, using election day registration for the first time, New Hampshire experienced a 9.85 percentage point increase in turnout, but Idaho's turnout increased by only 0.2 points. Both states were eventually declared exempt from the NVRA.[71]

Republican governor Pete Wilson of California sued the federal government over enforcement of the NVRA, challenging the constitutionality of the act on Tenth Amendment grounds, and was joined not long after by Virginia governor George Allen, a newly elected Republican. When four additional states—Illinois, Pennsylvania, South Carolina, and Michigan—raised the states' rights banner and refused to implement the NVRA, first the organizations that had fought for the act and then the Department of Justice brought suit against all six states. The U.S. district courts rejected all the state challenges to the NVRA. Those states that chose to appeal were defeated in the U.S. court of appeals as well. Although the Ninth Circuit Court unanimously rejected California's challenge, Governor Wilson unsuccessfully appealed to the Supreme Court (the Court denied certiorari in January 1996). The legal challenges were virtually finished twelve months after the law went into effect.

One important legal challenge remained in Mississippi, so often at the extreme in matters of race and politics in America. Alone among the states, Mississippi created a dual registration system for state and federal elections, implementing registration in motor vehicle and public assistance agencies *for federal elections only*. People registering at these agencies were not eligible to vote in state and local elections, because the state had failed to pass NVRA implementing legislation.[72] Heightening the racial disparity, people registering in motor vehicle agencies but not those registering in welfare agencies were routinely handed a state mail-in registration form. Voter registration activists and an unregistered recipient of public assistance sued Mississippi over the state's unwillingness to submit its dual registration plan for preclearance by the Justice Department. Even after losing in the Supreme Court, Governor Kirk Fordice vetoed legislation that would have created a unified registration system, requiring yet another lawsuit to finally bring Mississippi into compliance with the NVRA in 1998.

The early results of Motor Voter appeared promising. Human SERVE calculated that 20 million voter registration transactions took place in the first eighteen months of implementation. The Federal Election Commission's first biennial report on the impact of the NVRA showed 41 million transactions had taken place by November 1996. How much should we have expected registration to increase over this period? By noting which states had previously adopted mail-in registration, active or passive motor vehicle agency registration, and registration in other government agencies, Steven Knack estimated that the NVRA's mail and agency registration provisions would increase registration about 13 percentage points and turnout about half as much.[73] Since a complete driver's license renewal cycle is forty-eight months, and twenty-two months passed between January 1995 and November 1996, we should have expected 45 percent of the predicted increase, or 5.85 percentage points. The FEC report showed that registration climbed to 76.25 percent in 1996, 5.65 points over 1992 and 8.61 points over 1994. Despite the intransigence of a handful of states, the NVRA was having an impact.

Implementation in public-assistance and disability agencies was less promising. Human SERVE analyzed the state-by-state data every six months, and rang the alarm bells. Given the frequency of recertification interviews, Human SERVE estimated that 5 million public-assistance recipients should have registered to vote by the end of 1995, but only 1.3 million had. Eighteen months after implementation, 44 percent of the 20 million new registrants had registered at driver's license bureaus, and only 10 percent at public-assistance agencies. Less than half a percent had registered through disability agencies.

From the start, resistance from both national and state and local politicians, both Republican and Democratic, had been more insistent with regard to provisions requiring registration in welfare agencies where minorities and the poor would be reached. One result, as noted above, was that the NVRA required the voter registration application to be "part of the application" in driver's license bureaus, but in public assistance agencies the process was more unwieldy. Clients were to be given two additional pieces of paper, a voter registration form, and a declination form—a page of legal notices and a place for a client to sign if she declined to register to vote. These separate forms raised the possibility that agency staff would neglect to distribute them or clients would forget to fill them out, and they required duplicate information from the client, which the simultaneous motor vehicle application process did not. NVRA advocates were aware that this would lead to more effective registration in motor vehicle agencies than welfare agencies, but strong resistance in Congress to including agencies serving the poor had made it difficult to mandate a unified application form.

Furthermore, since the NVRA did not specify how the agency registration provisions should be enforced, only careful monitoring at the agencies would show whether voter registration was being derailed. Human SERVE staffers Dina Carreras and James Conley visited twenty-four welfare centers and public and private hospitals where registration should have been taking place in New York City and Westchester County. Eight months after the implementation deadline, fifteen of the agencies visited were doing registration, and nine were not. Although New York State had created new Medicaid, food stamp, and AFDC applications that included a voter registration application, Carreras and Conley found several agencies were still using the old forms.[74] Another Human SERVE monitor, Immanuel Ness, reported observing intake workers at public-assistance agencies tearing off and discarding the voter registration part of the application. At some sites, workers said they had never heard of the voter registration requirement; at the East Harlem Center, a worker said she had heard of voter registration in public-assistance agencies but that her center was simply not doing it.

ACORN and Project Vote evaluated implementation in public-assistance agencies in the first three quarters of 1995. While Missouri and Indiana were registering more than 30 percent of their food stamp applicants, fourteen states were registering less than 10 percent. On-site monitoring showed that the lack of a combined form, inadequate training, and the failure to require reporting were impeding registration. The experience in California was instructive: only three of the eleven Los Angeles County offices had attached the registration form to the application for aid, as required by a court order. In a Contra Costa office, applicants reported to ACORN interviewers that they were offered the opportunity to vote, and interviews with office staff showed why—employees were trained in voter registration procedures using a video, and the office supervisor refused to approve any application for aid that was not accompanied by a signed declination form.[75]

In sum, winning the NVRA required compromises that made the bill less effective. Same-day registration had to be abandoned, and purging provisions had to be introduced. The bill's supporters had to fight to include agencies serving the poor and disabled, those least likely to be registered at a motor vehicle agency, and they couldn't get language requiring registration procedures they knew were more effective.

Outright resistance greeted the newly signed federal law in the form of repeal efforts in Congress, lawsuits from Republican governors, and less than enthusiastic implementation in most of the country. Implementation in agencies serving the poor and disabled, never great, has only gotten worse. Two federal agencies bear the responsibility of seeing that the NVRA is faithfully executed: the Election Assistance Commission and the Department of Justice. Initially, the Department of Justice sued states that refused to implement the NVRA, defended the law against challenges by states, and generally made it clear that the law was to be obeyed. But after the first eight cases, the DOJ took no action against states that were inadequately implementing the bill. Under the Bush administration, while many states were still not complying with the public-assistance agency provisions, the DOJ has perversely focused its enforcement efforts on getting states to do more purging, further limiting the NVRA's effectiveness in achieving universal registration, as the next chapter will show.

As a result, the NVRA has disappointed its advocates. While millions have been offered the opportunity to register through NVRA-mandated agencies, millions more should have been offered that opportunity, and were not.[76] Applications, as reported by the states covered by the NVRA,[77] increased less than 20 percent, from 41.5 million in the difficult initial years of implementation, 1995–1996, to 49.6 million in 2003–4. Meanwhile, names deleted from the list climbed 45 percent, from 8.7 million in 1995–96 to 12.6 million in 2005–6. And yet, the Bush Justice Department sued states for not purging their voter lists aggressively enough, while ignoring inadequate implementation of the law in public-assistance agencies. Even before welfare reform, which sharply reduced the number of people who could be reached, registration was never effectively implemented in public-assistance agencies.[78] As the economy turned and economic conditions for working people worsened, several hundred thousand more Americans have signed up for food stamps, one of the largest public-assistance programs required to offer voter registration. Poor NVRA implementation has meant that few of these people are offered a chance to register to vote.[79] The hope that registration reform could continue and complete the work of the 1984 registration drives, erasing the participation gap between white and black, poor and rich, has not been fulfilled.

5

BEYOND RACE? THE PARTIES SEARCH FOR A "THIRD WAY"

The Chair now hands to the tellers the certificate of the electors for President and Vice President of the State of Florida . . . Is there objection?

—Vice President Al Gore, 2001

In the 1960s, as the black vote in the cities became more important, especially in presidential contests, national Democrats tried to reach out to blacks, not only with Great Society programs, but by supporting insurgent black candidates for mayor. Meanwhile, Republicans were taking advantage of the growing identification of blacks with the Democratic Party to lure white voters to Republican columns. By the 1980s, both parties were trying to mute their racial strategies, albeit for different reasons. For Democrats, there were two problems. Even while they had gained black votes, their losses of white voters in the South and of "Reagan Democrats" in the North were threatening the party's majority status. Just as important, their new black voter base was a solidly progressive bloc. In the 1980s, they sought to hold on to what remained of their voter constituency in the South and West by joining the Republicans in sending coded racial messages about blacks and ignoring or minimizing the needs of the black community, especially the segment that was poor. For the Republicans, the turn away from racial politics was less complete. On the one hand, the race politics of the past had worked and was continuing to work, especially in the South, where it had built the Republican base. On the other hand, the long-term demographic trends, and especially the growth of the Latino vote, argued the need to soften racist appeals.

The Democratic Leadership Council and the Third Way

The main force behind the Democratic Party's strategy was the Democratic Leadership Council (DLC), an organization created in 1985 by moderate and conservative Democratic elected officials mainly from the South and the Sunbelt. They were responding to both Ronald Reagan's forty-nine-state victory, particularly the Republican realignment of southern Democratic voters, and the Reverend Jesse Jackson's noisy, disruptive, grassroots-driven gamble for the 1984 Democratic presidential nomination (and the 1988 nomination as well). Jackson's Rainbow Coalition campaigns were an effort to pull the Democratic Party back to its populist New Deal roots, with the difference that minority voters would be in the lead. Nothing could be more alarming to the DLC. Its response was to call for policies that distanced the party from its New Deal and Great Society achievements, and to promote an electoral strategy that moved the party away from the constituencies that had made those achievements necessary. Race usually does not figure prominently in the story of the DLC's origins. But it is an important reason why leading Democrats, when faced with the defection of their southern base and of many white working-class voters in the North as well, moved to the right, toward the defectors, and not toward the wing of the party composed of liberals, progressive labor, and blacks. Instead of recruiting more blacks and their allies to challenge the Republicans' successful use of race to recruit whites, the Democrats developed their own version of the same strategy.

The conceit of the DLC, however, was that it was only a party-modernizing project. DLC rhetoric emphasized the importance of American economic competitiveness, concealing the extent to which the near-historic levels of black voter mobilization and Jesse Jackson's outsider run for the presidency in 1984 helped trigger its intraparty revolt.

Initially, the DLC focused on only three areas, the economy, defense, and crime, suggesting these were the only legitimate domains for governmental action. As Georgia senator Sam Nunn, a founding member of the DLC, put it, "There's no way that we can continue to hand the Republicans the military forces, the flag, and the keys to the jail and expect to win."[1] On the economy, the DLC veered sharply away from traditional Democratic positions on industrial policy and championed instead market-oriented strategies for economic growth. Its first report stressed the theme of America's waning international economic competitiveness and warned that our economy could not thrive in a globalizing marketplace by relying on government. The DLC criticized the Reagan administration's defense industry patronage for wasteful spending but adopted nearly all the rest of the Republicans' hard-line anticommunist foreign policy. In the late 1980s, DLC Democrats applauded Reagan's "evil empire" rhetoric, voted with Republicans for aid to the Nicaraguan Contras, and supported spending on missile defense. As for crime, they supported the death penalty, stiffer sentencing laws, and more money for local police forces. Social policies to deal with poverty and inequality were largely absent from the discussion.

Governor Charles Robb of Virginia signaled the sharp U-turn on race and social policy, ironically enough, in a speech at a 1986 DLC conference on the legacy of the Great Society. If anyone wondered how Robb, the son-in-law of Lyndon Johnson, felt about the Democrats' policy turn before he stepped up to the microphone, they had no doubt by the time he was through. Robb, who had just been chosen as the new chair of the DLC, announced that "[w]hile racial discrimination has by no means vanished from our society, it's time to shift the primary focus from racism—the traditional enemy without—to self-defeating patterns of behavior—the enemy within."[2] Social problems like poverty, racial discrimination, the miseducation of black youth, and the like were individual behavioral matters. What was needed was less whining about discrimination and more personal responsibility, a message more in tune with Reaganism than liberalism.

The DLC thus functioned like a Trojan horse inside the party, as one observer put it, successfully moving the party away from its historic New Deal– and Great Society–era commitments by ignoring issues of race and inequality in favor of arguments for a much more limited governmental role.[3] The language of the DLC was and is the language of a "third way" that eschews "big government" on the one side and completely unregulated capitalism on the other. It plants its flag in the soil of market competition, economic growth, and liberalized trade.

The electoral strategy of the DLC followed closely from its programmatic commitments. The challenge for the party was the white working-class male, the so-called Reagan Democrat, and how to get him to return to the party fold. The DLC's leaders claimed that the problem with the Democratic Party was its capture by "single-issue special interests" which hamstrung the party's ability to offer voters a coherent program addressing widely shared economic concerns. Their Southern Strategy, like its Republican counterpart, didn't explicitly target racial groups. How could it? Blacks were even more identified with the party than they had been in the 1960s, and party insiders worried that the DLC dissident faction "wants to take the cream of the party's leadership and leave [DNC chair Paul] Kirk with Jesse Jackson and the single-issue interest groups."[4] To avoid this possibility, DLC centrists argued for a deracialized, "smaller-government" national policy agenda focusing on bread-and-butter economic issues as a way to stanch the ongoing decay of support among lower-status and moderate whites in the burgeoning suburbs. Issues of racial equality so important to the party's black voter base were to be addressed obliquely through the promotion of economic-growth policies that promised to lift all boats.

The DLC thus became the vehicle of an intraparty revolt by regional conservatives who felt they were being electorally stymied by the party's commitment to government social programs and its inclusion of "shrill special interest" groups institutionalized by the party's caucus structure—women, blacks, Hispanics, liberal-progressives, and gays.[5] Party strategists knew that in 1984 blacks made up only about 11 percent of the electorate, while the white working class accounted for nearly 40 percent. They feared that Reagan's popularity, the ongoing Republican realignment in the South, and the growing appeal of the GOP among moderates in the Sunbelt might permanently end the ability of Democrats to compete for national office. Popular Sunbelt Democratic governors were reluctant to run for the Senate because, as one party strategist explained at the time, "when you run for the Senate you can count on losing eight to ten points [in popularity] just because you become identified with the national party."[6]

With its racial electoral strategy partly obscured, the DLC's perceived "special-interest" target was organized labor, and labor knew it.[7] Before the DLC was even formally organized, labor leaders smelled a rat. The AFL-CIO threatened to withhold support if the Democrats moved toward the Republican Party on trade and economic deregulation. Liberals responded too, distancing themselves from the organization. The California Democratic House delegation directed Representative Tony Coelho, chair of the Democratic Congressional Campaign Committee, to stay out of the group (which he did), and seventeen of the original forty Democratic elected officials who had signed on as founding members, concerned about the rumblings from the base, quietly withdrew their support when the group was first announced.[8]

The DLC was quickly forced to retool its image almost before it was launched. Instead of organizing as a formal party caucus group, it formed as a nonprofit corporation outside the party apparatus, openly courting women and minority elected officials to diversify its "red-faced white boy" appearance.[9] This seemed to appease the liberal old guard wary of the group's conservative agenda, including DNC chair Paul Kirk, a former aide to Senator Edward Kennedy. The DLC's electoral strategy focused on winning the presidency, and southern and Sunbelt politicians complained bitterly that party rules were locking them out of the nomination process. Kirk and traditional Democrats, who at the outset had viewed the DLC "as a kind of separatist movement of crypto-Republicans," agreed to implement some of the DLC's program for party reform, including reducing the number of special-interest caucuses and promising more seats to elected officials (the so-called superdelegates) among delegates to the 1988 convention.[10] Most important, the old guard signaled its agreement with the idea that Democrats could not win the presidency without a southern or Sunbelt politician on the ticket and embraced the DLC proposal for a southern regional primary for March 1988—on what is now known as Super Tuesday.

The disastrous election of 1988—the third straight defeat of the Democrats' presidential candidate—was a boon to the DLC, vindicating its criticism of the party as out of touch with the mainstream of American political life. The DLC became a bigger organization and proclaimed itself an "ideas movement" dedicated to rebuilding the Democratic Party. It expanded its donor base, attracted new membership, attempted to establish a grassroots network of state and local Democratic elected officials, and founded a think tank to develop its centrist policy agenda. The Dukakis drubbing "paved the way for the DLC's policy ideas to get a hearing inside the party."[11] An influential DLC policy paper by political scientists William Galston and Elaine Kamarck argued that

> [s]ince the late 1960s, the public has come to associate liberalism with tax and spend policies that contradict the interests of average families; with welfare policies that foster dependence rather than self-reliance; with softness toward the perpetrators of crime and indifference toward its victims; with ambivalence toward the assertion of American values and interest abroad; and with the adversarial stance toward mainstream moral and cultural values.[12]

Unless the Democrats could cease their obeisance to a rigid "liberal fundamentalism," Galston and Kamarck warned, a Republican realignment, delayed by Watergate, would become permanent.

Bill Clinton, the little-known governor of Arkansas, accepted the invitation to chair the now more prominent DLC in 1990. Later, his presidency would redefine the Democratic Party, moving its center of gravity to the right. DLC or "New" Democrats followed Clinton's strategy of out-Republicaning the Republicans, practicing what political consultant Dick Morris referred to as "triangulation," and campaigned by targeting swing white middle- and working-class voters with a program that emphasized economic growth over redistribution, and opportunity over equality. Clinton adopted most of the DLC's positions: reforming welfare "as we know it"; signing a major crime bill that put one hundred thousand new cops on the streets and expanded the federal death penalty; promoting investment in technological innovation; and advocating a balanced budget and lower interest rates to increase the value of the dollar and open new markets for American capital abroad. But since the Republicans were clearly much worse, the Democrats could take their captive black voters for granted.[13]

As discussed in chapter 4, the Clinton Justice Department litigated to enforce the National Voter Registration Act (NVRA), which Clinton signed into law in 1993. The department defended the NVRA against lawsuits from the Republican governors of California and Virginia, who claimed the law was an unconstitutional infringement on states' rights, and it brought suit against Illinois, Pennsylvania, Michigan, South Carolina, and Mississippi, in most cases joining or following cases brought by voting rights groups. All these lawsuits were filed in 1995, the first year the NVRA was effective. In 1996, the Justice Department sued New York for poor implementation of NVRA "in state-subsidized agencies that provide services for public assistance recipients, Medicaid recipients and the disabled."[14] All of these suits were successful, even though the Mississippi case was not resolved until 1998. Presumably, the states would now act to meet the requirements of the NVRA.

Nevertheless, Democratic ambivalence about the full enfranchisement of African Americans was still evident. After an initial wave of litigation, the Clinton Justice Department brought no more suits to enforce the NVRA, despite the administration's own data collection, which showed that implementation of the law was weak, and not improving. As required by the NVRA, the Federal Election Commission (FEC) surveyed the states biennially to report on the impact of the NVRA. Data from the 1997–98 report to Congress by the FEC showed that the number of voter registration applications was falling. Even the modest 10 percent increase in numbers regis-

Table 6

Sources of Voter Registration Applications, 1995–1998

Source	1995–1996		1997–1998	
	Number of Applications	% of Total	Number of Applications	% of Total
Motor Vehicle Offices	13,722,233	33.1	15,175,653	42.9%
By Mail	12,330,015	29.74	8,792,200	24.86
Public Assistance	2,602,748	6.28	1,546,671	4.37
Disability Services	178,015	0.43	247,764	0.70
Armed Forces	76,008	0.18	22,608	0.06
State-Designated Sites	1,732,475	4.18	1,092,526	3.09
All Other Sources	10,810,934	26.08	8,765,163	24.78
Total	41,452,428		35,372,213	

SOURCE: Federal Election Commission, "The Impact of the National Voter Registration Act of 1993 on the Administration of Elections for Federal Office, 1995–1996: A Report to the 105th Congress," 1997, table 2, p. 12; Federal Election Commission, "The Impact of the National Voter Registration Act of 1993 on the Administration of Elections for Federal Office, 1997–1998: A Report to the 106th Congress," 1999, table 2, p. 12.

tered at motor vehicle bureaus was disturbing, given that during most of the earlier 1995–96 cycle, eight states were still in litigation with the federal government.

Herb Stone, who worked on the NVRA for Senator Wendell Ford, spoke of "a certain foot-dragging" on the NVRA.[15] A bigger problem, perhaps, was the way the Clinton administration had neutralized the Justice Department. Stone remembered, "I had this meeting at the White House [about enforcing the NVRA], and I said, where's Justice? And everybody looked at me and said, they can't come to this meeting, this is a political meeting. . . . I'm still stunned. All these people will be out of a job if you idiots don't implement this law. What do you mean they're not here?" [16]

The Federal Election Commission under Clinton took little advantage of its NVRA-assigned responsibilities to maximize registration under the act. In its required 1995–96 and 1997–98 reports to Congress on state implementation, the FEC simply drew on recommendations made by state election officials themselves, passing up the opportunity to make their own recommendations for better implementation. [17]

Meanwhile, the capacity or willingness of the groups who had advocated for the Motor Voter law to press for vigorous implementation was declining. The major civil rights organizations, which have always been multi-issue organizations, turned their attention to other concerns. Human SERVE, which had long intended to close its doors once the bill became law, shut down its operations in 1997.

The flaws in NVRA implementation added to the chaos of the contested 2000 presidential election. In Illinois, the *Chicago Sun-Times* reported that "thousands" of Du Page County residents, and a smaller number of people from Cook County (which includes Chicago), did not appear on the voter registration lists, although they said they had registered at the motor vehicle bureau. [18] A review of news stories shortly after the 2000 election showed the same complaint voiced in Louisiana, Maryland, California, Nebraska, and Virginia. In a tiny suburb of Omaha, Nebraska, election officials collected seventy conditional ballots from voters who claimed to have registered at the motor vehicle bureau but whose registrations were not found. "Officials said most likely those people were mistaken, that their registrations were lost between the Motor Vehicles Department and their local election office, or those people failed to respond after receiving notice from the election office of errors on their application." [19] While none of these examples are from the battleground states of the 2000 election, the failure to implement the

NVRA did extend to at least one state where party competition was intense; Florida—the "mother of all battleground states."[20]

Black Disenfranchisement in the 2000 Election

The story of black disenfranchisement in the 2000 presidential election has been relegated to a footnote in much of the postelection academic literature analyzing that astonishing political event. Some journalists have done better in grasping the central lesson. For example, writing in *The Nation* about the record turnout of black Floridians in 2000, and the disproportionately high black ballot spoilage rate, John Nichols observed,

> That pile of discarded ballots formed a heartbreaking footnote to the great lost political story of Florida in 2000: A record turnout of new voters, many of them African American from Miami's Liberty City to rural counties on the Panhandle, radically altered the political landscape in a state that was supposed to be securely Republican. News organizations that could not see beyond dimpled chads, and a Gore legal team that failed to recognize where and how most Democratic votes were lost, generally missed that story.[21]

Greg Palast, reporting for the BBC, was the first to break the story of how Republican election officials in Florida produced deliberately inaccurate felon voter purge lists that disproportionately targeted African Americans for voter challenge campaigns at the polls (discussed in more detail in chapter 6).[22] And David Margolick and his colleagues in a major *Vanity Fair* cover story titled "The Path to Florida" similarly point out that "[a]mid the media frenzy after the election, one story went untold. . . . In fact, thousands of African-Americans in Florida *had* been stripped of their right to vote."[23]

Nonetheless, in popular lore, black vote denial, which we think is the main factor explaining the Florida 2000 election outcome, has been subordinated to the drama of the recount and the question of "Who really won?" Constitutional and legal scholars have been more interested in the role of the judiciary in deciding the election, and in whether the Supreme Court's majority opinion in *Bush v. Gore* was "rightly" or "wrongly" decided. Political scientists have focused on the technical issues to better understand voting patterns, ballot spoilage rates, equipment disparities, and the like, grappling with the empirical problems and statistical modeling challenges these problems present. To be sure, a number of important accounts have highlighted the claim that blacks faced higher hurdles and were less likely to have their votes counted than other groups, and political scientists have found racially disparate effects of what some observers have called "voter disenfranchisement by bureaucracy." But in general, the tale of how highly partisan Republican elected officials and state government employees manipulated election administration in Florida, *targeting blacks* in order to suppress their votes and aid George W. Bush's victory in the state, is usually relegated to the dustbin of "responsible" reporting or "objective" empirical analysis.

For example, in his otherwise lively report on the Florida recount, *Too Close to Call*, Jeffrey Toobin downplays the issue of race and black disenfranchisement, calling the notion that black votes were suppressed in Florida in 2000 "a kind of folklore."[24] He dismisses the allegation that roadblocks had been set up in black neighborhoods to obstruct and intimidate black voters trying to get to the polls, citing the U.S. Commission on Civil Rights' finding of only one such roadblock in the entire state, which had been set up as part of an existing traffic enforcement program in Tallahassee (and lasted only ninety minutes).[25] He finds "no credible evidence" of an organized attempt to keep blacks from the polls or to discourage them at the polls with procedural delays or deliberate equipment problems, conceding only, "To be sure, voting facilities are government services, and as such, they are generally worse in poor areas, where many minority citizens live."[26] And he dismisses the "conspiracy theories" about Florida Secretary of State Katherine Harris's felon purge lists, blaming instead ineptitude. "[T]he commonly made accusation that DBT [the private firm hired to collate the lists]—or the state of Florida or Katherine Harris—disenfranchised 'thousands' of black voters seems baseless."[27]

Nearly 180,000 ballots were cast but not counted in the 2000 election in Florida, more than half of these by blacks, who make up only 12 percent of the state's population. But this disproportionately high ballot-spoilage rate is usually attributed to any number of explanations that discount racism and the deliberate partisan manipulation of the electoral process. Preexisting social and economic inequalities underlying poor election administration—the quality of election machinery used by voters to cast ballots and to count those ballots, the ease of use and accessibility of that equipment, the quality of training given to local election officials and precinct workers, and the accountability for performance of local elections officials—are seen as "unfortunate" but politically neutral causes of black voter disenfranchisement. Poor election administration is explained as a consequence of local control over elections (usually seen as either constitutionally required or a reflection of the value Americans place on federalism), and an inevitable consequence of local control is that poorer communities will have less-adequate election administration. Such inequalities and their impact are rarely connected to the legacy of centuries of racial exclusion shaping American electoral institutions and popular electoral politics.

How does the story of black vote suppression and disenfranchisement in the Florida 2000 election stack up against our theory that electoral demobilization is a central feature of party competition in the United States, and that race is its fulcrum? The evidence from Florida couldn't be clearer. Black vote suppression was central to the winning strategy of the Republicans, and the Democrats, now led by DLC politicians Al Gore, Joseph Lieberman, and Bill Clinton, were stymied in their resistance by the bald fact that the stolen election was about blacks. But first, some background on Florida politics leading up to the 2000 presidential election.

Two important developments in Florida before the 2000 election place black disenfranchisement in context: (1) the bleak long-term prospects for Republican dominance of state politics given the demographic trends under way in the state since the 1990s;[28] and (2) the antiblack policies of the newly elected Republican governor, Jeb

Bush, which stimulated a large and successful voter registration and voter mobilization campaign in 1999 and 2000 among blacks, who feared the governor's brother, presidential candidate George W. Bush, would follow the same path.

Jeb Bush first ran for governor of Florida against incumbent Democrat Lawton Chiles in 1994. Bush lost that race in no small part due to a large black vote against him stimulated by his now-infamous response when he was asked what he would do for Florida's black community if elected governor. The gubernatorial hopeful answered with a stock conservative coded response straight out of the anti–affirmative action playbook: "It's time to strive for a society where there's equality of opportunity, not equality of results. So I'm going to answer your question by saying: probably nothing." [29] Chastened by defeat, Bush spent the next several years following his brother's lead as the newly elected governor of Texas, carving out a political identity as a "compassionate conservative." Both Bush brothers attempted to blaze a new trail for the Republican Party on the issue of race. Along with national Republican Party leaders like Ken Mehlman, George and Jeb Bush advocated for repudiation by the party of cruder versions of the old-style Southern Strategy, and for new approaches to building party support among people of color. [30] As baby boomers, they understood what the previous political generation of Republican Party leaders perhaps did not, that the Republican Party will not thrive as an all-white party. "Compassionate" conservatives still manipulate racial images and messages to divide and conquer Democrats, but they do not engage in overt race-baiting, and they show their comfort with people of color by appealing to the class interests of middle- and upper-class minorities, and by elevating a handful to visible and prominent positions of power inside the party and in government.

As governor of Texas, for example, George W. Bush tested the new Republican political formula by appealing to Latinos and embracing "sensible" immigration reform, and by building a reform agenda for the Republican Party in the area of public education. Jeb Bush also cultivated an image as a racial moderate. Stung by the damage done to his image by the "probably nothing" remark, he set about building a political machine in Florida that would help him mount another attempt at winning the governor's office. He needed an issue that would allow him to meld his conservative principles with a modest appeal to racial minorities that didn't also alienate whites. Taking a page from his brother's successful campaign in Texas, the wedge issue he chose was public education reform.

By now, the cant of market solutions to social problems is familiar, as is its success in the electoral arena. Such is the rhetoric of the school "choice" movement into which Jeb Bush threw himself after his humiliating electoral defeat. As a private citizen, he lobbied lawmakers in the state capitol to pass a charter-school law and founded a think tank, the Foundation for Florida's Future, which promoted the idea of school choice. He reached out to independent black leaders like T. Willard Fair, the president of the Urban League of Greater Miami and a disaffected former Democrat who voted for Bush in 1994, to test support for school choice among traditional black leaders. He searched for cracks in the Democratic Party's hold on socially conservative black voters, fissures that polling data suggested could be opened by a "compassionate conservative" Republican candidate who embraced school choice.

With school integration gone the way of the dinosaur as a solution for public school failure, the promise of school choice for black parents is understandable. At the same time, with government now out of the business of forcing integration by judicial fiat, conservative politicians have lost a reliable "race-neutral" way of communicating with a racially resentful white voter base by being "antibusing." School choice thus serves the new Republican formula well because it signals racial moderation and potential responsiveness to blacks while at the same time promising little change to anxious whites in the way of neighborhood or school integration. Unlike the traditional Southern Strategy, the school-choice mantra does not carry with it the stigma that has come to be attached to coded racial appeals—the school-choice message targets teachers' unions rather than unruly or inferior blacks. Once the Republican-controlled Florida state legislature passed Jeb Bush's school-choice bill, he and Fair created one of the state's first charter schools in the black Miami ghetto known as Liberty City. The school, where the students wear red, white, and blue uniforms and the teachers are permitted to inflict corporal punishment, was advertised as achieving early success and served as a symbol of Jeb Bush's newfound commitment to improving opportunities for low-income blacks as he headed into the 1998 election.

With the state Democratic Party split by a factional dispute over the dumping of a black state legislator from its leadership team, the Republicans buried the Democrats in the 1998 election, maintaining their dominance in both houses of the state legislature (picking up seven more seats in the House), winning the governor's mansion, and controlling the elected cabinet. Bush gained the endorsement of several black Democrats and increased his share of the black vote to 14 percent from 6 percent just four years before, though he and the state GOP had hoped he'd do better, some predicting he would get at least 20 percent of the black vote. His support among urban blacks was particularly disappointing to the GOP at about 8 percent.[31] Leon Russell, state president of the NAACP, explained, "Obviously he went to black churches this time, and to black neighborhoods. But he didn't present any campaign issues that would attract black voters. Yeah, it's new that you came. But you came and you didn't bring anything. You blew in and you blew out."[32] As pollster Jim Kane observed, "[Bush was] sending a message as much to moderate white voters who once thought him an extremist. As a political strategy, the effort they put into black voters was to gain white moderates and keep [his Democratic opponent, Buddy] MacKay off balance."[33]

As Florida's sixty-day legislative session got under way, Bush's proposals did not reflect his campaign rhetoric, which had painted him as a moderate. Black leaders worried that blacks would be hurt by the new governor's support for a $1.2 billion tax cut, state-funded private school tuition vouchers, and tougher sentencing laws. Bush's potential political problems were further complicated by the arrival in the state of wealthy black California businessman and affirmative action foe Ward Connerly, who targeted Florida after winning petition campaigns in California and Washington State. Connerly planned to gather enough signatures to put up to four anti-affirmative action initiatives on the 2000 ballot. His actions were unanticipated and not welcome by Bush and the state GOP, because they threatened to throw a wrench into the party machine as it geared up to deliver Florida's twenty-five Electoral College votes to the governor's brother. State Republican Party leaders met with party donors and traditional GOP advocacy groups and asked them not to contribute to Connerly's Florida Civil Rights Initiative. Republicans were careful not to criticize the goal of eliminating affirmative action, and Bush managed to avoid taking a clear position on the issue, but he continued to oppose Connerly, suggesting his methods would "create confusion."[34] GOP state party chair Al Cardenas worried that a protracted anti–affirmative action ballot initiative campaign would only hurt the Republican Party in Florida as it had done in California. "Not only did the entire state suffer socially," said Cardenas, "but the Republican Party took a nosedive."[35] State representative Chris Smith, a black Democrat who had supported Bush in the governor's race, put it plainly when he told a reporter, "This thing on the ballot in Florida helps Al Gore and [Democratic U.S. Senate candidate] Bill Nelson. It will galvanize black voters, increase minority turnout tremendously."[36]

To preempt Connerly, Bush worked quickly to come up with his own anti–affirmative action initiative that would keep the question off the 2000 ballot. He directed his staff to begin a top-to-bottom review of the state's affirmative action policies and to make recommendations to him on how the policies should be modified. While mandatory court review of any proposed ballot initiative language stalled Connerly's petitioning, Bush signed an executive order in November 1999, eliminating the consideration of race or ethnicity in state university admissions practices and barring racial set-asides in state contracting, saying his new "One Florida" plan "transcended" affirmative action.[37] This move was surprising to many, including the handful of black state legislators who had crossed party lines to endorse him for governor. Bush proposed to replace racial preferences in university admissions with a program modeled on the one his brother had adopted in Texas guaranteeing admission to a state university to the top 20 percent of each Florida high school's graduating class. In addition, Bush proposed a modest increase in state financial aid, and promised to ease regulations governing state certification of minority-owned businesses.

But Jeb Bush miscalculated. If he had hoped to stanch black voter mobilization against his brother's presidential bid by throwing the black community a bone and telling them it "transcended" a bone, he misjudged the ability of blacks to know when they were being insulted and used. U.S. Representative Corrine Brown of Jacksonville emerged as one of the fiercest critics of Bush's actions. A week after the governor signed his executive order, Brown called a press conference with other black elected officials to express their outrage. She turned the controversy into an opportunity for electoral payback, urging minority voters to retaliate at the polls and warning, "His brother is running, and we're going to deal with his brother." [38]

By the New Year, it was clear that Bush's strategy was backfiring. Representative Brown, along with Florida's two other African American congressional representatives, Carrie Meek and Alcee Hastings, asked the Clinton administration to investigate Bush's One Florida plan and its ban on race as a consideration in public higher education admissions. They alleged that Bush's plan violated a partnership agreement between the state and the U.S. Department of Education's Office for Civil Rights signed the year before, which built on a 1978 desegregation order and required Florida to provide admissions to minorities under an "alternative plan." Meanwhile, two young black state representatives, Representative Tony Hill of Jacksonville and Senator Kendrick Meek of Miami, along with Barbara DeVane, a fifty-seven-year old Tallahassee grandmother and member of the National Organization for Women, staged a twenty-five-hour protest in the office of Lieutenant Governor Frank Brogan demanding that Bush rescind the One Florida plan. Following the governor's admonition to an aide to "kick their asses out," [39] more than a dozen agents from the Florida Department of Law Enforcement (FDLE) eventually expelled reporters and dragged DeVane from the room, but allowed Hill and Meek to continue their protest. Outside the capitol building, about a hundred people demonstrated, singing civil rights songs and giving speeches. One of the speech makers was Representative Carrie Meek, Kendrick Meek's mother. "We are here to say to the governor, 'There is no way we're going to go down without a struggle,' " she told the crowd. Through Brogan's window, they could see Hill holding up an envelope on which he had scribbled, "Keep the Dream Alive."[40] The sit-in ended with a compromise when Bush agreed to delay the consideration of his education plan until the state's board of regents could meet with the black caucus, and hold three hearings on his plan before a fifteen-member legislative committee convened in Tallahassee, Tampa, and Miami to allow the public to express their views.

The public hearings were raucous events. Over six hundred people showed up at the first one at the Hillsborough Community College auditorium, where they "bombard[ed] legislators with scathing criticism of Bush's plan."[41] Most who spoke criticized not only the plan but how Bush put it together, without any input from the public, from civil rights groups, or from black lawmakers. When Republican co-chair of the legislative committee Senator Jack Latvala calmly interrupted a woman who had grabbed the microphone and was speaking for several minutes to ask her, "Anything specific you want to address about the One Florida plan?" she shouted back, "It stinks!" and the crowd erupted in cheers.[42]

Bush, who had not appeared at the first hearing, attended the second one in Miami three days later. He must have wished he hadn't. More than 4,000 people streamed through a downtown theater that had a seating capacity of 1,700. Lines snaked outside the door and down the street for blocks as people waited patiently in the soft afternoon rain. Bodies flowed through the auditorium for over seven hours, the shifting crowds regulated by fire marshals. Inside, it was another raucous hearing. *Miami Herald* writer Steve Bousquet was there and filed this report:

> As the governor listened from the front row, one speaker after another blasted his decision to wipe out state government racial and gender set-asides by executive order last November. Most of the more than 100 who spoke for three minutes apiece were black or Hispanic. Many were women. Most seemed determined

to get the governor to back down. A man who urged the crowd to "give Governor Bush a chance" was drowned out by thundering jeers. "We have been bought, sold, killed, beaten, raped, executed, exploited, excluded, shamed and scorned for a very long time," said Peggy Demon. . . . "The word unfair is not a fair description of our plight."[43]

Senator Latvala said he would push for a slowdown until the plan could go through a legislative review. "You can't sit through two or three hours of this and not be moved by the concerns. . . . Bush needs to appreciate the necessity of listening to people once in a while and learn to compromise a little bit."[44] Latvala seemed to appreciate what Bush didn't, that anger in the black community was escalating. People were upset by Bush's arrogance and his assumption that he could court their votes and then dump them once winning office, ending affirmative action with the stroke of a pen.

Inside and outside the auditorium volunteers set up tables to register people to vote and enlist their support for a massive protest march in Tallahassee planned for the first day of the legislative session, March 7—a day that was also the thirty-fifth anniversary of the famous civil rights march over the Edmund Pettus Bridge on the road to Selma, Alabama. Michelle Davis Hines, who had waited for two hours to get into the hearing and then four hours more before she could speak her mind, "brought the crowd to its feet, shouting: 'Let your voice be heard! Vote anyone and everyone out of office who does not support affirmative action!' "[45] Something big was stirring among the people in the packed auditorium, and newspaper columnist William Cooper could feel it rumble as he looked out over the faces in the crowd. "A pastor, retired school teachers, a state probation officer and social workers, to name a few. By looking at some of the people who attended the hearing, it's easy to see how the common person can turn a moment into a movement."[46]

The next week, another 1,200 people attended the third and final hearing in Tallahassee while Governor Bush skipped out. Again Bush's lieutenant governor promoted the One Florida plan, and again he praised the way it would "expand diversity and opportunity." Again the more than one hundred people who spoke were overwhelmingly against it. After the regents and the cabinet approved the new "race-neutral" admissions policy, Bush made a tactical retreat and removed other parts of the plan that required legislative approval. Instead of pushing for the elimination of affirmative action from all state contracting, which would have required two months of hearings and legislation, Bush wiped out affirmative action in only the fifteen state agencies directly under his control. Through his single-minded determination to outmaneuver Connerly, Florida became the first state in the nation to voluntarily ban race and gender preferences in college admissions. One Republican official expressed some relief that the episode was finally over. "Sometimes the best thing to do is retreat. We don't lose anything. The university portion is still in effect. We get most of what we want for state contracts. And they don't get a chance to keep beating on us." He added, prematurely, "I think it's going to be very hard for them to keep this issue alive after March 7." [47]

Black leaders began organizing in earnest for the March 7, 2000, demonstration. Kendrick Meek and Tony Hill, the two young state legislators who staged the sit-in in Lieutenant Governor Brogan's office and sparked the growing movement to oppose any "turning back of the clock" on civil rights in Florida, launched a weeklong bus tour to promote the upcoming rally in Tallahassee. They planned to crisscross the state, with stops in Tampa, West Palm Beach, Fort Lauderdale, Daytona, Orlando, Pensacola, Cocoa Beach, and Lakeland, among others. In a church parking lot, the two spoke at a rally organized to send them off as about a hundred people chanted, "We're not going back!" [48]

On the night before the march, about two hundred people crowded into the park across the street from the governor's mansion. They held a prayer vigil and sang hymns to raise spirits for the march. Alma Colson of Tallahassee was there with her eight-year old nephew, Toran Davis. "You've got to be fed first with the spiritual side before you go into the movement," she explained. One block away at one of the city's largest lobbying firms, a thousand lobbyists and legislators got sustenance from a different source. As they munched on chilled shrimp and drank champagne to celebrate the opening of the annual two-month legislative season, busloads of Floridians and supporters from out of state began the long journey to Tallahassee.[49] Many rode all night; others drove or walked.

The March 7 rally is considered one of the largest ever held in Florida's state capital, with estimates ranging from eleven thousand (by official sources) to over fifty thousand (by march organizers) in attendance. As the sun moved into the morning sky, people poured into Tallahassee saying they feared Governor Bush was taking away the gains blacks and other minorities had made since the days of the civil rights movement. Police closed the route to the capitol building, forcing many to disembark from their buses a mile away. When they marched into the city, they were greeted with police officers posted on nearly every corner near the capitol building.

Inside Bush was delivering his second State of the State address, reassuring Florida lawmakers that "the vast majority of Floridians favor the elimination of affirmative action programs," followed by a statement of his commitment to provide opportunities to all Floridians. But Bush didn't finish the sentence, because Republican legislators began clapping right after the "eliminating affirmative action" part, "leaving an embarrassed Bush to try to plow ahead through the inadvertent applause line."[50] Insulated from the sign-waving crowd assembling outside, their chants of "Shame on Bush! Shame on Bush!" ringing through the air on a hot afternoon, Bush asserted that under his One Florida plan, state universities would admit more minorities and state government would let more contracts to minority-owned businesses. He never acknowledged the protest. Mary Nesbitt, a nursing home employee, said she read Bush's One Florida plan and was concerned for her two great-grandchildren. "Affirmative action is gone," she said. "If [Bush's plan] doesn't work, what will we have? Back to square one. If he wanted to do something better, he could have improved what existed."[51]

Four hundred miles away in Miami, six hundred school bus drivers took the day off so that they could attend the rally, leaving thousands of students stranded.[52] Leon County schools gave students permission to skip classes to participate in the march. The faces of the young were everywhere. Melvin Wright, a senior at Florida A&M University, gave up his spring break to take part in the march. "It's a chance for us to have the opportunity for jobs and to get higher education," he said. "Spring break is every year, and I can go home any weekend I want. This is a once-in-a-lifetime deal."[53] Travis Thomas, a senior at Tallahassee's James Rickards High School, took the day off to attend the rally. "It affects us because not all of us are in the top 20 percent," he said. Shameeka Dixon was there with her mother, April Barlow. She told a reporter that she was risking getting an F from her South Fork High School English teacher. "I just like feeling like I'm taking action, standing up for what I believe in," she said. Her mother concurred: "She's making Florida history today."[54]

The Reverend Jesse Jackson, a speaker at the rally along with other national civil rights leaders like Martin Luther King III and NAACP president Kweisi Mfume, reiterated the sentiments of the crowd. "When you inherit the name, when you inherit legal protection, when you inherit the wealth, when you inherit skin color, when you inherit your parents' friends for advantage, you just don't understand," Jackson said.[55] Several speakers urged people to register to vote and linked the One Florida plan to the presidential candidacy of the governor's brother, the Republican front-runner, George W. Bush. Ion Sanchez, Leon County's supervisor of elections, sat at a small booth near the capitol. In less than four hours 170 people registered to vote, he reported, most of them Democrats and most of them students.[56] U.S. Representative Corrine Brown didn't beat around the bush when she came to the microphone. "Can you imagine what it would be like on November 8th to wake up and open the paper and see that George W. is president of the United States?" she roared. "That is my worst nightmare. We got to go to the polls and vote those Bushes out!"[57]

Through the spring and summer of 2000, black opposition mounted to both Connerly's ballot initiative effort and Bush's One Florida plan. A coalition of groups called Floridians Representing Equity and Equality (FREE) coordinated a series of meetings across the state to keep the issue on the front burner while the One Florida plan was under review by the courts.[58] They raised money for their own ballot initiative campaign to counter Connerly's in anticipation of his passing the required court review. In May, state legislators Kendrick Meek and Tony Hill announced new plans for yet another protest campaign against the elimination of affirmative action. They told reporters that they hoped to energize black voters and to encourage voter registration efforts among blacks and minorities across the state, calling on blacks to "Arrive with Five [more voters]" at the polls in November. The tactic was straight out of Harold Washington's 1983 playbook.[59] "Our job is to let people know there is an election coming," said Meek.[60] Term limits meant there would be some sixty-one open legislative seats on the ballot in addition to races for the presidency and other federal offices. Barbara DeVane, the National Organization for Women activist who had sat in with Meek and Hill at the capitol, planned to join them on their "Save Florida" walking tour. "The African American community in November can either be a hero or a zero," Hill told reporters. "We're going to educate people on the issues. We're going to tell them what happened in session, how mean-spirited they were," referring to both Republican-controlled chambers of the legislature.[61] They planned to meet at each stop with local leaders and ask prospective voters to sign pledge cards committing themselves to bringing five more voters to the polls. The group kicked off their walk on June 19, or Juneteenth, the 135th anniversary of the unofficial end of slavery, and over the course of the tour from Tallahassee to Miami, the two activists handed out over two hundred thousand voter registration cards.[62] Hill insisted, "Never again will the voters be left out of a crucial dialogue."[63]

Meek and Hill maintained that their walking tour was nonpartisan and that their aim was to highlight issues such as education, health care, and equal pay with the hope that the more voters learned about the issues, the more they'd be likely to vote. No Republicans joined them on the tour, and the response from Republican state officials was telling at a time when the party said it wanted to court black votes. Al Cardenas, state chair of the Republican Party, charged, "Apparently fear and anger is the theme of Democrats and these messengers [Meek and Hill] are experts (at) spewing venom." [64] The state Republican Party then put out a press release in which Cardenas called the statewide voter drive a "hate tour." Black leaders immediately called on Cardenas to retract the statement and appealed to Governor Bush to repudiate it. But Bush remained silent, and Jamie Wilson, the executive director of the Florida Republican Party, issued a statement avoiding the issue altogether by shifting the party's complaint from one about "hate" to one about "liberal causes." In it he said, "The Save Florida Tour is a line up of the who's who of liberal causes . . . a transparent attempt to mask an extremely liberal Democratic agenda." [65]

The NAACP's legal challenge to the One Florida plan delayed implementation of the plan's "Talented 20" component for state university admissions. Court proceedings produced evidence that at the University of North Florida (UNF) in Jacksonville, where affirmative action had been abandoned the decade before, black enrollment trailed that at other campuses in the state system. UNF assistant provost Lynda Lewis testified that since affirmative action had been abandoned at the 12,300-student campus in 1989, black enrollment had increased only 3 percentage points, from 6.9 percent to 9.9 percent in 1999, well below the state system's overall 14 percent and the 12 percent at Florida State University. UNF also trailed the University of South Florida, Florida Atlantic University, and Florida International University. "We're not using race for admission," Lewis told reporters. "If I were using race for admission I probably would be up near 24 percent, 25 percent." [66] Despite these findings, in July the court upheld the Talented 20 program's ban on the use of race in college admissions. One day later, the Florida Supreme Court concluded its review of Ward Connerly's anti–affirmative action ballot initiatives, denying ballot access on the grounds that the initiatives' language was too broad and could mislead voters. It was Connerly's first defeat, to the relief of Governor Bush, who called the court's decision "a good thing for our state." [67] Not so good for Republican Party fortunes, however, was the voter mobilization movement heating up in black communities across Florida and galvanized by opposition to the One Florida plan.

Watched by the national Democratic and Republican parties, but less visible to the media covering national campaigns, was the important role black voter turnout played across the South in 1998, but especially in states where Democrats eked out victories that year. In 1996, national black turnout in Bill Clinton's reelection victory over Republican senator Bob Dole declined to depressingly low levels, as did turnout among all groups. Two years later, however, partly in response to the Republican Party's assault on Bill Clinton and the impeachment charade, black turnout increased again, defying a national trend of declining turnout in congressional elections. White turnout declined between 1994 and 1998, from 50 percent to 47 percent, Hispanic turnout remained at 20 percent, and Asian and Pacific Islander turnout fell from 22 percent to 19 percent; but black turnout rose from 37 percent to 40 percent, a statistically significant increase of 3 percentage points.[68] Further analysis of turnout patterns by the Census Bureau found that controlling for standard socioeconomic factors that predict voting, blacks were more likely to vote in 1998 than nonblacks.[69] Targeted black voter mobilization campaigns for Democratic candidates in several states appeared to have made the difference. In Georgia, for example, black turnout went from 19 percent in 1994 to 29 percent in 1998; in South Carolina it climbed from 21 percent to 26 percent; and in both cases embattled Democratic candidates crested to victory on the strength of black turnout. Roy Barnes in Georgia was the beneficiary of massive black voter turnout in Fulton and DeKalb counties when he ran for governor, and in South Carolina, the increase in the black vote helped move Democrat Jim Hodges into the governor's mansion and to reelect Fritz Hollings to the U.S. Senate.

Republicans conceded that the Democrats generated impressive black turnout in 1998 and 1999 but dismissed their ability to drive black turnout any higher in 2000.[70] National Democratic Party strategists appeared to disagree. Al Gore hired Donna Brazile, the dynamic architect of the party's 1998 black mobilization effort in the

South, as his campaign manager.[71] This clearly signaled his understanding that black turnout in key swing states, including Illinois, Michigan, and New Jersey, might make or break his bid for the presidency. After the 2000 party conventions, the two standard-bearers, George W. Bush and Al Gore, were running neck and neck in as many as eighteen states. Campaigns to register and mobilize voters were picking up steam.

In Florida, where the polls were predicting a dead heat, political scientist Susan MacManus told the *St. Petersburg Times* that she'd never seen such an intense voter mobilization effort directed at Florida voters.[72] Both parties were separately spending about $800,000 a week on television ads in the state by October and pouring millions of dollars into their ground operations, outpacing the combined $2.5 million the national party organizations devoted to the state before September.[73]

Nationally, the black political leadership was active in get-out-the-vote campaigns in several of the battleground states, including Florida, where black voter turnout might swing the election. The national campaign had several components. With money from the Democratic Party, the Reverend Jesse Jackson toured cities with large black populations to lead rallies and encourage local voter registration drives. Advertisements were placed on movie screens of Magic Johnson Theaters and on Black Entertainment Television exhorting viewers to "Lift every voice and vote!" In Jacksonville, taxi driver Donald Duckett took ten minutes out of his day to register to vote at an unlikely place near his home, the Karpeles Manuscript Library Museum, telling a reporter that he learned about the opportunity to register while listening to *The Tom Joyner Show*.[74] In addition to these message campaigns, the NAACP mounted a multimillion-dollar drive called the National Voter Fund in July to energize its more than two thousand branches to register black voters and get them to the polls. A good deal of that money was spent on a get-out-the-vote campaign in Florida.[75] The Congressional Black Caucus sent its members out on the road on a bus tour to help local campaigns and drive up the black vote.[76] Floridians were experiencing the largest mobilization of black voters in the history of the state. On October

31, 2000, one week before the election, students from Florida A&M University led a "We Are Voting Early" march to the Leon County Courthouse echoing Hill and Meek's message to "Arrive with Five." Elections supervisor Ion Sanchez later announced that 780 people had voted early, and that 650 of them were students.[77]

Indeed, according to David Bosits, an expert on black voting at the Joint Center for Political and Economic Studies in Washington, D.C., the national voter mobilization effort in 2000 was "by far the largest and most expensive ever made to generate black turnout, with at least 10 times as much money being spent as in 1996."[78] By election day, as voters headed out to the polls, Florida was the largest state where Bush and Gore were still tied,[79] and the press was calling Florida "the mother of all battleground states."[80] What happened next reveals how the dynamics of voter mobilization and demobilization in American electoral politics turns on the axis of race.

By midday of election day 2000, the complaints from voters in several states, but especially Florida, were rolling in on a hotline established by the NAACP's national headquarters. NAACP national president Kweisi Mfume contacted the Justice Department, which sent an agent to the organization's Washington, D.C., office to monitor the nature of the complaints.[81] Other civil rights groups began hearing the same grievances from Florida voters—blacks who had never had any brush with the law were being told within earshot of other people waiting in line that they wouldn't be allowed to vote because they were felons; police were stopping people on their way to the polls in Daytona Beach and outside Tallahassee; elderly black voters showing up at their regular polling places were told that the polls had moved; blacks but not whites were being asked for multiple forms of identification and being denied their right to vote when they were unable to produce it, even though Florida law at the time said they could cast affidavit ballots;[82] machine breakdowns in Tallahassee had prevented black Florida A&M students from casting ballots.[83] Mfume and NAACP staff scrambled to send two hundred people from other states into Florida "because we were getting that many calls about irregularities."[84] On Friday, he flew to Miami to investigate for himself what was quickly beginning to look like a pattern of massive black voter disenfranchisement.

The NAACP held hearings on the weekend after the election and collected first-person evidence later used in a landmark class-action suit filed by six civil rights groups on behalf of thousands of black Floridians who were prevented from voting in 2000.[85] But national media attention was already being pulled away from the story of black disenfranchisement by the unfolding drama of the recount and the courtroom shootout between the two candidates' teams of lawyers. The Clinton administration's Justice Department failed to act swiftly, despite the preliminary data collected by the NAACP and other civil rights groups showing that there were very serious problems in Florida. As the evidence of an administrative meltdown continued to mount, Attorney General Janet Reno was nowhere to be found. The local media reported dozens of stories about people trying to vote and being thwarted by poll workers, inaccurate registration lists, and mechanical failure; tales of ballot cards that didn't fit into the machines and couldn't be punched properly; long lines made longer by confusion and misinformation about whether voters were going to be allowed to vote, where to vote, how to vote.

In Broward County dozens of people said they were unable to cast their ballots when poll workers checking on minor discrepancies in the records were unable to reach the main elections office. In Gadsden County, one of the poorest counties in the state and the only Florida county whose population is more than half African American, election officials recounting ballot cards said they often guessed at which candidate voters intended to cast votes for; at 12.4 percent, Gadsden had the highest ballot-discard rate of any county in the entire state.[86] Its elections supervisor, a white conservative Democrat named Denny Hutchinson, who spoke openly about giving money to George W. Bush, refused offers by county commissioners to station more polling places in neighborhoods to accommodate the increase in registration. Ed Dixon, one of those commissioners, said that Hutchinson liked things the way they were. He added, "In the only county that's a majority African American, you want a decreased turnout."[87] In Volusia County, a poll worker walked into the canvassing board office with a bag of uncounted ballots, prompting a judge to order the office sealed with crime scene yellow tape and guarded by the police after suspecting the poll worker may have tampered with the ballots.

The case of Duval County illuminates disenfranchisement by ballot design. There the elections supervisor, John Stafford, a white Republican, designed a ballot that spread the presidential candidates across two pages, something Duval voters had never seen before. The Duval ballot has since been called the "caterpillar" ballot because the list of presidential candidates crept down one side of the page and then up and down the other. Stafford placed a misleading sample ballot insert into a widely distributed local paper that failed to show the two-page feature of the presidential contest; the ad instructed citizens to make sure they "vote all pages." Calling the discrepancy between the sample ballot published in the newspaper and the actual ballot an "oversight," Stafford's spokeswoman, Susan Tucker Johnson, downplayed the impact of the misinformation on Duval's remarkably high spoiled-ballot rate.[88] On election day, when confused voters voted every page of their ballots, those ballots were invalidated. Nearly twenty-two thousand ballots were thrown out in Duval County because voters followed instructions and voted every page, including both pages of the presidential race.[89] Four years earlier, Stafford's presidential ballot had been one page long; turnout was only about 10 percent lower in that election, but the ballot-spoilage rate was a third of what it was in 2000.

The city of Jacksonville, which hosts a naval air base and an expanding financial center, encompasses most of Duval County thanks to the consolidation of the city and county in the 1960s. Despite the relative affluence of parts of the county, nearly half of the residents were judged to be functionally illiterate as late as 1993.[90] This could explain why some didn't know what to do when they found themselves in front of Stafford's unfamiliar caterpillar ballot. Local Democratic Party workers and get-out-the-vote volunteers had taken up the cry "vote every page" in their outreach efforts. With that cry in their heads, and the confusing caterpillar ballot before them, thousands of voters struggled with the instructions in the voting booth and mistakenly "overvoted." Some later complained that when they asked for help they didn't get it.[91]

Toobin writes that "the ballot in Duval County was probably a greater fiasco [for Gore] than Palm Beach's more notorious butterfly."[92] Just over a quarter of Duval County's population is African American and disproportionately poor. But about 42 percent of the invalidated ballots came from four Jacksonville city council districts that are Democratic and largely black.[93] An analysis of the statewide overvote problem by *USA Today* and Knight Ridder suggested that ballot design problems in Duval probably cost Gore at least 2,600 votes. When word got out that as many as 27,000 votes had been tossed (this number includes "undervotes" as well as "overvotes"), a few dozen protestors assembled and picketed the Duval County elections office. They called for a revote and carried signs demanding that John Stafford resign. A few Bush supporters heckled the protestors, telling them that if they didn't like the system, they should "go back to where you came from." According to Toobin, after the election in Florida, it was not uncommon to hear Republicans say that if people—meaning black people—were too dumb to follow the rules, it was only fair to exclude their ballots.[94] The views of some political conservatives concerning Duval's spoiled-ballot problem opens a window on their mean-spiritedness. Writing in the conservative magazine the *National Review*, John Derbyshire jokes:

> What seems to have happened [in Duval County] is that Democratic precinct workers had energetically registered, then transported to the polls, voters from wherever they could find them, without any regard to whether these voters had any interest in, or understanding of, the contest, or any familiarity with voting procedures. Yes, some Democrats are too dumb to vote. So are some Republicans. But people that dumb generally stay home on Election Day.[95]

In the days after the election, Mike Langton, the chair of the Gore campaign for northeast Florida, spent hours with John Stafford to determine what problems voters may have faced in Duval. The Gore campaign had only seventy-two hours after the closing of the polls to request a manual recount. Florida law requires candidates to file "protests" or requests for manual recounts by county, and each request must be justified by evidence suggesting problems with the machine count, so Langton needed to know whether Duval should be included on the Democrats' list of recount counties (it wasn't). Later, Langton told reporters that he asked Stafford how many ballots were "rejected" and that Stafford told him, "not many, perhaps 200 or 300." [96] Only after the deadline for filing protests did Stafford reveal that the number was closer to 27,000. "We have been, to put it bluntly," said Langton, "screwed." [97]

Two years after the contested 2000 election, when the Justice Department got around to filing lawsuits for violations of voters' rights in three Florida counties, those cases involved minor language-assistance issues. As reporter Steve Bousquet put it,

> after an 18-month investigation, nearly 11,000 complaints, discussions with [Florida] Attorney General Bob Butterworth's office and even a review of the NAACP's complaint logs, the federal government has determined that only certain minority voters were wronged. They were Hispanics in Orange and Osceola counties and Haitians in Miami-Dade. Not a single word from Justice about Katherine Harris' flawed purged voter list. Nothing, either, about the high number of discarded "overvotes" in areas with high concentrations of black voters, such as Jacksonville. [98]

Notably, all three counties the Justice Department threatened to sue had gone for Gore, and two of the three election supervisors were Democrats, while the other was a nonpartisan appointee of the county commission. Similarly misguided, when Congress got around to passing an election-reform bill, it focused on voting-technology issues, not partisan election administration, and funneled billions of precious taxpayer dollars to private voting-machine vendors, creating a mess that has yet to be cleaned up. There was, of course, another path, one that starts with the basic respect due the law and the civil rights of black people. As alleged in the NAACP class-action suit (*NAACP v. Smith*) and tacitly acknowledged by the state in settlement agreements resulting from that suit that require it to comply with the law, Florida violated the NVRA in a number of ways: by failing to properly process voter registration applications and changes of address in a timely manner, by illegally purging eligible voters from the registration rolls and failing to transfer the names of inactive voters to lists in a uniform and nondiscriminatory way, and by failing to allow voters who moved within their county to vote or update their registration, as required by federal law.[99]

If the Justice Department had been monitoring Florida's failure to properly implement the NVRA, and had acted to require it to comply, many of the problems faced by black voters in Florida could have been averted.[100] And yet, plenty of blacks had voted in the election, and they represented a larger share of Florida's active electorate than of the state's adult black population as a whole. U.S. attorney general Janet Reno, a Florida native, acknowledged the complaints flowing into her office, but urged caution. "We would have to look to see if there is a basis for a federal violation," she said, adding that she saw no reason for the federal government to "jump in" to the controversy.[101]

The U.S. Commission on Civil Rights, following up on the evidence presented at the NAACP hearings, held several days of its own hearings to investigate the complaints. A majority of the commissioners found a similar pattern to the NAACP findings. A statistical analysis conducted for the commission by voting rights expert Allan Lichtman showed large and significant racial disparities in ballot rejection rates (otherwise known as "lost votes," "spoiled ballots," etc.).[102] Lichtman's study found that one out of every ten ballots cast by black voters in Florida was set aside as invalid, compared with much smaller rates of ballot rejection for nonblacks. In some counties the rate was as high as one in five. If the rejection rates for blacks had been equal to those for nonblacks, Lichtman estimates that more than fifty thousand additional ballots cast by blacks would have been counted in the 2000 presidential election in Florida.[103]

• • •

Can we ever know if the Republican Party had a plan to disenfranchise black voters in Florida and "keep down" their votes? What would constitute proof? What we do know is that black turnout in Florida in 2000 was up a whopping 40 percent over 1996 levels, from about 527,000 to 925,000 votes.[104] We know that black Floridians gave 93 percent of their votes to Al Gore, increasing the share of black votes from 9 percent of the Democratic total in 1996 to 14 percent in 2000. We also know that African Americans in Florida's 2000 election at the very least experienced what civil rights lawyers call "structural disenfranchisement" overseen by state officials with close ties to the Republican candidate. This is essentially the major finding of the U.S. Commission on Civil Rights, which conducted an extensive probe of the Florida election.[105]

According to the racial justice organization Advancement Project, structural disenfranchisement is

> the modern equivalent of poll taxes, grandfather clauses, and literacy tests . . . [and] the cumulative effect of multiple problems and breakdowns in election systems. . . . there is no one guilty actor and rarely smoking gun evidence of discriminatory motive. Instead, inequity is built into the system. . . . structural disenfranchisement also includes the bureaucratic blunders, governmental indifference, and flagrant disregard for voting rights that produced and will continue to produce election day nightmares like Florida.[106]

Structural disenfranchisement can happen through the actions of election officials, as when election administrators prevent eligible voters from casting ballots due to inaccuracies in registration records.[107] It can result in "lost votes"—ballots cast but not counted because of voter error, voting machine failure, or administrative mistakes.

Partisan disenfranchisement "consists of tactics one political party uses to depress the turnout of another party's constituency."[108] For all practical purposes, the difference between the two forms of disenfranchisement is not a matter of motivation, since both are products of human intention. After all, in a democracy, if there is clear evidence that rules and procedures are preventing eligible voters from casting legitimate ballots, and those rules and procedures are then not modified to correct the problem, the failure should be considered intentional. Therefore, the main difference between structural and partisan disenfranchisement is not that the former is accidental and the latter intentional, as is often implied; it is the legality of the practices leading to blocked voting. In general, structural disenfranchisement is not illegal; rather, it is systemic and a function of historical and existing inequities in resources, the aftereffects of partisan manipulation of election rules and government indifference. Partisan disenfranchisement, which takes the form of outright voter suppression or intimidation, can be illegal.[109]

The amazing 2000 Florida presidential election, where nearly 180,000 votes were "lost," is the most scrutinized electoral contest in American history. It exposed the usually obscured ways in which *complex election rules open the way to partisan manipulation.* The underfunding of state bureaucracies responsible for election management and the lack of enforceable national standards were also manifest problems in Florida. But mechanical breakdowns, mismanagement, and manipulation are characteristic of American elections; they are not unique to one state or one election.[110] A number of important studies document the seriousness of the problems in 2000 (certainly not relieved by the enactment of the Help America Vote Act of 2002). For example, a nonpartisan analysis of voting technology by a team of computer scientists, mechanical engineers, and political scientists at the California Institute of Technology and MIT, for example, found that *4 million to 6 million votes* were lost in the 2000 election out of 111 million cast because ballots were poorly designed and confusing, voting equipment broke down on election day, or registration lists at the polls were inaccurate.[111] A postelection survey of local election officials by the General Accounting Office (GAO) found that approximately 57 percent of the nation's more than ten thousand voting jurisdictions had a major problem with election day operations, including maintaining accurate voter registration lists, voting machine breakdowns, processing absentee ballots, recruiting and training poll workers, and canvassing the vote.[112] And a series of investigative reports following both the 2000 and 2004 presidential elections from the office of U.S. Representative John Conyers, the chair of the House Judiciary Committee, document that well over 1 million voters were disenfranchised in those elections. In 2000, at least 1,276,916 voters in thirty-one states and the District of Columbia had their votes discarded, and in at least four states the number of unrecorded ballots was larger than the margin of victory. In 2004, possibly tens of thousands of voters in *just one state*, Ohio, were disenfranchised through what appears to be partisan manipulation of complex voting arrangements.[113]

The 2000 election in Florida was a circus. It was also a tragedy. The circus began when Jeb Bush tried to vault over racial politics by eliminating affirmative action in Florida in favor of his One Florida policy. The move precipitated a huge voter mobilization effort by blacks. And that effort in turn led to a reinvigorated campaign to suppress black voters. The tragedy, of course, is the corrosive effects of sustained racism and voter disenfranchisement on democracy. If there is one scene from the 2000 election that sums it all up, it must be the spectacle of Vice President Al Gore gaveling down African American House members, one after the other, as they rose to object to the counting of Florida's Electoral College votes during a joint session of Congress:

> VICE PRESIDENT GORE: The Chair now hands to the tellers the certificate of the electors for President and Vice President of the State of Florida. . . . Is there objection? . . . Is the objection in writing and signed by a Member of the House and by a Senator?
>
> REP. ALCEE HASTINGS OF FLORIDA: . . . I must object because of the overwhelming evidence of official misconduct, deliberate fraud, and an attempt to suppress voter turnout. . . . The objection is in writing, signed by a number of Members of the House of Representatives, but not by a Member of the Senate. . . .
>
> VICE PRESIDENT GORE: Since the present objection lacks the

signature of a Senator, accordingly, the objection may not be received. Are there other objections? . . .

REP. CARRIE MEEK OF FLORIDA: I have an objection. . . . it is in writing and signed by myself and several of my constituents from Florida. A Senator is missing. . . .

REP. CORRINE BROWN OF FLORIDA: I stand for the purpose of objecting to the counting of the vote from the State of Florida as read. . . . [The objection] is in writing and signed by several House colleagues on behalf of . . . the 27,000 voters of Duval County, of which 16,000 of them are African Americans that were disenfranchised in this last election. . . .

REP. EDDIE BERNICE JOHNSON OF TEXAS: I rise on behalf of the Congressional Black Caucus to object to the 25 electoral votes from Florida. . . . [The objection] is in writing, signed by a number of Members of Congress, and because we received hundreds of thousands of telegrams and e-mails and telephone calls, but we do not have a Senator. . . .

REP. SHEILA JACKSON-LEE OF TEXAS: I have an objection. . . . it is in writing, it is signed by myself on behalf of . . . the millions of Americans who have been disenfranchised by Florida's inaccurate vote count, along with my House colleagues . . . I do not have a Senator who has signed this objection. . . .

REP. MAXINE WATERS OF CALIFORNIA: I rise to object to the fraudulent 25 Florida electoral votes. . . . The objection is in writing, and I do not care that it is not signed by a Member of the Senate. . . . there are gross violations of the Voting Rights Act from Florida, and I object. . . .

VICE PRESIDENT AL GORE: On the basis previously stated, the objection may not be received. . . . May God bless our new President and our new Vice President, and may God bless the United States of America.[114]

Black lawmakers (and a few others) attempted twenty protests, and each time they were denied and refused debate by the vice president citing congressional rules of procedure. As some spoke, other members shouted them down, yelling, "Regular order!" to press Gore to cut them off. After several failed attempts by the black lawmakers to sever the meeting, Florida's Electoral College votes were added to George W. Bush's total, and the black caucus members walked out.[115]

Since then, a series of close national elections and continuing voter mobilization efforts have made the tactics of vote suppression, the subject of our next chapter, even more important.

6

KEEPING DOWN THE VOTE:
THE CONTEMPORARY REVIVAL OF
VOTE SUPPRESSION TACTICS

The attorney general admitted there was no fraud, that no ballot was altered. . . . But [Texas] Attorney General Greg Abbott charged me with a crime. . . . All I did was mail ballots for folks who couldn't get to a mailbox themselves, just like I've done for the past decade.

—Willie Ray, 2008[1]

The 2000 presidential election demonstrated how "hardball" party operatives continue to exploit electoral rules—themselves the crystallization of past vote suppression efforts—to "keep down the (black) vote." Like vote suppression since the days of Reconstruction, vote suppression today masquerades under the cover of party-run "ballot-security" campaigns to fight fraud, and is also embedded in the rigmarole of "prudent" election administration. Either way, formal and informal practices and campaign techniques that target minorities for vote suppression are usually justified as necessary to promote the "integrity" of the electoral process, a formulation that makes dirty politics look clean.

For the parties, the payoff for using vote suppression tactics increases when elections are tight, which is why we've seen their revival of late. The racial aspects of vote suppression are always publicly denied, but nevertheless implied in the reiterated argument that these practices are needed to clean up elections. The argument harkens back to the late nineteenth century and some of the debates over what to do about black suffrage in the "Redeemed" states of the former Confederacy. Proceedings from a number of the constitutional conventions of the time reveal a concern among white supremacists that the cost of stealing elections was becoming too high. The rise of the Populists had divided whites, and "white men have gotten to cheating each other until we don't have any honest elections," complained former governor William C. Oates at Alabama's 1901 convention.[2] A few years before, a "prominent Democrat" from Virginia expressed a similar view when he was quoted in a Virginia newspaper worrying that "[c]heating at elections is demoralizing our whole people. We are deteriorating as a people, and the principal cause of our deterioration is this idiotic nonsense about 'preserving white civilization' by cheating."[3] For the state constitution writers, observed the historian C. Vann Woodward, the remedy to all the fraud and demoralization of southern civilization "was the disfranchisement of the Negro."[4] A delegate to the Alabama convention explained: "We want to be relieved of purchasing the Negroes to carry elections. I want cheaper votes."[5] The paradox of taking away the black man's vote before it could be bought was clear enough to at least one white Republican delegate at Virginia's constitutional convention, who darkly mused, "The remedy suggested here is to punish the man who has been injured." Indeed, he observed, blacks were to be disenfranchised by the new constitutions of the Redeemer governments "to prevent the Democratic election officials from stealing their votes."[6]

It is tempting to tell story after story of how average American citizens trying to vote in recent national elections have been hassled and harassed by election officials or party operatives; had their names wrongly purged from the voter registration rolls; were improperly challenged about their eligibility and called to election board hearings to prove it; were photographed while standing in line to vote by campaign operatives trying to intimidate them by demanding to see identification; were subject to misinformation campaigns urging them to vote on the wrong day; were bullied by men with clipboards dressed to look like government officials, who drove in black sedans from one polling place to another to intimidate more voters; were told their college dormitory was not a legal voting address despite a court order finding that it was; were wrongly accused of fraud or of being a felon barred from voting—the list goes on and on. Note that in such instances a suppressed vote becomes a non-event. A discouraged voter leaves no evidence behind, making it difficult to develop tallies of the numbers of votes lost. Moreover, there are myriad ways to suppress votes through a range of campaign tactics and through the assiduous application of detailed rules to disqualify voters. But, we don't need to know the total number of votes suppressed to understand the strategic uses of demobilization. This is the lesson of the 2000 Florida election, where the presidency turned on a margin of 537 votes.

Instead of the litany of stories, we will delineate the current methods of keeping the vote down: the arsenal of strategies, techniques, and plain old dirty tricks used by partisan election officials, party operatives, and campaign workers to demobilize some portion of the electorate in order to win elections. We give a few instances of the main types of vote suppression below.

None of the strategies for keeping down the vote are new. Many, as noted, have antecedents as far back as the late nineteenth century. This is so because the basic legal framework for administering elections—personal registration systems, residency requirements, partisan election administration, decentralized authority and non-uniform rules across the states, felon disenfranchisement, and the like—has not changed much since then, despite the passage of landmark legislation and federal intervention to protect voting rights over the last forty years. The tactics used by political campaigns exploit the rules for what they are: the crystallization and institutionalization of past efforts to keep down the vote. Without laws that strip citizens convicted of felonies of their right to vote, there can be no felon purge list. And the flawed felon purge list is more easily used when the political parties are allowed to run elections, often under the screen of "bipartisan" election administration. For every story of a deliberately false campaign flyer circulated in a black neighborhood, or of a purge knocking eligible black voters off the registration rolls, or even of an officially sanctioned voter fraud investigation finding no fraud but keeping the myth of voter fraud alive, there are many others.

Misinformation Campaigns and "Deceptive Practices"

In the run-up to the 2004 election, Republican pollster Tony Fabrizio, an adviser to the 1996 presidential campaign of Bob Dole, admitted to a reporter that vote suppression tactics "conducted off the radar of national politics" in the form of flyers and clandestine telephone misinformation campaigns are "harsher than you can ever be in a TV ad." He explained, "If they're [the recipient of a deceptive flyer or telephone call] a Bush voter anyway, nothing lost. If it gets [others] to stay home, that's just as good."[7] Spreading misinformation to dampen turnout among targeted groups is not uncommon in American electoral campaigns, and no federal law specifically criminalizes deliberately giving false information to the public about the requirements to register or vote, or misinforming voters about polling place locations, or the dates of elections, or the hours polling sites are open.[8] If a campaign practice is not explicitly illegal, and it "keeps down the vote" on the opponent's side, there is a good chance it will be used.[9] There are numerous examples from recent elections. In 2002, flyers were circulated in Louisiana advising "Vote!!! Bad Weather? No problem!!! If the weather is uncomfortable on election day, remember you can wait and cast your ballot on Tuesday, December 10th," three days *after* the election.[10] The same year, flyers appeared in black neighborhoods in Baltimore stating, "URGENT NOTICE. Come out to vote on November 6th. Before you come to vote make sure you pay your parking tickets, motor vehicle tickets, overdue rent and most important any warrants."[11]

Campaigns also use phone banking to deliver messages they hope will convince voters to stay home. National NAACP president Kweisi Mfume testified before the Congressional Black Caucus in September 2001 that the weekend preceding the 2000 presidential election, black households received electronically generated phone calls from a person alleging to represent the NAACP urging voters to cast their ballots for George W. Bush.[12] The organization attempted to obtain a cease and desist order to stop the calls but failed. To combat the spread of false information—the NAACP did not endorse George W. Bush—the organization mounted an urgent radio campaign to inform voters of the truth.[13]

In one of the few cases of vote suppression actually prosecuted by the Bush Justice Department, officials with the New Hampshire and national Republican parties and their campaign consultants were charged with crimes involving a conspiracy to block a get-out-the-vote effort by the Democrats in the hard-fought 2002 New Hampshire U.S. Senate race between Republican John Sununu and Democrat Jeanne Shaheen. This incident did not especially target African Americans except to the degree that they were Democrats living in Manchester, Rochester, Nashua, or Claremont, New Hampshire. It is an important example of deceptive campaign practices because it points to the weaknesses of laws protecting voters from campaign and party vote suppression tactics, especially when the party doing the suppressing is also in control of enforcing the laws that do exist.

In the week before the 2002 election, the Democrats advertised a transportation program put together with help from the Manchester Professional Firefighters Association to provide free rides to the polls.[14] On the morning of election day, beginning at about 7:45 a.m., Democratic party workers and volunteers with the Manchester firefighters began receiving hundreds of hang-up calls that tied up their telephone lines and made it impossible for them to call voters to offer or schedule rides or receive requests for assistance.[15] The problem persisted for an hour and a half, and by then, hundreds of New Hampshire voters in Manchester, Nashua, and other towns may have missed their opportunity to vote.[16]

The long-drawn-out federal investigation and the timing of the indictments and guilty pleas eventually obtained by the federal government suggest the pattern of politicized law enforcement at the Justice Department that first came to light at the end of 2006 in the U.S. attorney–purge scandal.[17] At the center of the New Hampshire phone-jamming case was James Tobin, a longtime Republican Party operative, who in 2002 was the New England political director for the RNC.[18] Three other men involved in the scheme would eventually plead guilty to various felony crimes, but Tobin, who avoided federal investigation for two years, appeared to be receiving protection from high-ranking Republican Party operatives reaching well into the White House.[19] Two men, Charles McGee, the executive director of the New Hampshire Republican State Committee, who cooked up the scheme; and Allen Raymond, the Virginia-based consultant contracted by McGee to implement it, both pleaded guilty and implicated Tobin as the party official who authorized jamming the Democrats' phones, ultimately arranging for Raymond to be paid $15,600 for the job. Tobin denied any wrongdoing. He was later tried and convicted of felony telephone harassment charges, but acquitted of a conspiracy charge alleging he had injured the free exercise of the right to vote.

Federal prosecutors have few modern tools to use in combating the wide variety of vote suppression tactics dreamed up by party operatives. Instead, they rely mainly on what is left of the Enforcement Act of 1870, known as Section 241 or the "conspiracy of rights" law passed by Congress after the Civil War to ensure the enforcement of the Fourteenth and Fifteenth amendments.[20] As a civil rights law, Section 241 makes it a crime to deprive a person of a right guaranteed by the Constitution or laws of the United States; it does not itself guarantee any substantive rights. Tobin was able to convince a jury that this law had never before been applied to the crime he was charged with, telephone harassment. In March 2007, a federal appeals court overturned Tobin's conviction on the remaining charges, taking issue with some of the finer points of the meaning of "harassed" and finding that the district court had misled the jury by issuing an overbroad legal definition.[21] The case was remanded to the district court. So far, the Republican National Committee has paid out over $6 million to high-powered Washington, D.C., law firms to cover Tobin's legal fees.[22]

"Caging" and Challenging Voters

Since taking the presidency in 2000, the Republican Party has stepped up efforts to root out what the party depicts as an epidemic of voter fraud. In 2002 and 2003, the Republicans' multipronged "antifraud" strategy included poll-watcher campaigns and the use of challengers at the polls. Like many of the modern-day tactics used to keep down the vote, the use of voter challengers is legal in most states and is not new. As an up-and-coming young lawyer in Phoenix, Arizona, in the late 1950s and early 1960s, William Rehnquist, who went on to become chief justice of the U.S. Supreme Court, coordinated the GOP's ballot-security program in Phoenix, in which minority voters were allegedly singled out for challenge.[23] The party has continued to use challengers selectively in close elections to suppress the minority vote in order to help tip the election to the Republican candidate.[24] For example, in 2002, in Arkansas, the Republicans were in tight races for governor, the U.S. House, and the U.S. Senate. In Jefferson County, at the core of a Democratic district where African Americans are 40 percent of the population, a group of predominantly black voters went to the county courthouse to cast their votes at the beginning of the early voting period. They were confronted there by Republican poll watchers who photographed them and demanded to see identification. One poll watcher walked behind the counter in the clerk's office and photographed voter information on the clerk's computer screen. Democratic Party officials rushed in and accused Republicans of "Gestapo" tactics aimed at intimidating and harassing likely Democratic voters. Republican Party officials, in turn, accused the Democrats of committing egregious acts of voter fraud in their desperation to win and claimed Republicans were only trying to secure a free and fair election by ensuring voters were who they said they were and eligible to vote.[25]

In Philadelphia that same year, when an African American incumbent mayor, John Street, faced a tough reelection fight, three hundred black sedans bearing decals similar to those used by federal law enforcement agencies roamed the city's African American neighborhoods, dispatching men carrying clipboards to ask prospective voters for their identification. One of Street's campaign consultants was Tom Lindenfeld, an experienced Democratic Party operative who had run a counterintimidation campaign for former Charlotte, North Carolina, mayor Harvey Gantt in his 1990 U.S. Senate race against Jesse Helms. There the GOP and the Helms campaign attempted to keep down the vote for Gantt with a postcard mailing to 125,000 voters, 97 percent of them black, which spread false information about voter eligibility and warned voters of criminal penalties for voter fraud. With that experience in his background, Lindenfeld told reporters, "What occurred in Philadelphia was much more expansive and expensive than anything I'd seen before, and I'd seen a lot."[26] Frederick L. Voigt, a longtime election monitor with the nonpartisan good government group Committee of Seventy, concurred. "Much worse than in past elections" was how he summed up what the *Philadelphia Inquirer* called a racially charged "chaotic [election] day" of street fighting, disturbances, threats, harassment, and vandalism. At the close of the polls, the district attorney had recorded 171 serious complaints, four times the number of incidents reported four years before when the same two candidates ran for mayor. Common pleas court judges, who spent the day fielding allegations of intimidation, shoving, and fighting, issued orders to both Democrats and Republicans to cease the harassment and prohibited Republican poll watchers from demanding registration or identification from voters at at least two city polling places.[27]

As Chandler Davidson and his colleagues have documented, challenging minority voters in order to intimidate them or to invalidate their votes can backfire.[28] When plans are discovered beforehand they can stimulate a countermobilization achieving the opposite of what the vote suppression architects intend: increased turnout for the other side. This is what happened in Louisville, Kentucky, in 2003. In what was expected to be a tight race for governor between Republican Ernie Fletcher and Democrat Ben Chandler, the Jefferson County Republicans developed a plan to station challengers at 59 of Louisville's 483 voting precincts, all of them in predominantly black and low-income neighborhoods. A flyer recruiting challengers warned that the Democratic National Committee, the A. Philip Randolph Institute of the AFL-CIO, and the NAACP were a "militant" force in Louisville encouraging voter fraud.[29] After a firestorm of protest by the city's African American leadership and by the Democrats, the Republicans backed down and reduced the number of precincts where it would send challengers to 18. Fletcher went on to win the gubernatorial contest by a 10-point margin statewide. The preelection publicity about the Republican challenge plan had had an effect: as generally might be expected in a nonfederal election year, turnout in Louisville's predominantly white precincts slid by about 7 percent from 2002 levels. But in the black precincts citywide, turnout held steady, and actually rose in 21 of the 59 precincts originally targeted with challengers by the Republican Party. Democrat Chandler won Jefferson County on the strength of black turnout in Louisville.[30]

The partisan manipulation of election administration in the 2000 election was a warm-up for what would come in the next presidential election, this time in the swing state of Ohio. Republican secretary of state J. Kenneth Blackwell used the power of his office to "suppress Democratic voter registration, thwart likely Democratic voters from casting ballots, keep 'alternative' or provisional ballots from being counted, and skew the 2004 presidential vote in favor of Republicans," in the words of Bob Fitrakis, Steven Rosenfeld, and Harvey Wasserman.[31] The cumulative effect of Blackwell's multiple last-minute directives to county election officials was to create mass confusion, invalidating legitimate registration records and ballots across the state, but especially in Ohio's big cities, where Democrats and African Americans are concentrated.

Blackwell's record of deliberate disruption of the voting process among Democratic-leaning voters was appalling. In the summer of 2004, the secretary issued election-administration directives dictating the weight of the paper to be used for registration applications—applications from voters printed on any paper stock other than 80 pound weight were to be rejected. A storm of controversy engulfed Blackwell and he modified the rules, but only partly, informing county boards to accept applications on lighter-weight paper, but also directing them to call offending applicants to resubmit their applications on the correct paper or risk being challenged at the polls. No one knows how many eligible voters had their registrations thrown out in the confusion, but the estimates are in the thousands. While voters were trying to get on Ohio's rolls, selective purging by elections officials was throwing more of them off. Between 2000 and 2004, some 168,000 voters in Cuyahoga County, where the state's largest city, Cleveland, is located, or nearly one-fifth of the county's voters, were purged under an aggressive interpretation of the National Voter Registration Act's list-maintenance provisions. Required by the Help America Vote Act of 2002 to computerize registration records statewide, elections officials in Cuyahoga County lost another 10,000 records in the transition to the statewide system. Ohio election law does not require voter registration list purges. In Hamilton County, where Cincinnati is located, election officials reviewing registration records moved some 12 percent of registered voters from active to inactive status. A person whose registration record was flagged as inactive was required to show identification in order to vote (this was not a requirement of registered voters at the time); if poll workers were not satisfied with the identification presented, those voters were given a provisional ballot.[32] Records later indicated that nearly all of the provisional ballots voted in Hamilton County were from the city of Cincinnati. And here Blackwell weighed in again, issuing yet another order directing that any provisional ballot cast outside the voter's precinct was to be rejected. Ohio attorney Bob Fitrakis and his colleagues describe the chaos that ensued:

> [T]he secretary of state effectively engendered a classic "catch-22" situation: as BOEs [boards of election] changed long-standing Democratic precinct locations shortly before the elections, Blackwell simultaneously disseminated out-of-date voter rolls to county officials, ensuring that many new voters would not be on precinct lists given to poll workers. Then, to people who were confused as a result and did not end up at the correct precinct, he offered provisional ballots, but subsequently refused to count provisional ballots cast in the wrong precinct—

which was often simply the wrong table in the correct building and room. He also instructed vote counters to disqualify provisional ballots submitted without properly labeled voter identification envelopes, after issuing conflicting directives about labeling requirements.[33]

With help like that inside government, the Republican Party hardly needed a campaign strategy to win Ohio. But Ohio was too important to leave in the hands of a single scheming state official. The party revved up its voter challenge operation to help take the Ohio election in for a landing.[34]

Using a technique the Republican Party has perfected over many decades with the help of computers and a lot of money, the Ohio Republican Party mailed over two hundred thousand nonforwardable letters to newly registered Ohio voters encouraging them to vote Republican. About thirty thousand of these letters were returned to them as undeliverable. IT (information technology) party staff, in coordination with the Bush-Cheney campaign, went to work, compiling a list of voters to be challenged at the polls by Republican eagle eyes. Nearly 35,000 unsuspecting Ohio voters, most of them black, were about to be caged.

"Caging" is a common procedure used in the marketing business and refers to the practice of sorting responses generated by a direct-mail appeal, usually in a fund-raising campaign, and analyzing those responses to determine the effectiveness of the mailing. There are different accounts of the origin of the term. One dates to the late nineteenth century and the U.S. Postal Service's practice of sorting mail into wire cages; another claims the term is synonymous with a direct-mail industry practice known as "cashiering," by which money raised by a fund-raising letter is processed by staff who, in the early days of the industry, were locked in cages for security purposes.

Voter caging, however, is less benign than its marketing cousin. With respect to direct mail, having a bad address is usually beneficial for the addressee, saving a person from receiving one more piece of junk mail. Caged bad addresses may be researched for corrections or discarded as useless for purposes of the mailing list because they are nonproductive. Nobody gets hurt, and direct-mail caging doesn't lead to the abrogation of civil rights. In the context of political campaigns or an election, however, having a bad address on a political party's list can taint a voter as a potential criminal. Lists are compiled of voters who were not reached by a mailing, whether from a political party or even a local election board, or who chose not to respond to the mailing. These voters are then challenged at the polls, in some states directly by party workers, in others by poll workers. We noted in chapter 3 how in 1967, Lake County Democratic machine operatives working as election officials attempted to cage over five thousand legitimate African American voters in Gary, Indiana, by mailing out a letter that demanded an impossible response. In that instance, voters whose eligibility to vote was questioned by the board of elections—under false pretenses—were instructed to send the letter back through registered mail attesting to their eligibility and the accuracy of their address information. The caging letter was mailed just before Gary's mayoral election, which Richard Hatcher would go on to win, but not before a federal court ordered the names restored.

Voter caging made a recent appearance in 2004, when muckraking journalist Greg Palast came into possession of caging lists prepared by Republican Party operatives.[35] One of the lists contained the names of 1,833 voters in Duval County, Florida (the vast majority of addresses were in Duval's largest city, Jacksonville). A careful analysis by staff writers for the Web site ePluribus Media matched almost all of the caged voters on the list with the 2004 Duval County voter registration file and found nearly half were black in a county where blacks were only 30 percent of the population.[36] Caged addresses were identified in nearly all of Duval's sixty majority-black precincts, compared to only 56 percent of the county's other precincts (and some of these precincts contained only one caged address). As ePluribus Media correctly concludes, "black citizens were disproportionately represented in the caging lists."[37]

Palast seemed to think that the lists were part of a larger Republican Party scheme to challenge and intimidate likely Democrats at the polls, but his story was completely ignored by influential U.S. media outlets at the time. Nevertheless, the Republican Party's state campaign spokeswoman, Mindy Tucker Fletcher, felt the need to respond to Palast's report. In an e-mail to the editor of Palast's news program, she first explained that "caging is a commonly used term in the political process by which someone opens a large amount of mail and logs it into a database." She went on to claim that the Duval County list was created simply to update the Republican National Committee mailing list.[38]

Caging prepares the way for discriminatory list purging, a longstanding practice the National Voter Registration Act sought to eliminate. In 1878, the Florida legislature passed a law that gave local registrars the power to "correct" the registration lists by striking the names of voters who had died or moved away from the county in the preceding year. The cunning Democrats knew how to use the law. A correspondent for the *New York Times* reported,

> Under this law the Commissioners in those counties where the negroes are in the majority claim to have arbitrary power to examine and purge the registration lists, and are striking off the names of Republican voters in sufficient numbers to carry out the Democratic plan to secure the defeat of . . . the Republican candidates for Congress. . . . In Leon County alone, where the negroes largely outnumber the whites, over 2,000 names are reported to have been stricken from the registration lists. . . . As in the other Gulf States, the election in Florida promises to be entirely harmonious and almost entirely unanimous. The Southern Democrats are at last conciliated.[39]

Bob Fitrakis and his colleagues argue that the Republicans' voter caging and challenge operation in Ohio was a beard for the real scam perpetrated on voters, especially new and low-income voters—vote suppression resulting from the deliberate disruption of the voting process orchestrated by partisan election officials. They may be right. But this doesn't explain why the party put so much effort into defending its right to challenge voters at the polls.

Many states have laws allowing for voter challenges, though the laws are complex and differ across the states with respect to who can serve as a challenger, how far in advance of an election a challenge may be lodged, how a challenge is made, the procedures poll workers must follow in dealing with challenges, and so on.[40] From the perspective of the challenger, Ohio's voter challenge law is relatively liberal. Perhaps this is due to the once permissive grounds for allowing challenges in Ohio on the basis of a voter's suspected African ancestry.[41] Before the passage of the Fifteenth Amendment, black voters in Ohio could be challenged upon a "visible admixture of African blood," or whether the voter's community classified him as white or colored.[42] Today Ohio law allows any qualified voter to challenge the eligibility of any other qualified voter, and to do so either before an election or on election day, though challengers do need to register before election day.[43] If the challenge is made before election day and the county election board is not able to determine definitively the status of the challenged voter, that person must appear at a hearing on as little as three days' notice. Challengers themselves are not required to act in good faith, nor are they required to base their challenge on personal knowledge of a voter's ineligibility. In Ohio, challenged voters can be denied a ballot "if for any other reason a majority of the [precinct] judges believes the person is not entitled to vote."[44]

As the 2004 election approached, both the Democrats and the Republicans revealed plans to send thousands of poll watchers and lawyers into battleground states to monitor voting at the polling place. The Republican effort included thousands of recruits paid $100 a day to challenge the credentials of voters caged as a result of Republican mailings. Most of the voters on the Republicans' challenge lists were new registrants, and they were disproportionately minority. In the months before the 2004 election voter registration had soared in Ohio, up 250 percent over 2000 levels, much of it from heavily African American urban areas. The expansion of the rolls in Ohio fit a pattern observed around the country: in Jacksonville, Florida, new voters in black neighborhoods were registering to vote at a pace two-thirds faster than four years before, and in Philadelphia, election officials reported that voter registration surged to its highest peak in twenty-one years, much of it stemming from African American areas.[45]

Indeed, the surge in registration was part of "the biggest and most aggressive voter mobilization drives in the history of presidential politics," according to Dan Balz and Thomas B. Edsall of the *Washington Post*, stimulated no doubt by the conservative policies and polarizing presidency of George W. Bush.[46] Though there are no hard-and-fast numbers on the partisan swing of all these new voters, given the demographic profile of the new registrants, they more than likely favored the Democrats, and the Democrats were grateful, more than doubling their spending on election day operations over 2000. The Republicans, on the other hand, saw a tsunami of opposition mobilizing against Bush; they tripled their previous election day operations budget. Republicans saw the specter of widespread voter fraud in the intensive voter registration activity and ramped up a voter challenge campaign. "The organized left's efforts to, quote unquote, register voters—I call them ringers—have created these problems," said James P. Trakas, a co-chair of the Republican Party in Cuyahoga County.[47] In defending the party's plan to put 3,600 challengers inside precincts serving mostly black voters, and to object to the voter eligibility of some 23,000 legally registered Ohioans, Trakas's colleague, Mark Weaver, counsel to the Ohio Republican Party, echoed the view that expanding registration rolls and voter turnout are evidence of fraud: "The goal of the Ohio Republican Party is to guarantee a fair election for everyone. Each time the Democrats remove an additional safeguard," presumably, like making it possible to register to vote when applying for a driver's license, "the potential for voter fraud increases."[48]

In the week before the election, two civil rights activists and then a class of voters from Cleveland whose names erroneously appeared on the Republicans' voter challenge list as ineligible or questionable voters sued in federal court to stop the ballot-security program from moving forward. Two federal judges in Ohio and one in New Jersey found the challenge program constitutionally unacceptable and shut it down, though these decisions were quickly and successfully appealed. The Republicans, however, were unable to implement their program as planned because the appeals court decisions were handed down too close to election day. Few voters appear to have been challenged.

Manipulation of Registration Records and Lists

The story of how in 2000 and 2004, partisan election officials in Florida manipulated the state's ban on voting by people convicted of felony crimes is familiar. It illustrates a number of enduring weaknesses in election administration that allow something as simple as an inaccurate list to stand between a citizen and his or her right to vote. National election reform has only incrementally and incompletely dealt with this problem. The NVRA sought to establish national standards to guide the nondiscriminatory purging of registration records by local registrars. It also called for a means of fail-safe voting for those voters denied the right to vote when their registration records were mishandled. The Help America Vote Act of 2002 mandates fail-safe voting (in the form of provisional balloting) for the same reason. When these laws are violated or not enforced, voters whose registration records are mishandled can be deprived of their right to vote.

In chapter 4 we discuss the efforts of registration-reform advocates in the 1980s to ensure that national standards in the National Voter Registration Act would put an end to the discriminatory purging of registration lists. Prior to the NVRA, states and localities established their own standards for purging voter files, and some removed voters from voting rolls for failure to vote. The NVRA requires states to keep voter rolls up-to-date but restricts their ability to purge voters, permitting purges only upon a voter's request, death, felony conviction, or mental incompetence, or upon relocation.

Critics of the NVRA's restrictions on list purges, and of the increased cost of purging due to the NVRA's requirement that preemptory mailings must go out to determine a voter's status before a record can be deleted, point to the considerable amount of "deadwood" (ineligible voters) that remains on voting rolls. They argue that deadwood either is evidence of voter fraud or will lead to voter fraud. Indeed, as the states came into compliance with the NVRA's list-maintenance and antipurging requirements, the number of "inactive" registrants, or records where the voter's eligibility status may have changed from eligible to ineligible, increased from 1.6 million in 1994 to over 18 million in 2000, or 11 percent of the total number of registered voters reported that year. Moreover, as purges have become more costly, registrants have grown to outnumber the voting-age population in some areas.

The NVRA permits the maintenance of inactive lists, or lists of voters who have failed to respond to an address-verification notice sent by the voter registrar confirming a change of address. Inactive lists are bound to include some inaccurate information given how frequently Americans move.[49] Under the NVRA, "inactive voters" can be left on such lists for as long as two and a half years before they are purged entirely from the rolls. Contrary to popular belief, however, for about half of the forty states that purged voters for failing to vote prior to the enactment of the NVRA (as Indiana did when Richard Hatcher ran for mayor of Gary), this represents a *decrease* in the length of time a voter can remain inactive before being deleted entirely from the rolls (Indiana law allowed for purging only in January following a presidential election).[50] Moreover, the NVRA permits deletions from the rolls in eight states that did not formerly utilize the nonvoting purge.[51] In the 2004–6 federal election cycle, 12 million to 13 million registration records were purged under the guidelines of the NVRA in the forty-two states reporting data to the U.S. Election Assistance Commission.

The problem with the NVRA is not, as critics like Senator Christopher "Kit" Bond of Missouri have charged, that it has "caused sloppy voter rolls, [and] . . . actually facilitated organized vote fraud";[52] or, as Deborah Phillips of the now-defunct Voting Integrity Project testified before Congress, that it "has tied the hands of election directors to protect the rights of legitimate voters from the dilution of vote fraud";[53] or that it has "left the voter rolls in a shambles in many states," breeding mistrust in the electoral process and "foment[ing] 'the appearance of corruption,' that has, fairly or not, done real damage to American government," as John Samples alleges;[54] or even that it has, as Todd Graziano has charged, "create[d] the most inaccurate voting rolls in our history."[55] It has done none of these things. The problem with the NVRA rests with the failure of the states to fully and properly implement the provisions that widen opportunities for registration, and with the federal government for not routinely enforcing it.

An example from a recent election is in order. In the months leading up to the 2000 presidential election, African American leaders in St. Louis became concerned that the recent removal of more than thirty thousand names from the registration rolls to an inactive list would create problems at the polls on election day. State senator William Lacy Clay Jr., a candidate for a seat in the U.S. House of Representatives, gave a speech the day before the election in which he warned that if eligible voters were prohibited from voting at the polls because of inaccurate registration records, lawsuits would be brought to keep the polls open past their legal closing time of 7 P.M.[56] As it happened, hundreds of eligible St. Louis voters were unable to vote because their names had been put on inactive lists that were then not distributed to St. Louis's more than 250 polling places. Poll workers were told to call headquarters to verify the eligibility of voters whose names were not on their regular lists, but the problems were so extensive that the phone lines were jammed for most of the day. When poll workers were unable to get through, they told voters to go down to the election board's main office to plead their case. Hundreds of people tried to cram into the board's office at 300 North Tucker Boulevard. Many were still standing in line at 10 P.M., demanding their right to vote.

As Senator Clay had threatened, the Democrats filed suit in St. Louis City Circuit Court to keep the polls open late so that registered voters whose records had been mishandled by the board could vote. A sympathetic judge issued an order to extend voting hours, but the Missouri Court of Appeals quickly overruled her. The polls in St. Louis shut down at 7:45 P.M., with only about a hundred additional votes cast after the official 7 P.M. poll closing time.[57]

Republicans alleged fraud.[58] Senator Kit Bond led the charge calling for a federal investigation, accusing Democrats of engaging in a criminal conspiracy to extend polling place hours. Newly elected Representative Clay joined Senator Bond in calling for an investigation, but for Clay the issue was voter suppression. The ensuing FBI investigation subpoenaed all of the registration and voting records from the St. Louis City Elections Board for the month preceding the election.[59] To the surprise of Bond and others insisting fraud was responsible for the Democrats' surprisingly good showing statewide, the Justice Department threatened the board with a lawsuit for abusing the voting rights of thousands of eligible St. Louis voters by illegally purging their registration records in violation of the NVRA. It was these illegal purges that created much of the chaos on election day. The resulting federal court consent decree stipulated that the St. Louis Board of Election Commissioners would change its policies and procedures for maintaining accurate registration records and that it would comply with federal requirements for notifying voters of their registration status and handling voter lists on election day. The alleged voter fraud conspiracy in St. Louis was nothing more than a case of managerial ineptitude, administrative underfunding, and poor implementation of the NVRA on the part of St. Louis and Missouri election officials—made all the worse by partisan rancor and racial politics in a highly competitive election.

The failure to implement and enforce the NVRA has other negative ramifications on electoral participation. Implementation of the NVRA in agencies serving the poor and disabled, never good, has fallen off dramatically over time. As table 7 shows, the numbers of applications in public assistance and disability agencies during presidential election cycles have fallen precipitously since 1995–96, while registration by other methods has increased or remained steady. Voter registration applications in public-assistance agencies are only 40 percent of what they were in that cycle, and even then the rates were low. Registration in disability agencies has plummeted to less than 25 percent of the number achieved in 1996.

Early in the battle for a voter registration reform bill, Linda Davidoff, then executive director of Human SERVE, said of the effort of some congressional representatives to include provisions for list cleaning, "No matter how substantial an administrative problem

Table 7

Sources of Voter Registration Applications
Presidential Election Cycles, 1996, 2000, 2004

Source	1995–1996 Number of Apps	% of Total	1999–2000 Number of Apps	% of Total	2003–2004 Number of Apps	% of Total
Motor Vehicle Offices	13,722,233	33.1	17,393,814	38.1	16,120,091	32.8
By Mail	12,330,015	29.74	14,150,732	31	16,095,770	32.4
Public Assistance	2,602,748	6.28	1,314,500	2.88	1,050,479	2.2
Disability Services	178,015	0.43	190,009	0.42	106,615	0.2
Armed Forces	76,008	0.18	74,038	0.16	94,007	0.2
State-Designated Sites	1,732,475	4.18	1,881,984	4.12	3,771,620	8.4
All Other Sources	10,810,934	26.08	10,943,962	23.97	11,373,749	25.4
Total	41,452,428		45,654,673		49,674,098	

SOURCE: Federal Election Commission, "The Impact of the National Voter Registration Act of 1993 on the Administration of Elections for Federal Office, 1995–1996: A Report to the 105th Congress," 1997. Federal Election Commission, "The Impact of the National Voter Registration Act of 1993 on the Administration of Elections for Federal Office, 1999–2000; A Report to the 107th Congress," 2001. Election Assistance Commission, "The Impact of the National Voter Registration Act of 1993 on the Administration of Elections for Federal Office, 2003–2004: A Report to the 109th Congress;" 2005.

[deadwood] is, it's not the kind of problem that [the] inability to vote in our democracy is. We have to make sure we don't get efficient purging and inefficient registration out of this." [60] Reform advocates warned over and over again during the campaign to pass the NVRA that when large-scale purges of voter lists occur, legitimate voters are inevitably caught in the snares, and cut from the rolls. Under the

Table 8

Deletions from the Voter Registration Lists Compared to Total Applications

	Deletions	Applications	Percent Deleted
1995–1996	8,723,301	41,452,428	21.0
1997–1998	9,063,326	35,372,213	25.6
1999–2000	13,014,912	45,654,673	28.5
2001–2002	15,009,935	37,473,694	40.1
2003–2004	12,566,907	49,674,098	25.3
2005–2006	13,026,752	36,277,749	35.9

SOURCES: Federal Election Commission, "The Impact of the National Voter Registration Act of 1993 on the Administration of Elections for Federal Office, 1995–1996: A Report to the 105th Congress," 1997; Federal Election Commission, "The Impact of the National Voter Registration Act of 1993 on the Administration of Elections for Federal Office, 1997–1998: A Report to the 106th Congress," 1999; Federal Election Commission, "The Impact of the National Voter Registration Act of 1993 on the Administration of Elections for Federal Office, 1999–2000: A Report to the 107th Congress," 2001; Election Assistance Commission, "The Impact of the National Voter Registration Act of 1993 on the Administration of Elections for Federal Office, 2001–2002: A Report to the 108th Congress," 2003; Election Assistance Commission, "The Impact of the National Voter Registration Act of 1993 on the Administration of Elections for Federal Office, 2003–2004: A Report to the 109th Congress," 2005; Election Assistance Commission, "The Impact of the National Voter Registration Act of 1993 on the Administration of Elections for Federal Office, 2005–2006: A Report to the 110th Congress," 2007.

NVRA, we have certainly seen large-scale purges. Table 8 shows that between 2005 and 2006, the states removed more than 13 million people from the voter registration rolls, nearly 36 percent of the number of applications processed in that period. The magnitude of purging makes it reasonable to worry that the advocates were right.

How has the Bush administration responded to the states' backtracking on voter registration? Basically, it has ignored the violations of requirements to register voters, while pressuring states to purge more voters. Of the ten NVRA-related cases the Department of Justice has acted on during Bush's presidency, half claim that the states or localities are not purging enough voters from the rolls.[61] In the spring of 2007, the Justice Department sent preliminary letters to ten more states, putting them on notice that they were expected to do more to purge ineligible voters from their lists.[62] Meanwhile, voters in large numbers continued to report difficulties casting ballots due to registration problems. According to the biennial survey of the electorate conducted by the Census Bureau, 1.3 million registered voters were prevented from casting ballots in the 2000 election because of problems with their registration records. That number decreased slightly to 1.1 million in 2004, but then shot up by half a million more in the 2006 congressional election, when there were nearly *30 million fewer* ballots cast. As a percentage of all registered nonvoters, those unable to vote due to registration problems nearly doubled between 2004 and 2006.[63]

Demos and Project Vote called on the Department of Justice to enforce the NVRA, in particular the provisions requiring agency-based registration. They made this request in August 2004, and met with Justice Department officials in 2005, when it became clear that the department was energetically pursuing cases against states for not purging enough. "In January 2005, we had a 10-year report, which documented the 59 percent decline [in registrations] from 1995 through 2004," said Scott Novakowski, adding that Demos sent follow-up letters to the Justice Department, citing NVRA violations in Arizona, Connecticut, Florida, Massachusetts, Missouri, Montana, New Jersey, Pennsylvania, and Tennessee. "John Conyers (now the House Judiciary Committee chairman) and 29 other representatives asked Attorney General Alberto Gonzales to look into this, and there was no response."[64] The actions of the U.S. Election Assistance Commission (EAC) also reflect the Bush administration's hostility to the NVRA. The EAC was authorized by the Help America Vote Act in 2002, and took over the FEC's responsibility to report to Congress on the implementation of the NVRA. The EAC's 2005–6 report clearly indicates blatant state violations of the NVRA, without recommending any remedies. Five nonexempt states (Alabama, Connecticut, Massachusetts, New York, and South Carolina) report *zero* registrations in public-assistance agencies and disability agencies, and four additional states (Rhode Island, Tennessee, Utah, and West Virginia) and the District of Columbia report *zero* registrations in disability-services agencies.[65]

Voter Fraud Investigations

Three months into the presidency of George W. Bush, the Justice Department announced a new initiative to fight election fraud. Attorney General John Ashcroft shared the Republican Party's obsession with what they say is a wide-scale conspiracy on the part of the Democrats and their allies to win elections by committing fraud. He was, after all, a Missouri movement conservative and a recently ousted senator who lost his reelection bid in 2000 to a dead man amid allegations that blacks and Democrats stole the vote in St. Louis. With much fanfare, Ashcroft introduced a new "voting rights initiative," which would later take the name the Ballot Access and Voting Integrity Initiative (BAVII).[66] It would bring together experienced attorneys from the department's Civil Rights and Criminal divisions to train all U.S. attorneys and designated personnel at annual seminars in how to recognize, investigate, and prosecute voter fraud and voter intimidation.[67] The BAVII also upgraded the department's election day operation by designating deputy election officers in each U.S. attorney's office and publicizing their availability to receive complaints from the public of possible voter fraud, as well as allegations of voter intimidation. From this day forth the department would repeatedly insist that "under the ongoing initiative, election crimes are a high law enforcement priority of the Department."[68]

On paper the BAVII was mandated to investigate all kinds of corruption in voting—presumably, including the kind of disenfranchisement suffered by black voters in Florida in 2000, and perpetrated by Republican state election officials in their compilation and use of deliberately inaccurate felon purge lists. In reality, however, Ashcroft's BAVII was part of the "inside game" of using government authority to create the perception that voter fraud is rampant in American elections. As George W. Bush's top political adviser, Karl Rove, had learned some years before, the *perception* that fraud may have been committed in an election can be a very powerful tool for an election loser seeking to contest the results. Given the Republican Party's marginal grasp on power in Congress and the presidency, and the fact that demographic trends are against them, they need to master and use every trick in the book to delay their return to minority-party status. How Karl Rove learned about the tactical usefulness of specious voter fraud claims is a story worth telling because it presages so much of what has come later as the Republicans have pursued their strategy of vote suppression to try to hold on to power.

Rove experimented with these tactics while working on Perry O. Hooper Sr.'s 1994 campaign for chief judge of the Alabama Supreme Court. The race is a real education for any aspiring political consultant because long before the 2000 presidential election, it showed how an election can be flipped in the courts. The story began when the Business Council of Alabama persuaded the Texas-based Rove to help run a slate of Republican candidates for the state supreme court, where no Republican had won a seat in over a hundred years. They were impressed with Rove's recent victories reversing the political makeup of the Texas Supreme Court.[69] On the morning after election day, November 8, 1994, the Business Council's candidate, Hooper, was behind his Democratic opponent, incumbent Ernest "Sonny" Hornsby, by 698 votes.[70] The margin for Hornsby was eventually reduced to 304 out of more than 1.1 million votes cast, one of the closest elections in Alabama's history.[71] Rove immediately called for a recount. Joshua Green studied this election for the *Atlantic Monthly* and interviewed many of the people involved in the campaign. A former Rove staff person told Green that Rove rallied campaign staffers by telling them they had a good shot at turning the election around. The staffer explained Rove's strategy: "Our role was to try to keep people motivated about Perry Hooper's election and then to undermine the other side's support by casting them as liars, cheaters, stealers, immoral—all of that."[72] The Hooper campaign obtained a restraining order to preserve the ballots, while Rove hired investigators to observe the recount in every county of the state and to hunt for voter fraud. Rove promoted the idea that the Democrats were trying to steal the election by spreading rumors that votes were being cast in absentia for comatose nursing-home patients and that Democrats had been caught in a cemetery writing down the names of the dead, which they used to cast fraudulent absentee ballots.

Indeed, once in the courts, the election came down to two thousand disputed absentee ballots from heavily Democratic counties that had arrived late and had been set aside because they did not conform to the letter of the law (many had not been notarized or lacked the legally required witness signatures). The fate of these ballots was ultimately decided by federal judges nearly a year later. In the meantime, Rove and the Hooper campaign fought hard to convince the public of the notion that the Democrats were trying to steal the election with fraudulent absentee ballots. Hooper held a press conference three days after the election while the recount was going on and declared, "We have endured lies in this campaign, but I'll be damned if I will accept outright thievery," despite the fact that no thievery had come to light. His campaign sued every probate judge, circuit clerk, and sheriff in the state for "discrimination" and held rallies to keep the issue alive.[73] Business interests bought ads in newspapers across the state charging, "They steal elections they don't like," and Green reports that public opinion started to shift.

The propaganda campaign to plant the idea that fraud had been committed in the election was very important to the ultimate outcome of the contest. Alabama's absentee-ballot law, which in its present form dates to 1975, requires a signature on the absentee-ballot envelope from a notary or two witnesses attesting to the identity of the voter. Alabama state courts hearing contested absentee-ballot cases have ruled that in the absence of fraud, gross negligence, or intentional wrongdoing, "absentee ballots in substantial compliance with essential requirements of the absentee voting law should be counted if the irregularities do not adversely affect the sanctity of the ballot and the integrity of the election."[74] Rove understood that in order to convince the courts to strictly construe the signature requirements for valid absentee ballots and exclude those that did not conform, the idea that fraud was at work had to be hammered into the public's mind.

In a prelude to events that would take place in Florida six years later, the Hooper and Hornsby campaigns duked it out in the judicial arena, first in the state courts. When Rove got a ruling in a circuit court he didn't like, he didn't appeal; instead, he marched into federal court in search of a more sympathetic judge.[75] Meanwhile, the recount had narrowed Hornsby's initial lead to as little as nine votes, according to a tally taken on November 21.[76] The legal wrangling dragged out for nearly a year, and by mid-October 1995, a federal appeals court judge finally ruled that the disputed absentee ballots could not be counted, flipping the election outcome in favor of Hooper.[77] Hooper won, or perhaps we should say Rove and the Republican Party in Alabama won, by using modern vote suppression tactics, all of them legal. When a judge picks the winner, how much more legal can you get? Rove had turned Hooper's election around with a crafty propaganda campaign to keep rumors of fraud alive while the recount dragged on, softening up the ground for throwing out likely Democratic votes when those votes didn't meet the letter of the law.

Rove had learned a few lessons about what skillful lawyering could do in exploiting technicalities in the rules, which are themselves in place to make it harder for some citizens to vote. Rove took these lessons with him when he moved with George W. Bush to the White House. We can see their influence in many of the policy shifts of the Justice Department's Voting Section that have moved the department away from a fulsome embrace of voting rights. These shifts include questionable interpretations of federal voting rights laws that have had the opposite effect of what Congress originally intended by restricting rather than expanding the conditions under which legitimate ballots are cast and counted.[78] The Hooper-Hornsby race contained another important lesson for Rove, one that also appeared to guide subsequent electoral enforcement policy changes at the Bush Justice Department: spurious voter fraud allegations and criminal investigations create the appearance of corruption, which can be exploited to justify restrictive interpretations of electoral rules. Rove's experience in Alabama was a valuable reminder of the partisan advantages gained in creating a panic and stoking public distrust of settled election administration procedures. As later events would

confirm, this is especially true when the strategy is fortified by politicized election law enforcement.[79]

The Bush administration's efforts to quiet the public outcry over the
2000 election dispute took a number of forms. One of them was to
capitalize on the generally confused meaning of election "fraud," a
word used liberally by all sides in the battle over the disputed 2000
election. Where critics of Bush charged fraud in electoral procedures
that resulted in thousands of miscast and lost votes in Florida, supporters pointed to mix-ups that permitted felons to illegally vote.
Bush's new attorney general, John Ashcroft, sought to steer a path for
the Justice Department that spoke to Bush's critics by emphasizing a
(rhetorical) commitment to electoral integrity, while at the same
time appeased his supporters by putting in place a program dedicated to rooting out election crime, especially "voter fraud." In early
2002, Ashcroft announced what he claimed was a new direction for
the Justice Department's voting rights agenda. His Ballot Access and
Voting Integrity Initiative, however, was not a novel idea. It was re-
gurgitated from the Reagan era, when the department ran a program
with the same name and purpose: to use the power of the federal
government to help Republicans win elections by intimidating
voting rights activists, quashing voter registration activity in low-
income and minority communities, and suppressing voting. The
Reagan administration's politicization of legal policy, and through
that policy the Justice Department itself, certainly was also not new,
but it was carried out more systematically under Reagan than under
any previous administration.[80] Reagan, like Richard M. Nixon before
him and George W. Bush who would follow the same script later,
spoke to the right wing of his party by attacking "judicial activism"
through which the courts had become a partner in the extension of
minority rights and liberal social policy. According to political scientist Cornell Clayton, he appointed people "possessed [of] a thor-
oughly politicized view of the law and a sense of mission about how
it might be utilized for political reform."[81] Many saw themselves as
the vanguard of a new conservative legal movement to reorder priorities and reshape the institutions of government to protect their

political program. This had profound effects on Justice Department priorities at the time. Later, the strategy was resurrected under George W. Bush in the U.S. attorney purge scandal, in which a number of U.S. attorneys were unceremoniously fired, some, it is alleged, for failing to pursue specious voter fraud allegations.

In September of 1984, six weeks before a presidential election in which Ronald Reagan would win a second term, his attorney general announced a campaign to crack down on election fraud and abuse.[82] The House Judiciary Committee chair, Democrat Peter Rodino of New Jersey, wrote to Attorney General William French Smith to express concern that the campaign could undermine protections guaranteed by the Voting Rights Act. In particular, he mentioned his worry about safeguards afforded those engaged in assisting voters. An associate attorney general wrote back to Representative Rodino at the end of December 1984, well after Reagan's reelection, that departmental oversight rules would prevent any chilling effect. He noted that all election-fraud investigations and indictments must be "precleared" by the Public Integrity Section of the Criminal Division, implying they were carefully and cautiously handled.[83] What Justice Department officials failed to mention was that at least one politically charged fraud investigation was already well under way.

In the next year, that investigation, conducted at a cost of millions of dollars, led to 210 charges of vote fraud being brought against eight Alabama voting rights activists, seven of them black. Only one was found guilty (and on only four counts) before an all-white jury; later that conviction was overturned on appeal. Specifically, the federal government charged Albert Turner; his wife, Evelyn Turner; Spencer Hogue Jr.; Eutaw city councilman Spiver Whitney Gordon; James Colvin, the black mayor of the town of Union; and three civil rights workers with conspiracy, altering absentee ballots, voting more than once, and committing mail fraud. Turner and his wife were perhaps the most well known of the group, as they were long-time civil rights activists working in the Alabama Black Belt. In the early 1960s, the Turners had initiated the lawsuit that brought federal registrars to Perry County to help blacks register to vote.[84] Albert Turner also served as the Alabama director of Martin Luther

King Jr.'s Southern Christian Leadership Conference until 1972, when he left to work on local school-integration issues, among other civil rights causes. After that, the Turners and Hogue remained active in voter registration drives, legislative issues, and municipal representation through their community organization, the Perry County Civic League.

The federal investigations of the Turners and other black activists who worked to assist poor blacks in the mechanics of voting served several purposes and must be understood in the context of Reagan's reelection strategy, which involved consolidating Republican majorities in the South. The fraud prosecutions were a response to the black voter mobilization campaigns, which threatened the Reagan strategy. First and foremost, the Alabama prosecutions were meant to intimidate black voter activists and chill black voting in anticipation of the 1984 and 1986 federal elections. With Reagan's victory in 1980, the Republican Party was beginning to make inroads into Alabama politics. Jeremiah Denton became the first Republican to win a U.S. Senate race in Alabama in the twentieth century, riding on Reagan's coattails. But Denton's victory was precarious; he won by only a slim margin statewide, just 36,000 votes out of 1.25 million cast, and not in the Black Belt counties, where he lost in a landslide to his Democratic opponent. There were small towns in west Alabama where Denton got no votes at all. His prospects for reelection in 1986, therefore, were not good, because he wouldn't have Ronald Reagan on the top of the ticket.

The economically marginalized counties of the Black Belt were, nevertheless, places where blacks had gained some measure of political rights as a result of the struggles of the civil rights movement. By the early 1980s, registered black voters outnumbered whites in the Black Belt, and more than half of the local county elected officials in the ten western majority-black Alabama counties were black. But there remained stark reminders of the region's segregated past. In Selma and the surrounding county (Dallas), for example, where only about three hundred of over fifteen thousand eligible blacks were registered at the time of the passage of the Voting Rights Act, black registration rates approached white levels, but only one black had been elected to any office since Reconstruction. The progress of black political incorporation in other parts of the Black Belt meant that in some places, the struggle for local power would be between black candidates and between black party factions, some of whom were allied with the traditional white oligarchy against more progressive hold-overs from the civil rights era.[85]

When one such local black power struggle spilled over into the offices of two of Alabama's newly appointed U.S. attorneys, the Reagan Justice Department used the opportunity to intimidate the larger black electoral movement building in the Black Belt. Complaints of alleged absentee-ballot fraud by a handful of black elected officials provided the cause for an investigation, but ensuring the integrity of the ballot was not the motive for federal intervention. White local and state officials, including the powerful circuit clerk, Mary Aubmertin, and state district attorney Roy Johnson, had appealed to allies in the Reagan administration. Johnson sent a letter to Assistant Attorney General William Bradford Reynolds claiming that absentee-ballot fraud and voter intimidation at the polls in Perry County were "becoming explosive."[86] Just as opposition to Reagan was flaring among African Americans, lit up by the barnstorming candidacy of Jesse Jackson for the Democratic presidential nomination, the Justice Department unleashed its considerable prosecutorial apparatus against black activists to send a very clear message. One of these activists, Wendell Paris, later reflected,

> The local white powers and the feds have said that the Black Belt has gotten too politically strong. That's what this is about. This isn't really about a few absentee ballots. . . . Do you think that if they're going to come through here and put [black voter activists] in jail—and you think black folks would come back to the polls?[87]

To launch a fraud investigation into a purely state or local election, federal law would have to be bent. This was no small matter. In the summer before the fall 1984 primaries, Justice Department officials including the head of the Civil Rights Division, William Bradford Reynolds, crafted a new policy to accommodate the Black Belt prosecutions. Before 1984, the federal government deferred to local authorities in mixed state-federal elections where alleged election crimes had no impact on the outcome of an election. The new policy authorized federal law enforcement officials to investigate "political participants" who "seek out the elderly, socially disadvantaged, or the illiterate, for the purpose of subjugating their electoral will," or under whose "watchful eye" a voter happened to "mark his or her ballot." [88] This was just the kind of voter Black Belt activists had long assisted, and using one of the most important enfranchising tools in many rural black areas of the South, the absentee ballot.

Federal investigations of black voter activists in at least six and as many as ten west Alabama counties, including Greene, Lowndes, Macon, Perry, Sumter, and Wilcox, were initiated in the fall of 1984. Attorneys for the activists charged with fraud argued that their clients were entrapped in a government-sponsored sting operation that caught them assisting absentee-ballot voters in ways that violated Alabama law. According to evidence presented at trial, supporters of the Perry County Civic League's endorsed candidates in a primary for local office were misled through a government-coordinated mailing into voting for candidates *opposed* by the PCCL. When members of the PCCL then assisted these voters at the voters' request in correcting their mismarked ballots, the activists were apprehended and charged with fraud. The federal government's interest in this case was unprecedented. Between the September primary and the November general election, as many as fifty FBI agents interviewed upwards of a thousand people, sometimes at night; raided community offices; bugged the meetings of the Perry County Civic League; and conducted surveillance of the group's voter assistance activities. [89] In later questioning before the House Judiciary Subcommittee on Civil and Constitutional Rights, John Keeney, an official with the Justice Department's Criminal Division, conceded that the investigation and prosecutions could have cost the taxpayers as much as $1 million.

Part of the investigation, which occurred before there was any evidence at all that any crime had been committed, involved FBI agents who breached laws guarding the privacy of scores of black voters by obtaining a protective order allowing the registrar to secretly mark their absentee ballots so that the ballots could be traced back to the voters. To root out evidence of unlawful voter assistance, FBI agents then used these secretly marked ballots to interrogate the voters who cast them, often in an intimidating way, to suggest they had violated the law in voting absentee. Mamie Speight, sixty-four, filed an affidavit in the case in which she testified that two FBI agents knocked on her door and told her to wake up her seventy-two-year old husband, although he was ill. "One of the men asked him why he voted absentee," she said in her affidavit. "I told them he was sick and was not able to vote at the polls. The same man said 'didn't you know you were not supposed to vote absentee?' " Speight said the FBI agent then asked her husband whom he voted for. He told them "it was none of their business." [90]

Voters were harassed with repeated questions about their vote choices, political associations, and financial contributions. In some instances, FBI agents demanded to see membership lists of political organizations to which voters belonged. Following the interrogations, many elderly and housebound voters were subpoenaed to appear before a federal grand jury in Mobile, two hundred miles away from Perry County, despite the presence of a federal courthouse in Selma, less than fifty miles from where many of the voters lived. To make sure these witnesses, all of whom were black, appeared in Mobile,[91] they were ordered to appear at specific times and locations in Selma or Marion, where they were met by as many as a dozen armed federal agents who lined them up and boarded them on buses. In Marion, state and local law enforcement officers "with guns in their hands," according to one witness, blocked off the streets around the courthouse where people were getting on the bus. The buses then journeyed to Mobile, with marked state trooper vehicles in front and behind as if the Greyhound occupants were dangerous rapists or serial killers. On board were twenty-five to thirty mostly elderly, frightened African Americans. The Reverend O.C. Dobynes, one of the witnesses to go before the Mobile grand jury, testified before a congressional committee investigating the Alabama prosecutions,

"When I got on the bus I experienced one of the most degrading experiences of my life. I saw these old people that were very confused. I saw young people who were frightened and confused. Most of these people were illiterate."[92] Among the witnesses were "a large number [who] had never left home before," according to Albert Turner. "The majority . . . was better than 70 years of age, and most of them had to have the assistance of doctors and nurses to go."[93] One ninety-three-year-old man was too sick to make the trip and didn't want to go, so a police car picked him up at home and drove him to Marion, where the authorities put him on the bus. Once he arrived in Mobile his health deteriorated so fast that he was rushed back home, where he suffered a stroke.[94] The other witnesses, though they had not been charged with any crime, were photographed and fingerprinted at the federal building. According to Allen Tullos, a journalist who covered the prosecutions extensively and wrote about them for the Southern Regional Council, "the Mobile ordeal has convinced some black citizens of Perry County never to vote again."[95]

Jefferson Beauregard Sessions III, currently an Alabama senator, had been Senator Denton's handpicked choice for the job of U.S. attorney for the Southern District of Alabama, headquartered in Mobile. On January 25, 1985, Sessions announced the indictment of long-time civil rights workers Albert and Evelyn Turner and Spencer Hogue Jr. for voting fraud, alleging they improperly assisted elderly, often illiterate, and bedridden black voters in casting absentee ballots. The evidence turned on just twenty-seven ballots allegedly altered by the "Marion Three." Confusing testimony given to the grand jury from the black witnesses bused to Mobile about whom they had voted for and who had helped them read and mark their ballots influenced the Selma jury of seven blacks and five whites to reject the government's case.

The Turners and Hogue were acquitted after less than three hours of deliberation. In all, not one of the 210 fraud charges against the eight grassroots black leaders held up in court. But the Justice Department's assault on black voting rights did not end in the Alabama Black Belt. Over the next several years, the tactics authorized by the Justice Department in Alabama and the targeting of black absentee voting were used in Arkansas and Texas in the wake of unprecedented upswings in black electoral activity. Followed with alarm by civil rights advocates at the time, the Black Belt prosecutions are largely forgotten today, but there is no question they were politically motivated. By the time of Reagan's reelection the Justice Department had been transformed into an arm of the White House's political operation. It is difficult to overstate the appalling symbolism of bringing the full weight of the federal government down on working-class black electoral activity in the South. The prosecution of black voter activists in rural Perry and Greene counties in 1984–85 was meant to send a message to both those blacks in the rural South who were still fighting for voting rights, and to southern white Democrats still looking for a reason to vote Republican at the local level. Representative Rodino's concern that the attorney general's new antifraud initiative might lead to abuse of the rights of those providing assistance to voters protected by the Voting Rights Act was not unfounded.

In response to the upsurge in voter registration activity and the threat that mobilization "from below" represents for Republican Party dominance, the George W. Bush administration's Justice Department has revived the use of politically motivated voter fraud investigations. Since at least the 1960s, voter registration drives have played a central role in black politics and broader efforts to engage the electoral participation of low-income groups, waxing and waning in intensity.[96] By 2004, according to Census Bureau figures, approximately 12 million registered voters (or 8.5 percent of all registered voters), disproportionately lower-income minorities, had registered recently as a result of voter registration drives.[97] This is far higher than the number of people registering at public social service agencies mandated by the NVRA to provide registration opportunities.[98] Millions of eligible American citizens would be left out of the electoral process were it not for the groups that raise money and pound the pavement to register and encourage people to vote.

The use of thousands of volunteers and temporary workers who do the hard work of canvassing and trolling for unregistered eligible voters at little or no pay contributes to the potential for mistakes and duplication in the registration process. This is one of the consequences of a personal registration system that "outsources" voter registration work to the public at large rather than placing the burden of registration on government, as is done in many of the European democracies.[99]

The recent upsurge in voter registration activity has brought more media attention to the handful of cases in which drives have been accused of submitting fraudulent registration applications to local elections officials. The blogosphere exaggerates these accusations with wild charges that voter fraud "is breaking out all over"[100] as a result of "a coordinated effort by members of some organizations to rig the electoral system through voter registration fraud" that put "thousands of fictional voters"[101] on the rolls. Such charges are unsupported by any credible evidence anyone has been able to present. In fact, the suspicions about a vast "left-wing" or "liberal Democrat–sponsored" conspiracy to commit voter registration fraud would border on the paranoid if the partisan purposes of fraud claims were ignored. According to available government statistics, the federal government indicted just forty-two people for various misdemeanor and felony crimes related to election fraud *that could also have involved registration fraud* between October 2002 and September 2005.[102] All but two of the people indicted were accused of falsifying information about *their own* eligibility to vote, or of otherwise voting illegally, including: twenty-one people in four states who were prosecuted for registering or voting but who were ineligible under state law because they lacked U.S. citizenship; ten people who voted in the 2004 presidential election in Milwaukee who were prosecuted for falsely certifying that they were eligible to vote when they were still under state supervision for felony convictions;[103] and nine people who were prosecuted for illegally casting two votes in a federal election. Fourteen of the forty-two, including five of the noncitizen cases, five of the felon cases, and four of the double-voting cases, were either acquitted of the charges against them or had their indictments dismissed.[104] Both of the other two people prosecuted for submitting falsified voter registration applications were Louisiana residents; one was a St. Martinville city councilwoman who pleaded guilty to charges stemming from a conspiracy to allow three supporters who lived outside her district to falsely register and vote, helping the woman win reelection in a close race. The other person, a registration canvasser, pleaded guilty to making false statements to a grand jury in connection with eleven fraudulent registration forms.[105]

The exaggerated charges of registration fraud have been used by Republican Party operatives and their conservative and business allies to justify a crackdown on groups like ACORN, America Coming Together, and the NAACP, which have registered millions of low-income Americans in recent years.[106] For example, in one preposterous lawsuit filed by two Ohio voters, one of whom, it was later revealed, had been "indemnified" by a now defunct Republican Party front group, plaintiffs charged America Coming Together, ACORN, the Ohio AFL-CIO, and the NAACP Voter Fund with engaging in a criminal conspiracy to traffic drugs in order to raise funds for their fraudulent voter registration activities. The case had to be withdrawn after the plaintiffs were deposed and found to grasp few of the details of the case or even why they had brought the litigation.[107] But this was not before the Republican-controlled state legislature passed a four-hundred-page election "reform" bill that the League of Women Voters of Ohio warned would result in voter "confusion, uncertainty, disenfranchisement, distrust, and an overburdened election system." Of particular concern were what the league called the bill's "suppression provisions," which required voters to show positive identification before casting a ballot, and mandated that paid registration canvassers must register in *each county* where they might work, opening up registration activists to criminal prosecution for failing to follow the letter of the law.[108]

In a number of states, lawmakers have since introduced and passed bills placing new restrictions on nonpartisan, not-for-profit organizations engaging in voter registration drives. For example, in two recent battleground states, Florida and Ohio, legislatures enacted laws that, among other things, required registration canvassers to register with the state and list their names and addresses on state agency Web sites; required those canvassers to submit completed applications within narrow time frames or face potential felony charges; and increased the paperwork to be submitted with each voter registration application. Court challenges led federal judges to strike the laws down on First Amendment grounds before they went into effect for the 2006 election. But new rules that create hurdles for voter registration drives in other states remain on the books.[109]

One emerging trend violates the intent of the NVRA's mandate that states permit the use of a standard federal voter registration form. Veteran advocates of the 1983–84 registration wars who helped shape the NVRA had insisted on federal standards for registration application forms because of their experience with registrars who refused to provide enough forms to canvassers, or required deputization and made that process onerous, or designed confusing forms that made it easy to disqualify applicants. By 2004, some of these older vote suppression practices were being revived. In 2005, new rules in Colorado required organizations providing voter registration assistance to file an annual "intent" form with the state. Before they can file the form, they must designate a Colorado resident an "agent" of the organization and provide for each canvasser to complete a state training program. Each organization filing an intent to engage in a voter registration drive is assigned a number by the secretary of state that must be provided to each person the organization registers and recorded on every registration form it submits. Because the federal form does not include a tear-off receipt or a box where this number can be filled in, the secretary of state dissuades organizations from using the federal registration form. Likewise, in Georgia, the secretary of state's office does not properly inform visitors to its Web site that the federal registration form will be accepted by county registrars. Instead, it implies that the federal form is appropriate only for out-of-state residents who might want or need to register to vote in their home state while traveling through Georgia.[110] Arizona is embroiled in a conflict with the U.S. Election Assistance Commission, the federal agency responsible for the content of the federal form, because the form does not mandate that registrants provide a copy of proof of citizenship, as is now required by Arizona law. As of December 2007, five other states—Colorado, Delaware, Georgia, New Jersey, and Rhode Island—also had requests for changes to the federal form pending before the EAC. Permitting the states to alter the federal form eviscerates the national minimum standards and voter protections mandated by the NVRA.

The Republican Party's obsession with what it purports to be rampant voter fraud and criminality on the part of Democrats has had a significant impact on the federal government's approach to voting rights since 2000, shifting policies and priorities for the Justice Department from the pursuit of election crimes involving conspiracies and strategic prosecutions geared to having larger preventive effects, to the prosecution of hapless individuals for dubious "fraud" crimes that had no impact on the outcome of any election. While policy was shifting at the Justice Department, the Republican Party expanded its long-standing ballot-security programs. Thus, in terms of vote suppression, it is possible to speak of an "inside" strategy mobilizing federal law enforcement resources to combat nonexistent voter fraud, and an "outside" strategy targeting blacks to reduce the Democratic vote at the polls.

The "outside" electoral strategy of vote suppression relies on the partisan uses of voter fraud allegations, which resonate easily with the public because they trigger deeply held beliefs about a widespread culture of corruption among politicians. Indeed, some, like Larry Sabato and Glenn Simpson, argue that despite periodic efforts to uproot it, corruption is endemic to American politics. They write, "Corruption is truly a staple of our Republic's existence, and its durable, undeniable persistence in the face of repeated, energetic attempts to eradicate it is darkly wondrous."[111] These general beliefs are given specific narrative shape by evoking the colorful folklore of electoral shenanigans in American history. Some people are appalled, but others, it must be said, secretly admire our outlaw history of stolen elections.[112] Either way, most of the time those who revive the old stories of ballot boxes floating down New York City's East River, or 147 percent turnout rates in Tammany wards, do so with a mischievous wink and a nod. Think of the lore about the Daley machine in Chicago and the alleged rigging of the 1960 presidential election in favor of John F. Kennedy. Or the ingenious way voters lined up in alphabetical order to cast their ballots for the young Lyndon Johnson and send him to the Senate in 1948. How many times have you heard these stories repeated by those making the charge that voter fraud is "rampant" today? The romantic invocation of the past covers up the fact that voter fraud allegations are often politically motivated; it also creates confusion about who is committing the fraud.

Today's alleged perpetrators of voter fraud crimes are similar to the kinds of people accused of fraud in the past—the marginalized and formerly disenfranchised, urban dwellers, immigrants, blacks, and lower-status citizens, indeed, the "discordant" voter for whom the stain of political exclusion has not yet been wiped away. Why is the alleged perpetrator of voter fraud always the discordant voter? Because groups at the economic margins of society are still vulnerable to political exclusion despite the progress resulting from the civil rights victories of the 1960s. It is indisputable that racial and class divisions continue to persist in American life, and may even be worsening. Social and economic divisions produce discordant voters whose inclusion in the political system is a threat to the status quo. Their demands for greater social justice, for protections from predatory markets, and for expanded opportunities would force a confrontation with powerful interests, and with a good many voters as well. The Democratic Party leanings of these discordant voters explains why the Republican Party is the party of vote suppression today.

And it is the Republican Party that has used Justice Department investigations to create the appearance of a ballot-security problem, justifying the party's (long-standing) "ballot-integrity" campaigns. The "inside/outside game" of using federal law enforcement power to generate exaggerated allegations about voter fraud, matched to Republican campaign tactics to "cage" voters and challenge their eligibility at the polls, is a winning combination. It is the myth of voter fraud that justifies the misleading argument that follows: access to the ballot must be balanced by measures guarding the integrity of the ballot.

The problem in American elections, however, isn't grasped by the familiar canard that easy access to the ballot sacrifices the integrity of the vote. The real problem is and has been access. The accumulated administrative practices and partisan strategies that combine to make access difficult go far to account for the stunted and misshapen American electoral universe.

EPILOGUE

There is a familiar litany of complaints about American democracy.[1] The list inevitably begins with the distorting influence of the out-of-control competition for campaign contributions. The *New York Times* reported that, by the end of May 2008, $900 million had been raised and spent by all the candidates of the two major parties combined, a whopping $470 million more than was spent during the 2000 primaries, when both major parties last had competitive primary battles.[2]

Then there are the distortions of a presidential primary system that usually gives tiny numbers of older and white Americans in New Hampshire and Iowa the privilege of pruning the field to a few frontrunners. Or consider the peculiar American method of counting votes through the Electoral College, a system arranged at the time of the writing of the Constitution to privilege the influence of the South, and that still functions to give smaller states more weight. Or in congressional elections, there is the overwhelming influence of incumbency. And then there are the mind-boggling possibilities of fixing elections by tampering with the virtually unregulated electronic machines that now record and count votes. These are the serious problems we usually think of when we worry about democracy in America.

But vote suppression as a permanent feature of our electoral system is at least as serious because it means that the direction of influence in American politics is reversed. Instead of voters choosing their political leaders, politicians and their parties strain to shape the administrative arrangements and campaign tactics that determine who will in fact exercise the right to vote. Politicians, in a word, campaign by choosing the voters, a process that has helped to determine election outcomes from the beginnings of the Republic. And African Americans have been at the fulcrum of these campaign tactics, particularly in the post–civil rights period, when blacks became an important political constituency.

We proposed at the outset that in tightly contested elections, the political parties are as likely, if not more so, to adopt strategies to block opposition voters as they are to work to attract new voters to their own candidates. Moreover, it is marginal groups, and given the American experience, African Americans, who are likely to be targeted for such caging strategies. In our time, Republican campaigns first weakened the Democrats by drawing away erstwhile Democratic white voters with race-based appeals, and then weakened the Democrats again by engaging in multiple stratagems to suppress the black vote. Democrats scarcely resisted, because they worried about racial fractures within the ranks of their own constituency, and also because they worried that black policy demands would alienate business supporters. So, instead of reaching out to mobilize their discordant voters, they responded weakly and ambivalently.

Meanwhile, with much of the electorate encouraged by contending political leaders to see the grand political issues of our time as having to do with blacks (and the coded invocations of welfare or crime or out-of-wedlock births attributed to blacks), business influence within both parties grew, although it grew more in the Republican than the Democratic Party. The result has been a domestic policy agenda of tax cuts for corporations and the affluent; privatization of public programs and institutions; the deregulation of business; environmental deregulation and despoliation; and the rollback of New Deal/Great Society labor protections, services, and income support. These policies have been hard on many Americans. But they have been hardest on blacks and Latinos. Overall official unemployment rates are rising, but they are rising much more for blacks (and especially for black youth), and more for Latinos as well. The subprime mortgage crisis affects many of the less-well-off, but when African Americans and Latinos lose their homes, it wipes out the little wealth that these communities have accumulated, and they are also much harder hit by credit card debt.[3] Within minority communities, economic differentiation is increasing, and poverty is rising.[4] In 2005, 25 percent of African Americans lived in poverty, compared to 8.3 percent of whites.[5] Moreover, there is reason to worry about the economic prospects of minorities over time.[6] A recent Brookings Institution study fastened on the prospects of black children:

> Whereas children of white middle-income parents tend to exceed their parents in income, a majority of black children of middle-income parents fall below their parents in income and economic status. ... Startlingly, almost half (45 percent) of black children whose parents were solidly middle class (in 1968) end up falling to the bottom of the income distribution, compared to only 16 percent of white children.[7]

Moreover, poverty is never just an economic condition, especially when those who are poor are surrounded by affluence, and are deluged by media depictions that amplify affluence. Poverty bars people in multiple ways from participating in the social life of a rich nation like ours, and it also strips them of the respect and self-respect that all human beings require. The isolation of those who fall below our standards of material comfort makes conceivable what should be inconceivable, the incarceration of millions of largely minority people, for example, or the iconic tragedy of Hurricane Katrina and its aftermath. A majority-black city was destroyed not by a storm, but by the wanton greed and neglect that underlay the failed public infrastructures, and then underlay the failure to save the victims or restore them to their city. No wonder blacks are pessimistic about the state of their progress, and no wonder that they see a widening gap between the attitudes of the black poor and the black middle class.[8]

The pall of economic depression and social stigmatization that American society casts over African Americans increasingly envelops Latino immigrants. It is a truism that race is a social construction, and other groups can be painted black, especially if they are without the resources to fight back. This is what happened to European immigrants in the late nineteenth and early twentieth centuries, and it allowed them to be made the targets of reformer campaigns that branded them as an inferior and corrupt race, and introduced new obstructions to their exercise of the franchise. Today, it is mainly Hispanics and Muslims who may be on the way to becoming black.

The parallels between the political situation of the people called immigrants today, which means mainly Latinos and Asians, and the political situation of blacks in the 1960s are striking. The numbers of Latinos are growing, they have become an important voting bloc in states that are key to winning the presidency, and they are increasingly leaning Democratic. To be sure, many Latinos do not vote, but many do. And remember, many blacks in the South did not have the vote in the early 1960s, although their civil rights protests did much to activate those blacks who were voters. Similarly, there is every reason to think that immigrant voting preferences are responsive to the claims raised by the immigrant rights movement.

Another parallel is also striking. Republican politicians with national ambitions are more alert to the losses they can suffer in key states if the turn to the Democrats among immigrant voters continues, and their rhetoric tends to be less inflammatory. But Republicans whose ambitions are bounded by local races or by congressional districts with few Latinos are free to be boldly anti-immigrant. An ad from Bob Latta, a Republican running to hold a congressional seat in Ohio's 96 percent white Fifth District, is an example: "Broken borders, and Washington does nothing. Had enough? Bob Latta wants to get tough." And also consistent with race politics in the past, Robin Weirauch, the Democratic challenger in the district, tries to change the subject to trade and health care.[9]

There are signs, in other words, of a revival of the Republican two-pronged strategy, this time also directed against a group now pejoratively called "immigrants." On the one hand, reminiscent of the Southern Strategy, the rhetoric reviling immigrants and invoking fears that the swarm of newcomers will swamp white America is escalating among Republicans and their allies.[10] Yet we also see a revival of the second prong in a battery of vote suppression tactics targeted not only at blacks but also at the increasingly Democratic-leaning Latino vote. For example, Arizona now requires all applicants for registration to show documentary proof of citizenship, and in the

2007–8 legislative session, nineteen other states introduced bills that would have the same effect.[11]

We began this book by pointing to the tension or contradiction between democratic rights and social inequality, especially the caste-like inequality marked by race. Historically, that tension has been managed by vote suppression, itself the result of a complex apparatus of voting rules and administrative practices, and also the result of the chicanery of political parties that compete by warding off voters instead of mobilizing them. The remarkable transformations of the second half of the twentieth century that made African Americans an important social movement and a voting bloc was met by a battery of vote suppression tactics. But it was not as simple as that. Blacks fought back, and their passion and resilience more or less sustained what is called the voting rights revolution. The culminating result was Barack Obama's historic candidacy for the presidency.

Can this forward motion be reversed? Across the country, Republicans tried to do just that. Between 2002 and 2008, eleven states with Republican-dominated legislatures and governors adopted stricter voter identification laws. Efforts to keep down the vote escalated in the final months of the 2008 campaign, including misinformation campaigns and the piling on of more requirements for registration and voting. Increasingly, party tactics have been embedded in state election law. For example, in 2006 the Ohio state legislature passed a law that requires county boards of election to send a piece of registered mail with election information to every registered voter sixty days before an election. The boards must maintain a list of all voters whose mail is returned as undeliverable and make that list available to the public, including to party organizations. In effect, county governments are now required to do a mailing that can be used to "cage" voters.[12] In Florida, a new law that went into effect in September 2008 requires an exact match between a voter registration applicant's identifying information and state or federal government databases. When the law was first implemented, at least thirteen thousand eligible Florida citizens were barred from registering.[13] At about the same time in Virginia, the Montgomery County election director announced (falsely) that students who registered to vote at their college addresses could no longer be claimed as dependents on their parents' tax returns.[14]

The consequences of vote suppression go beyond the impact on minority groups. We are all the victims of the policies that vote suppression makes possible because we all live in a society where the protective and regulatory role of government has collapsed. The consequences are soaring inequalities, crumbling infrastructure, families and communities where most people work harder for less and where decent health care is a privilege, and a society where financial institutions are free to wage aggressive and predatory lending campaigns that bankrupt innocents. If we lift our eyes from our own country, it gets worse. The corruption of American electoral procedures has not only been dangerous for us, it has also been dangerous for the world because it has shored up national leaders who ignored environmental threats and international financial instabilities even while they launched murderous wars to gain political advantage and business profit. Democratic rights do matter.

NOTES

Introduction

1. Lee Atwater in a 1981 interview with Alexander P. Lamis, reported in Lamis's book, *Southern Politics in the 1990s* (Baton Rouge: Louisiana State University Press, 1999), 8, and cited by Bob Herbert, "Impossible, Ridiculous, Repugnant," *New York Times*, October 6, 2005, 37 and Bob Herbert, "The Ugly Side of the G.O.P.," *New York Times*, September 25, 2007, 31.

1. The Party Logic of Voter Demobilization

1. W.E.B. Du Bois, "Kicking Us Out," *Crisis* 24 (May 1922), 11.

2. See Judith Sklar, *American Citizenship: The Quest for Inclusion* (Cambridge, MA: Harvard University Press, 1991), 25–62. J. Morgan Kousser discusses the psychological impact of disenfranchisement as ritual status degradation in the South. See his book, *The Shaping of Southern Politics: Suffrage Restriction and the Establishment of the One-Party South* (New Haven, CT: Yale University Press, 1974), 263–64. Kousser discusses the impact on poor whites, but Sheldon Hackney makes the point that the disenfranchisement of blacks in Alabama at the end of the nineteenth century was a reaction to the fear that Negroes were "succeeding too well." See Hackney, *Populism to Progressivism in Alabama* (Princeton, NJ: Princeton University Press, 1969), 180.

3. A.D. Grambling to Stephen Duncan, August 10, 1873, Stephen Duncan Papers, Natchez Trace Collection, University of Texas, cited in Eric Foner, *Reconstruction: America's Unfinished Revolution, 1863–1877* (New York: Harper & Row, 1988), 291.

4. Foner, *Reconstruction*, 291, citing *Cincinnati Commercial* in the newspaper *American Freedman*, February 1868, 373.

5. Most but not all of Fannie Lou Hamer's story of her beating in a Winona, Mississippi, jail cell was aired live. Worried about the impact any testimony from MFDP delegates could have on public opinion, President Johnson conducted a hastily organized diversion campaign by alerting the

media to a planned meeting at the White House with thirty Democratic governors. Johnson deliberately misled the press into assuming that an announcement of his vice presidential choice was imminent. As Mrs. Hamer neared the end of her statement, NBC broke away to cover the president's press conference. Johnson used up as much time as he could without making any announcements or revealing any news, dodged reporters' questions, and then retreated back to his meeting with the governors. The remaining testimony from four witnesses, including from the Reverend Dr. Martin Luther King, in favor of seating the MFDP delegation was not aired. See Taylor Branch, *Pillar of Fire: America in the King Years, 1963–1965* (New York: Simon & Schuster, 1998), 458–62.

6. Testimony of Fannie Lou Hamer Before the Credentials Committee, Democratic National Convention, Atlantic City, New Jersey, August 22, 1964. See also Chana Kai Lee, *For Freedom's Sake: The Life of Fannie Lou Hamer* (Chicago: University of Illinois Press, 2000), especially chap. 5.

7. The familiar example is the fact than a voter in Alaska carries a hundred times more weight than a voter in California in electing a senator.

8. V.O. Key, "A Theory of Critical Elections," *Journal of Politics* 17:1 (February 1955), 3.

9. Chilton Williamson, *American Suffrage: From Property to Democracy, 1760–1860* (Princeton, NJ: Princeton University Press, 1960), 38; Alexander Keyssar, *The Right to Vote: The Contested History of Democracy in the United States* (New York: Basic Books, 2000), 5–7.

10. John A. Phillips, "Popular Politics in Unreformed England," *Journal of Modern History* 52:4 (December 1980), 624.

11. President George W. Bush, "President Bush Signs Voting Rights Act Reauthorization and Amendments Act of 2006," July 27, 2006, www.whitehouse.gov/news/releases/2006/07/20060727.html.

12. Steven Rosenfeld, "Voter Purging: A Legal Way for Republicans to Swing Elections?" *Alternet*, September 11, 2007, http://www.alternet.org/rights/62133/?page=2.

13. E.E. Schattschneider, *Party Government* (New York: Holt, Rinehart & Winston, 1942), 47. The argument is of even longer standing. In 1928, Harvard historian and political scientist William Munro asserted that "the history of American suffrage has been one of steady and irresistible expansion." Munro, *The Government of American Cities*, 4th ed. (New York: Macmillan, 1928), 147–48, quoted in Keyssar, *The Right to Vote*, xvii.

14. Schattschneider, *Party Government*, 1.

15. Edward S. Greenberg and Benjamin I. Page, *The Struggle for Democracy*, 7th ed. (New York: Pearson / Longman, 2005), 242.

16. Robert Dahl, *Pluralist Democracy in the United States* (Chicago: Rand McNally, 1967), 245.

17. Steven J. Rosenstone and John Mark Hansen, *Mobilization, Participation, and Democracy in America* (New York: Macmillan, 1993), 161.

18. See also Richard M. Valelly, *Two Reconstructions: The Struggle for Black Enfranchisement* (Chicago: University of Chicago Press, 2004), and Paul Frymer, *Uneasy Alliances: Race and Party Competition in America* (Princeton, NJ: Princeton University Press, 1999), regarding the "logic" of party competition, although Frymer thinks that African Americans are a special case.

19. This view of the parties derives from the "responsible-party" school of thought that dominated American political science after World War II and was sounded in the influential 1950 report of the American Political Science Association, "Toward a More Responsible Two-Party System." It puts mass-based, programmatic parties at the center of democracy, emphasizing their importance in facilitating broad political participation and in building consensus. Parties are "responsible" when they compete for votes by making policy commitments to the electorate that they are able to carry out in office. It follows that party competition relying on rational incentives to voters will only drive up turnout. E.E. Schattschneider served as the chair of the committee that wrote the APSA report. See American Political Science Association, "Toward a More Responsible Two-Party System: A Report of the Committee on Political Parties," *American Political Science Review* 44:3, pt. 2 (September 1950), Supplement.

20. Walter Dean Burnham, who follows Schattschneider in most respects, nevertheless attributes the atrophy of the mass parties and the decline of voter participation to the longer-running trend of rising industrial capitalism. See Burnham, "The Changing Shape of the American Electoral Universe," *American Political Science Review* 59:1 (March 1965), 7–28. See also William E. Dugan and William A. Taggart, "The Changing Shape of the American Political Universe, Revisited," *Journal of Politics* 57:2 (May 1995), 469–82.

21. Sidney Milkis, "Franklin D. Roosevelt and the Transcendence of Partisan Politics," *Political Science Quarterly* 100:3 (Fall 1985), 502, cited in Philip Klinkner, *The Losing Parties: Out-Party National Committees, 1956–1993* (New Haven, CT: Yale University Press, 1994), 3.

22. Frymer, *Uneasy Alliances*, 8.

23. Stanley Kelley Jr., Richard Ayers, and William G. Bowen, "Registration and Voting: Putting First Things First," *American Political Science Review* 67 (1967), 375.

24. To an extent, the idea of the party, its unity and durability, gained credibility because the party allegiances of voters had a certain durability. Allegiances inherited from parents or formed during youth tended to endure. But this may be a thing of the past. See Matt Bai, *The Argument: Billionaires, Bloggers, and the Battle to Remake Democratic Politics* (New York: Penguin Press, 2007). For an opposing view and an update of the Michigan School's findings on the salience of party identification, see Donald Green, Bradley Palmquist, and Eric Schickler, *Partisan Hearts and Minds* (New Haven, CT: Yale University Press, 2002).

25. Sidney Milkis and Jesse Rhodes, "George W. Bush, the Republican Party, and the 'New' American Party System," *Perspectives on Politics* 5:3 (September 2007), 471–75. Milkis and Rhodes think that the centralized Republican Party led by George W. Bush and Karl Rove reflects the emergence of a national party system centered on the presidency. Time will tell, but the plummeting popularity of the Bush regime, and rising conflict within the party, suggest otherwise.

26. See Frances Fox Piven, *Challenging Authority: How Ordinary Americans Change America* (New York: Rowman & Littlefield, 2006), 55–80.

27. Schattschneider, *Party Government*, 38.

28. See Richard P. McCormick, "The Party Period and Public Policy: An Explanatory Hypothesis," *Journal of American History* 66:2 (September 1979), 295.

29. Martin Shefter, *Political Parties and the State* (Princeton, NJ: Princeton University Press, 1993).

30. The evidence is anecdotal despite the fact that the literature on the party history of the nineteenth century is vast; representative works include Richard Hofstadter, *The Idea of a Party System: The Rise of Legitimate Opposition in the United States, 1780–1840* (Berkeley: University of California Press, 1969); Paul Kleppner, *The Third Electoral System, 1853–1892: Parties, Voters, and Political Cultures* (Chapel Hill: University of North Carolina, 1979); Richard P. McCormick, *The Second American Party System: Party Formation in the Jacksonian Era* (Chapel Hill: University of North Carolina Press, 1960), and *From Realignment to Reform: Political Change in New York State, 1893–1910* (Ithaca, NY: Cornell University Press, 1981); Michael E. McGerr, *The Decline of Popular Politics: The American North, 1865–1928* (New York: Oxford University Press, 1986); Keith J. Polakoff, *Political Parties in American History* (New York: Alfred A. Knopf, 1981); and John H. Aldrich, *Why Parties? The Origin and Transformation of Political Parties in America* (Chicago: University of Chicago Press, 1995); see also Richard Franklin Bensel, *The American Ballot Box in the Mid-Nineteenth Century* (New York: Cambridge University Press, 2004) for a fascinating and ex-

tended discussion of the actual practice of voting and election administration in the antebellum period, including the role of "party agents" in enticing and intimidating voters.

31. See Christopher Malone, *Between Freedom and Bondage: Race, Party, and Voting Rights in the Antebellum North* (New York: Routledge, 2007).

32. Ibid., 41.

33. Ibid., 52.

34. The mobilization and demobilization of the black vote, or, as Malone puts it, the disenfranchisement and reenfranchisement of blacks, also played a role in the complex and convoluted events of Dorr's Rebellion in Rhode Island. See Malone, *Between Freedom and Bondage*, chap. 4. In Massachusetts, where the black population was always small and declined in density as the years wore on, and where the abolitionist movement was stronger, racial targeting did not occur in this period.

35. Foner, *Reconstruction*, 282.

36. Ibid., 283.

37. Frymer, *Uneasy Alliances*, 15.

38. Kleppner, *The Third Electoral System*, 93.

39. See Peyton McCrary, Jerome A. Gray, Edward Still, and Huey L. Perry, "Alabama," in Chandler Davidson and Bernard Grofman, eds., *Quiet Revolution in the South: The Impact of the Voting Rights Act, 1965–1990* (Princeton, NJ: Princeton University Press, 1994), 41 (citing Malcolm C. McMillan, *Constitutional Development in Alabama, 1798–1901: A Study in Politics, the Negro, and Sectionalism* (Chapel Hill: University of North Carolina Press, 1955), 110–13, 124–33, 151–56, 169–74.

40. See Valelly, *Two Reconstructions*, 23–46. See also Nathan Newman and J.J. Gass, "A New Birth of Freedom: The Forgotten History of the 13th, 14th, and 15th Amendments," Judicial Independence Series (New York: Brennan Center for Justice at New York University School of Law, 2004).

41. Leon F. Litwack, *Been in the Storm So Long: The Aftermath of Slavery* (New York: Vintage, 1979), 547.

42. Valelly reports estimates of African American turnout of 80 percent in the ratification of the new Mississippi constitution in 1868, and turnout rates in 1876 that were higher than they are today in Louisiana and South Carolina. In 1875 and 1876, 55 percent of Louisiana's registered voters were African American, and about 75 to 78 percent of black registrants voted in 1876. See Valelly, *Two Reconstructions*, 76.

43. Ibid., 79. There were two black senators, both from Mississippi, and fourteen congressmen.

44. Ibid., 79–87.

45. Frances Fox Piven and Richard A. Cloward, *Why Americans Still Don't Vote, and Why Politicians Want It That Way* (Boston: Beacon Press, 2000), 82.

46. McCrary et al. "Alabama," 43. The authors go on to describe the restrictive voter registration and election laws and practices that followed in Alabama in the 1890s, which dramatically reduced black voting.

47. Frymer, *Uneasy Alliances*, 49–86.

48. Hackney in his study of Alabama suggests that physical violence against blacks was roughly correlated with the salience of the disenfranchisement issue. See Hackney, *Populism to Progressivism in Alabama*, 180–208.

49. Two-thirds of the freedmen were illiterate, in no small measure because in most slave states before the war, it was a crime to teach blacks to read or write. The Supreme Court recognized the purpose of the literacy test in the South during this period. In *South Carolina v. Katzenbach* (383 U.S. 301), which upheld the constitutionality of the Voting Rights Act of 1965, the Court noted that "Senator Ben Tillman frankly explained to the [South Carolina] state delegates the aim of the new literacy test: '[T]he only thing we can do as patriots and as statesmen is to take from [the "ignorant blacks"] every ballot that we can under the laws of our national government.' "

50. J. Morgan Kousser analyzes the impact of suffrage restriction in the South on turnout. See especially Kousser's correlations of suffrage restriction and turnout, *The Shaping of Southern Politics*, 241–42. Kousser also argues a correlation between positions on disenfranchisement and wealth; see 246–53.

51. Quoted in Hackney, *Populism to Progressivism*, 206–7.

52. "The Close of the Canvass," *New York Times*, November 7, 1876, 1.

53. Walter Dean Burnham, "The System of 1896: An Analysis," in Paul Kleppner et al., eds., *The Evolution of American Electoral Systems* (Westport, CT: Greenwood Press, 1981), 100.

54. Piven and Cloward, *Why Americans Still Don't Vote*, 82.

55. Keyssar, *The Right to Vote*, 118–59.

56. F.G. Crawford, "The New York State Literacy Test," *American Political Science Review* 17:2 (May 1923), 260.

57. Lincoln Steffens, *The Shame of the Cities* (New York: Sagamore Press, 1957), 139.

58. Piven and Cloward, *Why Americans Still Don't Vote*, chap. 4; Joseph P. Harris, *Registration of Voters in the United States* (Washington, D.C.: Brookings Institution, 1929).

59. See Harris, *Registration of Voters in the United States*, 65–92.

60. Quoted in Kousser, *The Shaping of Southern Politics*, 254.

61. Piven and Cloward, *Why Americans Still Don't Vote*, 72–93.

62. Philip E. Converse, "Change in the American Electorate," in Angus Campbell and Philip E. Converse, eds., *The Human Meaning of Social Change* (New York: Russell Sage Foundation, 1972); Philip E. Converse, "Comment on Burnham's 'Theory and Voting Research,'" *American Political Science Review* 68:3 (September 1974) 1024–1027.

63. Burnham, "The System of 1896," 100. Burnham's calculations are based on estimates of all citizens eligible to vote, aliens excluded.

2. Race and Party Competition in Post–World War II America

1. Cited in Vincent Gordon Harding, "Wrestling Toward the Dawn: The Afro-American Freedom Movement and the Changing Constitution," *Journal of American History* 74:3 (December 1987), 718.

2. Steven F. Lawson, *Black Ballots: Voting Rights in the South, 1944–1969* (New York: Columbia University Press, 1976), 151.

3. Ibid., 152.

4. Democrats won the presidency in 1912 only because Theodore Roosevelt, disappointed at the failure of his party to nominate him for another term, formed a third-party slate.

5. See Walter Dean Burnham, "The System of 1896: An Analysis," in Paul Kleppner et al., eds., *The Evolution of American Electoral Systems* (Westport, CT: Greenwood Press, 1981), 100, table 1.

6. *Smith v. Allwright*, 321 U.S. 649 (1944); see Charles L. Zelden, *The Battle for the Black Ballot: Smith v. Allwright and the Defeat of the Texas All-White Primary* (Lawrence: University Press of Kansas, 2004).

7. David J. Garrow, *Protest at Selma: Martin Luther King, Jr., and the Voting Rights Act of 1965* (New Haven, CT: Yale University Press, 1978), 7.

8. On the concentration of blacks in agriculture and domestic service, see Arthur M. Ross, "The Negro in the American Economy," in Arthur M. Ross and Herbert Hill, eds., *Employment, Race, and Poverty* (New York: Harcourt, Brace & World, 1967), 3–48. See also Ira Katznelson, *When Affirmative Action Was White: An Untold History of Racial Inequality in Twentieth-Century America* (New York: W.W. Norton, 2005) especially chap. 2 and 3. On southern relief practices, see Frances Fox Piven and Richard A. Cloward, *Regulating the Poor: The Functions of Public Relief* (New York: Pantheon Books, 1993), especially chap. 7.

9. Allen Yarnell, *Democrats and Progressives: The 1948 Presidential Election as a Test of Postwar Liberalism* (Berkeley: University of California Press, 1974), 35–69.

10. Quoted in Bert Cochran, *Adlai Stevenson: Patrician Among Politicians* (New York: Funk & Wagnalls, 1969), 230.

11. Numan V. Bartley, *The Rise of Massive Resistance: Race and Politics in the South During the 1950s* (Baton Rouge: Louisiana State University Press, 1969), 28–46; V.O. Key Jr., *Southern Politics in State and Nation*, new ed. (1949; Knoxville: University of Tennessee Press 1984), 329–44, 394–95; The Thurmond-Wright ticket was on the ballot in fewer than half the states and received only 2.4 percent of the nationwide vote. But in three of the four states won by the Dixiecrats, the majorities were huge—87 percent Mississippi, 80 percent in Alabama, and 72 percent in South Carolina (the Dixiecrats won 49 percent of the vote in Louisiana). See David Leip's Atlas of U.S. Presidential Elections, "1948 Presidential General Election Data—National by State," http://uselectionatlas.org/RESULTS/index.html (accessed June 2008).

12. See Samuel Lubell, *Revolt of the Moderates* (New York: Harper & Row, 1956); John B. Martin, *Adlai Stevenson of Illinois* (Garden City, NY: Doubleday, 1976).

13. Cochran, *Adlai Stevenson*, 222.

14. Ethel L. Payne, "How Ike Broke Back of South: New Vote Bloc Stuns Dixiecrats," *Daily Defender*, November 8, 1956, 1; Lawson, *Black Ballots*, 161–62.

15. Lawson, *Black Ballots*, 141; Taylor Branch, *Parting the Waters: America in the King Years, 1954–63* (New York: Simon & Schuster, 1988), 193.

16. Paul Kleppner, *Who Voted: The Dynamics of Electoral Turnout* (New York: Praeger, 1982), 116.

17. Frances Fox Piven and Richard A. Cloward, *Why Americans Still Don't Vote, and Why Politicians Want It That Way* (Boston: Beacon Press, 2000), 144.

18. See James Alt, "The Impact of the Voting Rights Act on Black and White Voter Registration in the South," in Chandler Davidson and Bernard Grofman, eds., *Quiet Revolution in the South: The Impact of the Voting Rights Act, 1965–1990* (Princeton, NJ, Princeton University Press, 1994), 368.

19. Ibid., 374, table 12.1. Alt also discusses the difficulties in making precise calculations of black voter registration levels.

20. Tali Mendelberg, *The Race Card: Campaign Strategy, Implicit Messages, and the Norm of Equality* (Princeton, NJ: Princeton University Press, 2001).

21. On the racial code developed by the Republicans (with the assistance of maverick George Wallace), see Carey L. Powers, " 'Hunting Where the Ducks Are': The Republican Racial Strategy in Post–Civil Rights Era Campaigns, 1960–2000" (Ph.D. diss., City University of New York, 2005).

22. Chandler Davidson, Tanya Dunlap, Gale Kenny, and Benjamin Wise, "Vote Caging as a Republican Ballot Security Technique," *William Mitchell Law Review* 34:2 (2008), 533–62.

23. Ibid., 34.

24. Ibid., 35.

25. Democratic National Committee, Press Release, October 27, 1964, quoted by Rick Perlstein, *Village Voice* blog, October 31, 2004, http://www.villagevoice.com/blogs/operationeagleeye/archives/2004/10/its_like_heavie.php.

26. Anthony York, "Eliminating Fraud—or Democrats?" *Salon.com*, December 8, 2000, http://archive.salon.com/politics/feature/2000/12/08/integrity/index.html.

27. See Dan T. Carter, *George Wallace, Richard Nixon, and the Transformation of American Politics*, Thirteenth Charles Edmondson Historical Lectures, Baylor University, Waco, Texas April 14–16, 1991 (Waco, TX: Baylor University Press, 1992), 19.

28. See Frances Fox Piven and Richard A. Cloward, *Poor People's Movements: Why They Succeed, How They Fail* (New York: Pantheon Books, 1977), 219–20.

29. According to Jeremy Mayer, an unofficial Democratic campaign flyer showed Nixon "in various poses of affection and affinity with Negroes. Some were in American business suits and some in African tribal regalia." See Jeremy Mayer, *Running on Race* (New York: Random House, 2002), 32.

30. James Farmer, *Freedom—When?* (New York: Random House, 1965), 40.

31. See Carter, *George Wallace, Richard Nixon*, 15.

32. Ibid., 37. Analyzing the significance of the 1968 election for the two major parties, Phillips argued, "Negroes are slowly but surely taking over the apparatus of the Democratic Party in a growing number of Deep Southern Black Belt counties, and this cannot help but push whites into the alternative major party structure—that of the GOP." For this reason, he urged that "maintenance of Negro voting rights is essential to the GOP." See Kevin P. Phillips, *The Emerging Republican Majority* (Garden City, NY: Anchor Books, 1970), 287.

33. Carter, *George Wallace, Richard Nixon*, 43.

34. Kevin A. Pirch reports that studies of campaign outreach show that

the percentage of African Americans contacted by Democratic campaigns between 1952 and 1996 was roughly representative of their numbers in the population. Given that those blacks who voted favored the Democrats by roughly 90 percent, Democratic turnout efforts should have favored blacks as well. Meanwhile, of course, Republicans were much less likely to contact blacks. See Pirch, "War and Morality: An Examination of African Americans, the Republican Party, and the 2004 Presidential Election: A Research Note," *National Political Science Review* 11 (2007), 368.

3. Black Voting Power in the Cities

1. Bayard Rustin, "From Protest to Politics: The Future of the Civil Rights Movement," *Commentary* 39:1 (January 1965), 29.

2. Ibid., 25–31.

3. See William E. Nelson Jr., "Cleveland: The Rise and Fall of the New Black Politics," in Michael B. Preston, Lenneal J. Henderson Jr., and Paul Puryear, eds., *The New Black Politics: The Search for Political Power* (New York: Longman, 1982), 187. See also Eddie N. Williams, "Black Political Progress in the 1970s: The Electoral Arena," in Michael B. Preston et al., *The New Black Politics*, 73–108.

4. The classic statement on this phenomenon, later called into question, is Nathan Glazer and Daniel Patrick Moynihan, *Beyond the Melting Pot: The Negroes, Puerto Ricans, Jews, Italians, and Irish of New York City* (Cambridge, MA: MIT Press, 1963).

5. For a review of these several developments, see William E. Nelson Jr. and Philip J. Meranto, *Electing Black Mayors: Political Action in the Black Community* (Columbus: Ohio State University Press, 1977), especially 335–81.

6. Ibid., 67–107.

7. "Richard G. Hatcher," *New York Times*, November 9, 1967, 33.

8. Gene Roberts, "Latin Residents Hold Pivotal Role in Gary Election," *New York Times*, September 3, 1967, 39.

9. Wallace garnered only about 30 percent of the vote in the Republican-leaning state, but his victories in Lake and Porter counties were troubling signs to national Democrats, who worried now that their support for a civil rights bill could cause defections among northern congressional Democrats. The day after the election, a disappointed editor of the state's largest newspaper, the *Indianapolis Star*, wrote, "If any responsible official had suggested six months ago that a segregationist from the deep South could poll such a vote in Indiana, he would have been hooted into silence and shuffled quietly into obscurity." Quoted in Dan T. Carter, *The Politics of Rage: George*

Wallace, the Origins of the New Conservatism, and the Transformation of American Politics, 2nd ed. (1995; Baton Rouge: Louisiana State University Press, 2000), 211; see also, Roberts, "Latin Residents," 39, and Donald Janson, "Suit Is Expected in Gary," *New York Times,* November 9, 1967, 1.

10. One gimmick involved putting campaign cards under door-to-door milk deliveries. When water condensed on the cold bottles of milk, the card would stick to the bottom and be delivered into the house along with the milk. See Nelson and Meranto, *Electing Black Mayors,* 234–35.

11. Ibid., 238.

12. Ibid., 240.

13. Ibid., 249.

14. Greer did not work on Hatcher's campaign, arriving in the city five months after Hatcher was elected. See Edward Greer, "The 'Liberation' of Gary, Indiana," *Trans-Action* 8:3 (January 1971), 30–39, reprinted in Alan Shank, ed., *Political Power and the Urban Crisis,* 2nd ed. (Boston: Holbrook Press, 1974), 324; and Greer's reflections on and analysis of the limits of black electoral power in *Big Steel: Black Politics and Corporate Power in Gary, Indiana* (New York: Monthly Review Press, 1979).

15. The following account is taken from Nelson and Meranto, *Electing Black Mayors,* 259–68.

16. Jon C. Teaford, " 'King Richard' Hatcher: Mayor of Gary," *Journal of Negro History* 77:3 (Summer 1992), 126–40.

17. Ibid., 129.

18. Donald Janson, "First Negro Mayor Is Elected in Gary After Bitter Contest," *New York Times,* November 8, 1967, 1.

19. Donald Janson, "Tension High As Gary Election Nears," *New York Times,* November 5, 1967, 80. Ed Greer claims that "—it was a Gary tradition for the Democratic machine to contribute $1,500 each week to a black ministers' alliance for them to distribute to needy parishioners—with the tacit understanding that when elections came around they would help deliver the vote." And in Hatcher's primary, "the machine spent an estimated $500,000 in cash on buying black support alone." See Greer, "The 'Liberation' of Gary, Indiana," 324. Similarly, Nelson and Meranto found that to maintain their grip on the black vote, the Democratic Party machine typically used payoffs to black leaders and politicians; Hatcher's primary was no different, with the machine dropping "nearly $100,000 in the black community" in the last two weeks before the election (see *Electing Black Mayors,* 255).

20. The ad ran on page 29 of the August 24, 1967, edition of the *Times,* and simultaneously in the *Gary Post-Tribune.* See also Associated Press, "Ads Bringing Funds to Negro Candidate," *New York Times,* August 26, 1967, 15.

21. The ad cost $6,960 in the *Times* and $860 in the *Post-Tribune.* See

Martin Arnold, "Negro Candidate Asks Funds in Ads," *New York Times*, August 24, 1967, 26.

22. *Info*, September 7, 1967, cited in Nelson and Meranto, *Electing Black Mayors*, 290–91.

23. "Humphrey to Help Negro Run," *New York Times*, September 2, 1967, 24.

24. In 1962, Mayor George Chacharis was forced to resign when he was convicted of federal tax evasion. Chacharis went to prison for failing to report nearly a quarter of a million dollars in kickbacks he received from contractors doing business with the city; he returned to Gary to help Martin Katz run his unsuccessful reelection campaign. See Martin Arnold, "Negro Candidate Asks Funds in Ads," 26; Associated Press, "Ads Bringing Funds to Negro Candidate," 15; Clayton Knowles, "Negro Candidate in Gary Is Feted," *New York Times*, October 22, 1967, 48.

25. The backing of high-profile national Democrats, in turn, also brought the support of the governor of Indiana and the Indiana Democratic Party, despite the intransigent opposition of the Lake County organization.

26. Mrs. Marion Tokarski, quoted in the *Chicago Sun Times*, November 19, 1967, cited in Nelson and Meranto, *Electing Black Mayors*, 304.

27. Ethel L. Payne, "FBI Denies Getting Hatcher Vote Fraud Complaint Wire," *Chicago Daily Defender*, October 31, 1967, 1. Hatcher told the press that black voters were being purged because "they're supposedly dead." He added, "I assure you they're alive and kicking. Most have been voting at their addresses for years." See Arnold Rosenzweig, "Hatcher's Court Plea Could Delay Election," *Chicago Daily Defender*, November 1, 1967, 1.

28. "Asks U.S. to Prevent Vote Fraud in Gary," *Chicago Tribune*, October 27, 1967, A14. For the content of the telegram, see Ethel L. Payne, "FBI Denies Getting Hatcher Vote Fraud Complaint Wire," 1; see also Thomas Connor, "Dem Worker Held in Gary Vote Frauds," *Chicago Tribune*, December 31, 1967, 3.

29. Charles H. Levine and Clifford Kaufman, "Urban Conflict as a Constraint on Mayoral Leadership: Lessons from Gary and Cleveland," *American Politics Quarterly* 2:1 (January 1974), 78–106, 99.

30. Quoted in Nelson and Meranto, *Electing Black Mayors*, 306.

31. A day after Hatcher sent his telegram, a Justice Department spokesman told the press that the department could not send in federal observers to oversee a municipal election as requested by the Hatcher campaign. He said the Voting Rights Act provided for observers only in low-registration situations in certain states or political jurisdictions that did not apply to Gary. "Justice Department Shuns Gary, Ind., Observer Role," *New York Times*, October 28, 1967, S25. Three days later, Dean St. Dennis of the Justice

Department's Office of Public Information told the *Chicago Defender* that a check of the records showed no receipt of a telegram to Attorney General Ramsey Clark from the Hatcher campaign. Ethel L. Payne, "FBI Denies Getting Hatcher Vote Fraud Complaint Wire," 1.

32. "Court to Hear Hatcher Fraud Suit Monday," *Chicago Tribune*, November 1, 1967, D6.

33. Ethel L. Payne, "Hatcher's Plea Triggers Dramatic Action in Capital," *Chicago Defender*, November 7, 1967, 8.

34. Ibid.

35. John Elmer, "Pick Gary Mayor Today; Bitter Campaigning Ends; Troops Poised," *Chicago Tribune*, November 7, 1967, 1.

36. Nelson and Meranto, *Electing Black Mayors*, 308–9.

37. Ibid., 310.

38. Betty Washington, "Hatcher Fears Election Steal; Fraud Admitted," *Chicago Defender*, November 7, 1967, 1; Donald Janson, "Court Acts to Bar Gary Vote Fraud," *New York Times*, November 7, 1967, 1.

39. Elmer, "Pick Gary Mayor Today," 1.

40. In a bid to head off litigation, Krupa had already restored most of the names after county attorneys informed him that his actions violated Indiana election law. The voters, however, were not notified that their registration status had been restored.

41. "Gary Election: What the Court Ruled," *Chicago Defender*, November 7, 1967, 1.

42. Governor Branigin, responding to a request from outgoing mayor Katz, said he was acting on information indicating "imminent danger" to the peace in Gary. The Hatcher campaign saw this as another effort at intimidating black voters and worried that the presence of the Guard might scare some African Americans from coming out to vote. Hatcher worried the Guard's presence would be seen as a provocation and said he was "absolutely unaware" of any danger to the peace. See Donald Janson, "Guard Is Alerted for Vote in Gary," *New York Times*, November 3, 1967, 30.

43. See Betty Washington, "Irregularities Charged During Gary Balloting," *Chicago Defender*, November 8, 1967, 4.

44. James B. Lane, "Black Political Power and Its Limits: Gary Mayor Richard G. Hatcher's Administration, 1968–87," in Colburn and Adler, eds., *African American Mayors*, 61.

45. See Lane, "Black Political Power," 73.

46. Nelson and Meranto, *Electing Black Mayors*, 96–97.

47. Ibid., 101.

48. Leonard Moore reports that "[Stokes's] supporters urged him to ask for a recount when they heard rumors of voter fraud in predominantly

white precincts. . . . [M]any . . . concluded that white voting registrars stole the election. Their suspicion was confirmed when it was learned that a white police officer had been dispatched to bring in 'a bag of missing votes' two hours after the polls had closed." See Leonard N. Moore, *Carl B. Stokes and the Rise of Black Political Power* (Urbana: University of Illinois Press, 2002), 43.

49. Nelson and Meranto, *Electing Black Mayors*, 105.

50. Ibid., 104.

51. U.S. Commission on Civil Rights, *Children in Need: A Study of a Federally Assisted Program of Aid to Needy Families with Children in Cleveland and Cuyahoga County, Ohio* (Washington, DC: GPO, 1966).

52. Moore, *Carl B. Stokes*, 47.

53. Michael D. Roberts, "The Riot and the Bad Address," *Cleveland Magazine*, July 2006.

54. Nelson and Meranto, *Electing Black Mayors*, 109. See also Jeffrey K. Hadden, Louis H. Masotti, and Victor Thiessen, "The Making of the Negro Mayors, 1967," in August Meier, ed., *The Transformation of Activism* (Chicago: Trans-action Books/Aldine, 1970), 95; and Carl B. Stokes, *Promises of Power: A Political Autobiography* (New York: Simon & Schuster, 1973), 94. Two years later rioting erupted again in the Cleveland neighborhood of Glenville, and this time it took a form resembling guerrilla warfare. See Louis H. Masotti and Jerome R. Corsi, *Shoot-out in Cleveland: Black Militants and the Police* (New York: Praeger, 1969).

55. Roldo S. Bartimole and Murray Gruber, "Cleveland: Recipe for Violence," *The Nation*, June 26, 1967, 814.

56. Roldo Bartimole, "Ralph Locher, a Dose of 1960s History, or Why Cleveland Mayors Are Expendable," *CoolCleveland.com*, www.cool cleveland.com/index.php?n=Main.Ralph:Loucher (accessed June 2008).

57. Ibid.

58. Nelson and Meranto report that "[s]ome Clevelanders began to circulate the suggestion that the city's slogan be changed from 'The Best Location in the Nation' to 'The Mistake on the Lake.' Among the businessmen who traveled extensively, some 'were becoming ashamed to admit that they lived in Cleveland.' " See *Electing Black Mayors*, 112.

59. Moore, *Carl B. Stokes*, 44.

60. Ibid., 28–37.

61. Nelson and Meranto, *Electing Black Mayors*, 123.

62. Ibid., 121.

63. The grant was to cover activities that included voter registration, youth leadership training, and community organization. See Karen Ferguson, "Organizing the Ghetto: The Ford Foundation, CORE, and White

Power in the Black Power Era, 1967–1969," *Journal of Urban History* 34:1 (November 2007), 67–100; see also August Meier and Elliott Rudwick, *CORE: A Study in the Civil Rights Movement, 1942–1968* (Urbana: University of Illinois Press, 1975), 420.

64. Moore, *Carl B. Stokes*, 57.

65. Stokes, *Promises of Power*, 95–96.

66. Bartimole, "Ralph Locher."

67. Tamar Jacoby, "McGeorge Bundy: How the Establishment's Man Tackled America's Problem with Race," *APF Reporter* 13:3 (1990), www.aliciapatterson.org/APF1303/Jacoby/Jacoby.html. Historian Karen Ferguson sees this as part of a pattern of action by Ford as it sought to use its grants to find ways to peacefully incorporate rural black migrants into the urban political economy. See "Organizing the Ghetto," 70.

68. Kenneth G. Weinberg, *Black Victory: Carl Stokes and the Winning of Cleveland* (Chicago: Quadrangle Books, 1968), 199.

69. Hadden et al., "The Making of the Negro Mayors, 1967," 103.

70. See Moore, *Carl B. Stokes*, 60.

71. Ibid., 38–39.

72. Richard M. Peery and Paul Shepard, "*Carl Stokes; 1927–1996*," *Cleveland Plain Dealer*, April 4, 1996, A1.

73. See Dennis McIlnay, "Philanthropy at 50: Four Moments in Time," *Foundation News and Commentary* 39:5 (September–October 1998), www.foundationnews.org/CME/article.cfm?ID=1053. Ferguson also says that the new federal tax regulations for foundations were imposed in part because of "controversy arising from accusations of pro-Stokes partisanship in the CORE grant's voter registration activities"("Organizing the Ghetto," 95).

74. A congressional report on the Tax Reform Act of 1969 acknowledged as much. In explaining the new rules on foundations, it stated, "In recent years, private foundations had become increasingly active in political and legislative activities. In several instances called to the Congress' attention, funds were spent in ways clearly designed to favor certain candidates. In some cases, this was done by financing registration campaigns in limited geographical areas." The joint committee was headed by the longtime segregationist from Louisiana, Senator Russell Long, and the Dixiecrat from Arkansas, Representative Wilbur Mills. See U.S. Congress, Joint Committee on Internal Revenue Taxation, General Explanation of the Tax Reform Act of 1969, HR 13270, 91st Cong. PIL 91–172 (Washington, DC: GPO, December 3, 1970), 48.

75. Roy Wilkins, "Negro Voting Rights," Letter to the Editor, *New York Times*, August 8, 1969, 32.

76. Frank C. Porter, "Gist of Tax Reform Act's Provisions, Effects on Revenue," *Washington Post*, December 31, 1969, A4.

77. Paul Kleppner, *Chicago Divided: The Making of a Black Mayor* (DeKalb: Northern Illinois University Press, 1985), 144–46.

78. Ibid.; Ronald W. Walters, *Freedom Is Not Enough: Black Voters, Black Candidates, and American Presidential Politics* (New York: Rowman & Littlefield, 2005); Katherine Tate, "Black Political Participation in the 1984 and 1988 Presidential Election," *American Political Science Review* 85:4 (December 1991), 1159–76.

79. Studs Terkel, "The Chicago Machine Is Junk Heap," *New York Times*, April 17, 1983, quoted in Manning Marable, *Black American Politics: From the Washington Marches to Jesse Jackson* (London: Verso, 1985), 191.

80. Marable, *Black American Politics*, 206–9; for alternative views, see James R. Ralph Jr., *Northern Protest: Martin Luther King, Jr., Chicago, and the Civil Rights Movement* (Cambridge, MA: Harvard University Press, 1993); Adam Fairclough, *To Redeem the Soul of America: The Southern Christian Leadership Conference and Martin Luther King, Jr.* (Athens: University of Georgia Press, 1987); and David J. Garrow, *Bearing the Cross: Martin Luther King, Jr., and the Southern Christian Leadership Conference* (1987; New York: HarperPerennial, 1999).

81. Milton L. Rakove, *Don't Make No Waves, Don't Back No Losers: An Insider's Analysis of the Daley Machine* (Bloomington: Indiana University Press, 1975).

82. Steven P. Erie, *Rainbow's End: Irish-Americans and the Dilemmas of Urban Machine Politics, 1840–1985* (Los Angeles: University of California Press, 1988), 186.

83. Abdul Alkalimat and Doug Gills, *Harold Washington and the Crisis of Black Power in Chicago* (Chicago: Twenty-First Century Books and Publications, 1989), 80.

84. See, for example, James Q. Wilson, *Negro Politics: The Search for Leadership* (New York: Free Press, 1960); Dianne M. Pinderhughes, *Race and Ethnicity in Chicago Politics: A Reexamination of Pluralist Theory* (Chicago: University of Illinois Press, 1987); William J. Grimshaw, *Bitter Fruit: Black Politics and the Chicago Machine* (Chicago: University of Chicago Press, 1992).

85. Twiley W. Barker, "Political Mobilization of Black Chicago: Drafting a Candidate," *PS* 16:3 (Summer 1983), 482–85.

86. William J. Grimshaw, "Unraveling the Enigma: Mayor Harold Washington and the Black Political Tradition," *Urban Affairs Quarterly* 23:2 (December 1987), 193.

87. Quoted in Gary Rivlin, *Fire on the Prairie: Chicago's Harold Washington and the Politics of Race* (New York: Henry Holt, 1992), 13.

88. Mike Royko, *Boss: Richard J. Daley of Chicago* (New York: New American Library, Inc., 1971), 134. Similarly, in the early 1960s, even as black voters gave him their votes, Daley publicly resisted proposed solutions to the segregation of black children in inferior schools, backing his hapless schools superintendent's plan to relieve overcrowding with mobile trailers while black students living within blocks of underenrolled white schools were refused admission. Daley also loudly and forcefully opposed busing as a means of integration, and resisted a court-ordered scattered-site housing-desegregation plan that compelled the CHA to build public housing in white areas. He adamantly defended the discriminatory hiring and promotion practices in the Chicago Police Department, risking the loss of $95 million in federal funds for refusing to obey a court-ordered quota system imposed by a federal judge who condemned the city's "arrogant, contemptuous" behavior. Kleppner, *Chicago Divided*, 84–87.

89. Grimshaw, "Unraveling the Enigma," 195; and Grimshaw, *Bitter Fruit*, 115.

90. "Daley Hails Hatcher, Stokes Elections," *Daily Defender*, November 9, 1967, 4.

91. Michael B. Preston, "The Resurgence of Black Voting in Chicago: 1955–1983," in Melvin G. Holli and Paul M. Green, eds., *The Making of the Mayor: Chicago 1983* (Grand Rapids, MI: William B. Eerdmans, 1984), 39–51.

92. Kleppner, *Chicago Divided*, 75.

93. Paula P. Wilson, "Black Aldermen Search for New Power in Post-Daley Era," *Chicago Reported*, January 1978, 7; the quote is from Don Rose, cited in Kleppner, *Chicago Divided*, 97.

94. Grimshaw, "Unraveling the Enigma," 196.

95. Robert McClory, "Up from Obscurity: Harold Washington," in Holli and Green, eds. *The Making of the Mayor*, 3–16.

96. Michael B. Preston, "The Election of Harold Washington: Black Voting Patterns in the 1983 Chicago Mayoral Race," *PS* 16:3 (Summer 1983), 486–89.

97. Kleppner, *Chicago Divided*, 144.

98. Erie, *Rainbow's End*, 186.

99. Woods, "The Chicago Crusade," 19.

100. U.S. District Court, Northern District of Illinois, plaintiff's brief, *POWER v. Thompson*, case no. 82-C-5024.

101. The settlement reached in August 1982 was a compromise. It per-

mitted POWER to enter the waiting rooms to talk with people about registering to vote, but actual registration had to be conducted by board staff operating outside the offices at card tables or in unmarked vans supplied by POWER. POWER had to sue a second time to gain access to welfare and unemployment agencies for a drive before the 1983 mayoral primary and general election, and this time it won access to office waiting rooms conditioned on its agreement to reduce the length of the drive from 751 site-days to 231 site-days. See Woods, "The Chicago Crusade," 18–22; "Voter Registration Catches On," *Chicago Tribune*, December 15, 1982, 18.

102. Kleppner, *Chicago Divided*, 147 (quoting Chicago Board of Election Commissioners chair Michael Lavelle: "It's amazing. This is the best outreach year ever. I give credit to the outstanding efforts of the community groups for this success.").

103. Tim Franklin, "120,000 Voters File on Last Day," *Chicago Tribune*, January 27, 1983, 3.

104. Kleppner, *Chicago Divided*, 149.

105. Ibid.

106. Preelection polls were wildly off, predicting a 55 percent to 38 percent victory for Thompson over Stevenson on the eve of the election. See Richard Day and Kurt M. Becker, "Preelection Polling in the 1982 Illinois Gubernatorial Contest," *Public Opinion Quarterly* 48:3 (Fall 1984), 606–14.

107. As a percentage of the voting-age population, 52.3 percent of blacks in Chicago voted for Stevenson, compared to 30.6 percent of whites. See Kleppner, *Chicago Divided*, 150.

108. Robert Davis, "Vrdolyak's Day Started with a Bang, Got Better," *Chicago Tribune*, November 4, 1982, 15.

109. Two years earlier, the Women's Auxiliary of the Lu Palmer Foundation surveyed black Chicagoans to identify potential candidates. Out of this effort, the auxiliary pulled together a list of about ninety names and submitted them to over a thousand members of the Chicago Black United Communities (CBUC) organization for feedback. The CBUC pared the list down to twenty and in early May 1982 circulated the new list to over 17,500 people throughout black neighborhoods. Some 13,500 surveys were returned, and Harold Washington was the overwhelming choice of respondents. Palmer and others organized a mass meeting, and again, Washington was the choice of the over 1,000 people in attendance. See Rivlin, *Fire on the Prairie*, 21–61.

110. Barker, "Political Mobilization of Black Chicago," 484.

111. Paul M. Green, "The Primary: Some New Players—Same Old Rules," in Holli and Green, eds., *The Making of the Mayor*, 25.

112. Barker, "Political Mobilization of Black Chicago," 483.

113. Green, "The Primary," 30.

114. Douglas Frantz, "Daley Calls Campaign Leaflet a 'Filthy' Attempt to Split City," *Chicago Tribune*, February 20, 1983, 18; Vrdolyak denied he made the statements, but the damage was done. After Vrdolyak's remarks were publicized, Byrne's poll numbers dropped 7 percentage points among what little black support she had left. See Melvin G. Holli and Paul M. Green, eds., *Bashing Chicago's Traditions: Harold Washington's Last Campaign, Chicago, 1987* (Grand Rapids, MI: William B. Eerdmans, 1989), 8.

115. Green, "Primary," 31.

116. Alkalimat and Gills, *Harold Washington and the Crisis*, 73.

117. Kleppner, *Chicago Divided*, 177.

118. "Dear Mr. Ogilvie . . . ," *Chicago Tribune*, February 19, 1983, 6.

119. Grimshaw, "Unraveling the Enigma," 160–64.

120. Kleppner called their rivalry "an Irish blood feud." See Kleppner, *Chicago Divided*, 170.

121. Rivlin, *Fire on the Prairie*, 158–59.

122. Kleppner, *Chicago Divided*, 185.

123. Alkalimat and Gills, *Harold Washington and the Crisis*, 87.

124. Kleppner, *Chicago Divided*, 188.

125. Rivlin, *Fire on the Prairie*, 166.

126. Kleppner, *Chicago Divided*, 189.

127. Rivlin, *Fire on the Prairie*, 176.

128. Ibid., 169.

129. Alkalimat and Gills, *Harold Washington and the Crisis*, 86.

130. Don Rose, "How the 1983 Mayoral Election Was Won: Reform, Racism, and Rebellion," in Holli and Green, eds., *The Making of the Mayor*, 118; Kleppner, *Chicago Divided*, 196.

131. Kleppner, *Chicago Divided*, 191.

132. Ibid.

133. Ibid., 229.

134. Grimshaw, "Unraveling the Enigma," 188; Kleppner, *Chicago Divided*, 208–9.

135. Kleppner, *Chicago Divided*, 211.

136. Alkalimat and Gills, *Harold Washington and the Crisis*, 89.

137. Rivlin, *Fire on the Prairie*, 187.

138. Kleppner, *Chicago Divided*, 187, 212.

139. Rose, "How the 1983 Election Was Won," 117–18.

140. Kleppner, *Chicago Divided*, 232.

141. Grimshaw, *Bitter Fruit*, 82.

142. Rivlin, *Fire on the Prairie*, 195.

143. Kleppner, *Chicago Divided*, 238; Rose, "How the 1983 Election Was Won," 101–24.

144. Kleppner, *Chicago Divided*, 223–24.

145. Tim Franklin, "Washington Win Spurs Blacks' Political Hopes," *Chicago Tribune*, April 26, 1983, B3.

146. Kleppner, *Chicago Divided*, 252–53.

4. Party Resistance to National Voter Registration Reform

1. Laughlin McDonald, "The Quiet Revolution in Minority Voting Rights," Symposium: The State of the Union: Civil Rights, *Vanderbilt Law Review* 42 (May 1989), 1293–96.

2. Pennsylvania, Debates of the Constitutional Convention, 1837, 3, 44; quoted in Joseph P. Harris, *Registration of Voters in the United States* (Washington, DC: Brookings Institution, 1929), 68.

3. J. Morgan Kousser, *The Shaping of Southern Politics: Suffrage Restriction and the Establishment of the One-Party South, 1880–1910* (New Haven, CT: Yale University Press, 1974).

4. Earl M. Lewis, "The Negro Voter in Mississippi," *Journal of Negro Education* 26:3 (Summer 1957), 338–39.

5. Joseph L. Bernd and Lynwood M. Holland, "Recent Restrictions upon Negro Suffrage: The Case of Georgia," *Journal of Politics* 21:3 (August 1959), 487–513.

6. Quoted in Brian K. Landsberg, *Free at Last to Vote: The Alabama Origins of the 1965 Voting Rights Act* (Lawrence: University Press of Kansas, 2007), 128.

7. See Kevin P. Phillips, *The Emerging Republican Majority* (Garden City, NY: Anchor Books, 1970).

8. Edward G. Carmines and James A. Stimson, *Issue Evolution: Race and the Transformation of American Politics* (Princeton, NJ: Princeton University, 1989), 54. See also Norman C. Amaker, *Civil Rights and the Reagan Administration* (Washington, DC: Urban Institute Press, 1988). Although Reagan's 9 percent share of the black vote was a record low for a Republican in 1984, George W. Bush has since broken it, winning only 8 percent of the black vote in 2000.

9. Frances Fox Piven and Richard A. Cloward, *Why Americans Still Don't Vote, and Why Politicians Want It That Way* (Boston: Beacon Press, 2000), 144.

10. "Gallup Report; Political Social and Economic Trends," report no. 199 (Princeton, NJ: Gallup Poll, 1982), 19.

11. "Gallup Report: Political Social and Economic Trends," report no. 213 (Princeton, NJ: Gallup Poll, 1983), 28.

12. Human SERVE fund-raising letter, undated, Human SERVE archives, Columbia University.

13. Sheila D. Collins, *The Rainbow Challenge: The Jackson Campaign and the Future of American Politics* (New York: Monthly Review Press, 1986), 96.

14. Sanford A. Newman, "Project VOTE! Tapping the Power of the Poor," *Social Policy* 13:3 (Winter 1983), 18. Before the introduction of Electronic Benefit Transfer, recipients had to pick up their food stamps once a month.

15. Hulbert James, Frances Fox Piven, and Richard Cloward, "The Continuing Struggle for the Franchise in the United States: Some Next Steps," a report on the accomplishments in 1984 and the proposed program and budget for 1985 (New York: Human SERVE Fund, 1984), 7–8.

16. Robert Pear, "Drive to Sign Up Poor for Voting Meets Resistance," *New York Times*, April 15, 1984, 1.

17. Jesse Jackson, "Speech at the Democratic Convention," *National Journal*, July 21, 1984, 25.

18. Jesse Jackson, "The Keys to a Democratic Victory in 1984" (speech before the 13th Annual Convention of Operation PUSH), *Black Scholar*, September–October 1984, 3.

19. James L. Guth, "The New Christian Right," in Robert C. Liebman and Robert Wuthnow, eds., *The New Christian Right: Mobilization and Legitimation* (New York: Aldine Publishing, 1983), 37; Kathy Sawyer, "Linking Politics and Religion," *Washington Post*, August 23, 1980, H1; Seymour Martin Lipset and Earl Raab, "The Election and the Evangelicals," *Commentary* 71 (March 1981), 25–32.

20. James Kilpatrick, "A Conservative View on the Need for GOP to Register Voters for 1984," *Staten Island Advance*, December 6, 1983.

21. Jane Perlez, "Does Voter Registration Cut Two Ways?" *New York Times*, May 13, 1984, sec. 4, p. 9.

22. Ibid.

23. "Campaign Notes: Voter Registration Curb in Cincinnati Challenged," *New York Times*, September 13, 1984, B14.

24. Pear, "Drive to Sign Up Poor."

25. Project Vote memo, undated.

26. Josh Barbanel, "Voting Board Struggles with Registration Load," *New York Times*, October 4, 1984, B1.

27. David W. Dunlap, "Goldin Clashes with the Mayor About a Letter," *New York Times*, September 21, 1984, B5.

28. Robin Leeds (Massachusetts field staff, Human SERVE), interview by Margaret Groarke, March 12, 1985.

29. Frances Fox Piven and Richard A. Cloward, *Why Americans Still Don't Vote* (New York: Pantheon, 1988), 178.

30. Operation Big Vote, "Report on 1984 Mobilization," unpublished, 1985.

31. Jo-Anne Chasnow (associate director, Human SERVE), interview by Margaret Groarke, 1996.

32. Linda Davidoff and Cynthia Williams, "Litigating the Right to Register and to Cast a Ballot: A Summary of Current Cases and Approaches," Human SERVE Campaign, unpublished (October 1986).

33. In March 1984, Democrat Edwin Edwards replaced Republican David Treen as governor of Louisiana.

34. Chasnow interview, 1996.

35. U.S. Bureau of the Census, Current Population Reports, ser. P-20, no. 405, "Voting and Registration in the Election of November 1984" (Washington, DC: GPO, 1986).

36. The "Ad Hoc Funders Committee for Voter Registration" comprised eighty-five foundations that had contributed $6.7 million to over a hundred groups organizing nonpartisan registration drives. See Interface, "Expanding Voter Participation: An Assessment of 1984 Non-Partisan Voter Registration Efforts" (New York: New York Interface Development Project, 1985), 6.

37. Piven and Cloward, *Why Americans Don't Vote*, 202. Peter D. Hart Research Associates surveyed 883 first-time registrants and 33 percent reported that they had been registered by organized drives. Piven and Cloward pointed out that another 22 percent of the respondents said that they had registered at tables staffed by volunteer registrars in churches, social agency waiting rooms, and other locations.

38. Francis Fox Piven and Richard A. Cloward, "The Registration Strategy: Trying to Break Down the Barriers," *The Nation*, November 2, 1985, 433–36.

39. As early as 1964, President Lyndon Johnson considered postal registration. In a January 15, 1965, private discussion between Johnson and the Reverend Martin Luther King Jr. about the need for federal voting rights legislation, Johnson told King that "we may have to put [voter registration] in the post office. Let the postmaster [do it]. That's a federal employee that I control. Who they can say is local . . . If he doesn't register everybody, I can put a new one in . . . I talked to the Attorney General and I've got them working on it." Quoted in Brian K. Landsberg, *Free at Last to Vote*, 156; conversation between Johnson and King reproduced in Michael Beschloss,

Reaching for Glory: Lyndon Johnson's Secret White House Tapes, 1964–1965 (New York: Simon & Schuster, 2001), 159–60.

40. Richard Moe (former chief of staff to Vice President Walter Mondale, 1977–1980), interview by Margaret Groarke, 1998.

41. Adam Clymer, "President Warned by House Democrats Against Water Projects Veto," *New York Times*, May 24, 1977, 16.

42. Sonia Jarvis (National Coalition on Black Voter Participation), interview by Margaret Groarke, 1990.

43. "Cranston the Right Stuff to Buck a Trend," *Los Angeles Times*, November 6, 1986, 1.

44. U.S. Public Interest Research Group, www.uspirg.org.

45. Letter, Gene Karpinski to endorsers, June 15, 1985.

46. Early participants included the NAACP, the League of Women Voters, the NAACP Legal Defense Fund, Project Vote, Public Citizen, the Midwest Voter Registration and Education Project, the Churches Committee for Voter Registration/Education, the Center for the Study of Responsive Law, People for the American Way, ACORN, AFL-CIO COPE, the Advocacy Institute, Citizen Action, MALDEF, the Southwest Voter Registration and Education Project, and Operation Big Vote. Human SERVE initiated coalition meetings and hired a staff person to coordinate coalition activities. The coalition long had no formal name—Human SERVE memos frequently refer to it as the "voter registration coalition." It would eventually take the name National Motor Voter Coalition and would grow to include roughly 150 additional organizations that endorsed the national reform effort.

47. House Committee on House Administration, "Voter Registration: Hearings Held Before the Subcommittee on Elections, 100th Cong., 2nd sess." April 19, May 10, and May 27, 1988, 263.

48. Chasnow interview, 1996.

49. Glenn E. Mitchell II and Christopher Wlezien, Voter Registration and Election Laws in the United States (a database of state laws), Michigan, Inter-University Consortium of Political and Social Research (ICPSR), 1995.

50. Committee for the Study of the American Electorate, "Creating the Opportunity: How Changes in Registration and Voting Law Can Enhance Voter Participation," Washington, D.C., October 1987.

51. Chandler Davidson, Tanya Dunlap, Gale Kenny, and Benjamin Wise, "Vote Caging as a Republican Ballot Security Technique," *William Mitchell Law Review* 34:2 (2008), 548–49.

52. U.S. Senate, "Equal Access to Voting Act of 1989: Hearings before the Subcommittee on the Constitution of the Committee of the Judiciary, One Hundred First Congress, First Session," May 10, 1989 (Washington,

DC: GPO, 1990), 29–30. See also Davidson et al., "Republican Ballot Security Programs," 60–62, which discusses the reopening and revision of the federal court consent decree originally negotiated in 1982 between the Democratic National Committee and the Republican National Committee.

53. Letter, Davidoff to Epstein, January 13, 1988, Human SERVE archives, Columbia University. Emphasis in original.

54. Mark Mackie (counsel to the [Republican] minority, Senate Rules Committee), interview by Margaret Groarke, 1990. Stevens had also helped lead the opposition to mail registration in the 1970s.

55. Abe Frank (Election Center), interview by Margaret Groarke, 1990.

56. Tamara Somerville (legislative assistant to Senator Mitch McConnell), interview by Margaret Groarke, 1990.

57. Tracy Campbell, *Deliver the Vote: A History of Election Fraud, an American Political Tradition, 1742–2004* (New York: Carroll & Graf, 2005).

58. House Committee on House Administration, "Voter Registration: Hearings," 768.

59. Al Swift (former congressman and chair of House Elections Subcommittee), interview by Margaret Groarke, 1999.

60. Cynthia Williams, "A National Legislative Reform Effort to Liberalize Voter Registration Procedures," unpublished paper, 1989, 23.

61. Swift interview, 1999.

62. Jarvis interview, 1990.

63. Edward Hailes, interview by Margaret Groarke, January 28, 1997.

64. President George H.W. Bush, "Message to the Senate Returning Without Approval the National Voter Registration Act of 1992," Museum at the George Bush Presidential Library, http://bushlibrary.tamu.edu/research/public_papers.php?id=4533&year=1992&month=7.

65. Elizabeth A. Palmer, "Democrats, Perot Criticize Bush for 'Motor Voter' Veto," *Congressional Quarterly Weekly Report* 50:27 (July 4, 1992), 1983.

66. Richard Sammon, "Motor Voter' Rides a Fast Track Through the House," *Congressional Quarterly Weekly Report* 51:6 (February 6, 1993), 264.

67. Paul Craig Roberts, "Citizenship Lost in the Ambuscade," *Washington Times*, May 28, 1993, F3.

68. *Congressional Record*, August 12, 1994, S 11424.

69. *Congressional Record* (January 4, 1995), Extensions, E4.

70. Although Democratic governor Evan Bayh of Indiana appeared willing to sign implementing legislation, the bill was tied up in a partisan disagreement in the legislature over when the proposed law would go into effect.

71. For more on the postpassage efforts to force implementation, see

League of Women Voters, "Voting Rights: The League's History," http://www
.lwv.org/AM/Template.cfm?Section=Democracy_Agenda&TEMPLATE=/
CM/ContentDisplay.cfm&CONTENTID=9995 (accessed December 10,
2007).

72. Mississippi had had a dual voter registration system since 1892, as
part of the "Mississippi Plan" to disenfranchise black voters, but the dual
system had been abolished by court order in 1984. Brenda Wright, "*Young v.
Fordice*: Challenging Dual Registration Under Section 5 of the Voting Rights
Act," *Mississippi College Law Review* 18 (Fall 1997), 67.

73. Stephen Knack, "Does 'Motor Voter' Work? An Empirical Analysis
of the National Voter Registration Act," unpublished paper, July 1993.

74. Dina M. Carreras and James Conley, "Survey of Voter Registration
in Medical and Public Assistance Agencies" (unpublished report by Human
SERVE), 1995, Human SERVE archives, Columbia University.

75. "Cheating Democracy: Discrimination in the Implementation of
Motor Voter Laws" (Report published by ACORN and Project Vote), December 4, 1995.

76. Douglas R. Hess and Scott Novakowski, "Unequal Access: Neglect-
ing the National Voter Registration Act, 1995–2007" (Report by Project Vote
and Demos), February 2008, http://www.demos.org/pub1531.cfm.

77. Six states were exempt from the NVRA over the two reporting peri-
ods because they either had no voter registration requirement (North
Dakota) or offered voters election day registration at the polls (Minnesota,
Wisconsin, Wyoming, Idaho, and New Hampshire).

78. A recent Heritage Foundation report argues that the decline in
TANF (welfare) caseloads "contributed substantially" to the decline in registration at public-assistance agencies, but the study does not include a measure of implementation, nor does it explain why state registration rates of
public-assistance applicants vary from 0 to 30 percent. See David B. Muhl-
hausen and Patrick Tyrrell, "Early Returns: Welfare Reform and the Drop in
Voter Registration at Public Assistance Offices," Heritage Foundation,
CDA08-03, June 11, 2008.

79. Hess and Novakowski, "Unequal Access."

5. Beyond Race? The Parties Search for a "Third Way"

1. Morton M. Kondracke, "Recriminations '88: Nunn's Story," *New Republic*, December 5, 1988, 15.

2. "Democratic Leadership Council," Right Web Profile (Silver City,
NM: International Relations Center, 2006), www.rightweb.irc-online.org/
profile/1463.

3. Robert Kuttner, "Red-Faced White Boys," *New Republic*, March 21, 1988, 9.

4. The comment was made to a reporter by a Democratic Party strategist who added, "Kirk needs these moderate elected officials for leverage in dealing with the interest groups and building the broad-based consensus he wants." See Phil Gailey, "Dissidents Defy Top Democrats; Council Formed," *New York Times*, March 1, 1985, A1.

5. On the DNC's coalitional structure and culture during the 1980s, see Jo Freeman, "The Political Culture of the Democratic and Republican Parties," *Political Science Quarterly* 101:3 (1986), 327–56.

6. George J. Church, "Moving Toward the Middle; Sick of Caucuses, Sunbelt Democrats for—What Else?–a Caucus," *Time*, March 18, 1985, 25; see also Jon F. Hale, "The Making of the New Democrats," *Political Science Quarterly* 110:2 (Summer 1995), 207–32.

7. The annual budget for the DLC during its first two years was $400,000, much of it raised in large contributions from corporate executives, lawyers, and lobbyists. By 1988, the annual budget had increased to over $2 million, largely on the strength of corporate sponsorships, with fifty-seven corporations among the DLC's one hundred Sustaining Members, and another twelve professional or trade associations in the energy, health care, insurance, pharmaceutical, retail, and tobacco industries represented. See Hale, "The Making of the New Democrats," 220.

8. Church, "Moving Toward the Middle," 25.

9. Ibid.; Kuttner, "Red-Faced White Boys," 8–9; Richard Stengel, "Rising Stars from the Sunbelt; the Democratic Leadership Council Is Redefining the Party," *Time*, March 31, 1986, 30.

10. Stengel, "Rising Stars from the Sunbelt," 30; Hale, "The Making of the New Democrats," 218.

11. Hale, "The Making of the New Democrats," 222.

12. William Galston and Elaine C. Kamarck, "The Politics of Evasion: Democrats and the Presidency" (Washington, D.C.: Progressive Policy Institute, 1989), 3–4.

13. For an astute analysis of how Clinton successfully managed the black-white divide over what to do about the race problem, see Claire Jean Kim, "Managing the Racial Breach: Clinton, Black-White Polarization, and the Race Initiative," *Political Science Quarterly* 117:1 (Spring 2002), 55–79.

14. American Bar Association of New York, www.abany.org.

15. Herb Stone, interview by Margaret Groarke, December 11, 1997.

16. Ibid.

17. The FEC makes the same three recommendations in both biennial reports: that states require all or part of an applicant's Social Security num-

ber, that states develop a statewide computerized registration database and integrate it with the agencies involved in registration, and that the U.S. Postal Service offer cheaper rates for "official election material" and provide space free of charge in their lobbies for voter registration materials. See Federal Election Commission, *The Impact of the National Voter Registration Act of 1993 on the Administration of Elections for Federal Office, 1995–1996* (Washington, DC: GPO, 1997); Federal Election Commission, *The Impact of the National Voter Registration Act of 1993 on the Administration of Elections for Federal Office, 1997–1998* (Washington, DC: GPO, 1999).

18. Dan Rozek, "DuPage Probing Voter Registration Problems," *Chicago Sun-Times*, November 10, 2000, 6.

19. Joe Dejka, "Close Tally Shows Flaws in Vote Law, Some Papillion Residents Who Thought They Were Registered Through 'Motor Voter' Weren't," *Omaha World-Herald*, November 14, 2000, 1.

20. Thomas C. Tobin and Leonora LaPeter, "State of Confusion: Voters Statewide Say They Had Poll Troubles," *St. Petersburg Times*, November 9, 2000, 1A.

21. John Nichols, "Could Turnout Turn Jeb Out?" *The Nation*, October 28, 2002, 20.

22. Gregory Palast, "Florida's 'Disappeared Voters': Disenfranchised by the GOP," *The Nation*, February 5, 2001, 20–23; see also Greg Palast, *The Best Democracy Money Can Buy: An Investigative Reporter Exposes the Truth about Globalization, Corporate Cons, and High Finance Fraudsters* (Sterling, VA: Pluto Press, 2002), 6–43.

23. David Margolick, Evgenia Peretz, and Michael Shnayerson, "The Path to Florida," *Vanity Fair*, October 2004, 359.

24. Jeffrey Toobin, *Too Close to Call: The Thirty-Six-Day Battle to Decide the 2000 Election* (New York: Random House, 2001), 168.

25. The U.S. Commission on Civil Rights heard testimony both from voters who filed complaints about the roadblock and from state highway officials. In their review, highway officials found policy violations occurred, but they did not find that any voter had been unreasonably delayed or prohibited from voting as a result. Florida's attorney general stated, "What we do know is that a check point on that date, Election Day, was absolutely not necessary for law enforcement purposes and similar check points should never again be implemented on Election Day. . . . No law enforcement barriers should be placed on Florida's roadways when people are going to and from voting." See Testimony of Florida Attorney General Robert Butterworth, January 21, 2001, Transcript, Hearing Before the U.S. Commission on Civil Rights, *Voting Irregularities in Florida During the 2000 Presidential Elections* (Washington, DC: U.S. Commission of Civil Rights, 2001), 199.

26. Toobin, *Too Close to Call*, 169.

27. Ibid.

28. Lance DeHaven-Smith, *The Battle for Florida: An Annotated Compendium of Materials from the 2000 Election* (Gainesville: University of Florida Press, 2005), 195–203.

29. Ellen Debenport, "GOP Candidates Glibly Hold Court," *St. Petersburg Times*, July 28, 1994. A coalition of African American groups opposed Bush on a range of issues, including his school voucher plan, his poor record of minority appointments when he was the state's commerce secretary, his views on welfare reform, and his get-tough talk on crime. See Bill Moss, "Black Groups Condemn Bush's Record," *St. Petersburg Times*, October 7, 1994, 4B. But the insensitivity of Bush's remark was particularly galling. State senator Matthew Meadow and the Florida Conference of Black State Legislators announced a massive statewide effort to get blacks to the polls. "That one statement made by Mr. Bush has truly angered the black community," said Meadows, "and we're going to show him on Election Day." See Diane Rado, "Bush Alienates Black Lawmakers," *St. Petersburg Times*, October 28, 1994, 2B.

30. Tom Hamburger and Peter Wallsten, *One Party Country: The Republican Plan for Dominance in the 21st Century* (Hoboken, NJ: John Wiley & Sons, 2006), 53–83. See also Adam Nagourney, "Lost Horizons," *New York Times Magazine*, September 24, 2006, 32ff.; Roger Stone, "How the G.O.P. Can Nail Down the Black Vote," *New York Times*, September 30, 1989, 23.

31. "Bush's Support Among Urban Blacks Lower Than GOP Projections," Associated Press State & Local Wire, November 22, 1998.

32. Ibid.

33. Ibid.

34. Quoting Jeb Bush, see Janet Marshall, "Bush Gets Jump on Affirmative-Action Foe: A Review of Florida's Policies May Defuse the Californian's Bid to Put His Initiative on the Ballot," *Sarasota Herald-Tribune*, August 19, 1999, 1B.

35. Peter Wallsten, "Anti-Preference Activists Ready," *St. Petersburg Times*, May 5, 1999, 1B.

36. William March and Michelle Pellemans, "Review Worries Affirmative Action Proponents," *Tampa Tribune*, August 18, 1999, 6.

37. David Mark, "Bush Bans Affirmative Action, Says He Has Found Another Way," Associated Press State & Local Wire, November 9, 1999.

38. Mike Schneider, "Black Politicians Denounce Bush's Affirmative Action Plan," Associated Press State & Local Wire, November 15, 1999.

39. Margolick et al., "The Path to Florida," 359.

40. Jim Saunders and Thomas B. Pfankuch, "Sit-in Leads to Affirmative Steps; Bush Agrees to One Florida Hearings, Puts Off Vote on University Admissions," *Florida Times-Union*, January 20, 2000, A1.

41. Letter to the Editor from Margaret Hyde, *St. Petersburg Times*, February 3, 2000, 17A.

42. Janet Marshall, "Audience Gets Vocal at First Public Hearing; the First Hearing on Gov. Bush's Plan Became Rowdy as a Majority of the Crowd Expressed Disagreement," *Sarasota Herald-Tribune*, January 29, 2000, 1B; Steve Bousquet, "Florida Governor Draws Opposition on Affirmative-Action Proposal," *Miami Herald*, February 1, 2000, 1A.

43. Steve Bousquet, "Florida Governor Listens to Critics of Plan to End Affirmative Action," *Miami Herald*, February 4, 2000, 1A.

44. Ibid.

45. Ibid.

46. William Cooper Jr., "Black Community Comes Together in Response to One Florida Issue," *Palm Beach Post*, February 5, 2000, 1B.

47. Brian E. Crowley, "Jeb Bush, GOP Not Hurt by Race Plan," *Palm Beach Post*, February 23, 2000, 1A.

48. Sandra Walewski, "Meek, Hill Set Off on Bus Tour; Opponents of Bush Initiative Rally," Associated Press State & Local Wire, February 29, 2000.

49. Marcia Gelbart, "200 Attend Vigil to Protest One Fla.," *Palm Beach Post*, March 7, 2000, 11A.

50. Marcia Gelbart and S.V. Date, "Thousands March on Capitol as Governor Opens Session; Protesters Say Bush Not Listening to Concerns," *Palm Beach Post*, March 8, 2000, 1A.

51. Michelle Pellemans and Ted Byrd, "Marchers Rally Against Plan," *Tampa Tribune*, March 8, 2000, 1.

52. Jounice L. Nealy, "On Bus from Pinellas to Capital, 'We're All as One,' " *St. Petersburg Times*, March 8, 2000, 7A.

53. Jim Saunders and Beth Kormanik, "2000 Florida Legislature Opens; Thousands Protest One Florida Plan State of State: Bush Proposes $500 Million Tax Cut, Adding $720 Million for Schools," *Florida Times-Union*, March 8, 2000, A1.

54. Gelbart and Date, "Thousands March on Capitol."

55. David Mark, "Thousands to Protest Bush's Affirmative Action Changes," Associated Press State & Local Wire, March 7, 2000.

56. Ibid.

57. Gelbart and Date, "Thousands March on Capitol."

58. Janet Marshall, "Opponents Haven't Given Up One Florida Fight," *Lakeland Ledger*, May 21, 2000, B1.

59. Jim DeFede, "The Untold Story: Guess Who's Coming to Vote? Guess Again," *Miami New Times*, November 30, 2000.

60. Marcia Gelbart, "One Florida Protest Organizers Turn Efforts Toward Voter Drive," *Palm Beach Post*, June 20, 2000, 2A.

61. Marcia Gelbart, "Statewide Trek by 2 Legislators to Encourage Minorities to Vote," *Palm Beach Post*, May 23, 2000, 7A.

62. DeFede, "The Untold Story."

63. Gelbart, "One Florida Protest Organizers."

64. Ibid.

65. Funds for the tour were raised through the group Coalition of Conscience, which had sponsored the March 7 rally in Tallahassee and included support from NOW, the People for the American Way Foundation, the Florida Education Association, the Florida chapter of the NAACP, and the AFL-CIO. See also Julie Hauserman, "GOP 'Hate Tour' Remarks Attacked," *St. Petersburg Times*, June 23, 2000, 1B.

66. Bill Kaczor, "Affirmative Action Hearing Concludes, Decision Expected in June," Associated Press State & Local Wire, April 26, 2000.

67. Diane Rado, "Court Bars Affirmative Action from 2000 Ballot," *St. Petersburg Times*, July 14, 2000, 4B.

68. U.S. Bureau of the Census, Public Information Office, "African Americans Defy Trend of Plunging Voter Turnout, Census Bureau Reports," Press Release, July 19, 2000.

69. Avalaura L. Gaither and Eric C. Newburger, "The Emerging American Voter: An Examination of the Increase in the Black Vote in November 1998," Population Division Working Paper No. 44 (Washington, DC: U.S. Census Bureau, Population Division, 2002).

70. Carl Hulse, "Black Voters Key to Democratic Hopes," *Lakeland Ledger*, June 12, 2000, A1.

71. "The African-American Firebrand Who Heads the Gore Campaign," *Journal of Blacks in Higher Education* 26 (Winter 1999–2000), 20–21.

72. Mary Jacoby and Susan Thurston, "It's Not How Many Vote, but Who Votes," *St. Petersburg Times*, October 28, 2000, 1A.

73. Ibid.

74. Alliniece T. Andino, "Radio Show Promotes Black Voter Registration Drive," *Florida Times-Union*, September 12, 2000, B3.

75. "NAACP President Headed to Florida to Investigate Voter Irregularities," Associated Press State & Local Wire, November 9, 2000; John Lantigua, "How the GOP Gamed the System in Florida," *The Nation*, April 30, 2001, 12.

76. Ronald W. Walters, *Freedom Is Not Enough: Black Voters, Black Can-*

didates, and American Presidential Politics (New York: Rowman & Littlefield, 2005), 94–95.

77. Advancement Project, "No Plans Have Been Written for Retreat: Documenting Black Political Power in Florida," n.d.; available online: www .advancementproject.org.

78. David Firestone, "The 2000 Campaign: The Turnout; Big Push Starts to Lift Turnout of Black Vote," *New York Times*, October 29, 2000.

79. Bill Adair and Tim Nickens, "Time to Decide: Florida May Be the Key to Vote; High Turnout Expected," *St. Petersburg Times*, November 7, 2000, 1A.

80. Tobin and LaPeter, "State of Confusion."

81. Walters, *Freedom Is Not Enough*, 97.

82. In Seminole County, the sister of Al Gore's campaign manager, Donna Brazile, was forced to show three forms of identification instead of the one required under Florida law before she was permitted to cast a ballot. See "No Justice in Florida," *Nation*, June 17, 2002, editorial, 3–4.

83. Walters, *Freedom Is Not Enough*, 98; See also Laura Conaway and James Ridgeway, "Democracy in Chains; Slavery's Legacy Shackled the Black Vote—and Cost Gore Thousands of Ballots," *Village Voice*, November 29–December 5, 2000, 41.

84. "NAACP President Headed to Florida to Investigate Voter Irregularity," Associated Press State & Local Wire, November 9, 2000.

85. Tom Bayles, "NAACP Questions Irregularities," *Sarasota Herald-Tribune*, November 11, 2000, A19; Allen G. Breed, "NAACP Hears Testimony of Florida Voting Irregularities," Associated Press State & Local Wire, November 11, 2000; see also *NAACP et al. v. Smith and Kast et al.*, U.S. District Court for the Southern District of Florida, Miami Division, No. 01-0120-civ-Gold (2001).

86. Advancement Project, "America's Modern Poll Tax," 21.

87. Margolick et al., "The Path to Florida," 360.

88. Leonora LaPeter, "Today Brings an Epilogue to Their Election Dramas; John Stafford, Jr., Duvall County Supervisor of Elections," *St. Petersburg Times*, January 20, 2001, 11A.

89. U.S. Supreme Court justice Sandra Day O'Connor would have appreciated Duval voters trying to follow instructions. During oral argument in *Bush v. Gore*, the case that stopped the Florida recount and decided the election for George W. Bush, she showed little sympathy for voters who didn't follow instructions and failed to punch out their chads. She asked Gore's lawyer, David Boies, what vote-counting standard should be used for determining the intent of the voter. Boies began to respond when O'Con-

nor, annoyed, asked, "Well, why isn't the standard the one that voters are instructed to follow, for goodness sakes? I mean, it couldn't be clearer." See Lani Guinier, "And to the C Students: The Lessons of *Bush v. Gore,*" in Ronald Dworkin, *A Badly Flawed Election: Debating* Bush v. Gore, *the Supreme Court, and American Democracy* (New York: The New Press, 2002), 238.

90. Conaway and Ridgeway, "Democracy in Chains," 42.

91. Bill Adair, "Duval Reveals Snapshot of Confusion, Inexperience," *St. Petersburg Times*, November 12, 2001, 1X; David DeCamp, "Ballot Confusion Still Simmering in Duval: Some Unsure of Their Vote," *Florida Times-Union*, November 22, 2000, A8.

92. Toobin, *Too Close to Call*, 173.

93. DeCamp, "Ballot Confusion Still Simmering," A8.

94. Toobin, *Too Close to Call*, 175.

95. John Derbyshire, "Too Dumb to Vote, and Too Smart, As Well," *National Review*, December 18, 2000, 26–28.

96. Mark Reynolds, "Gore Campaign Hopes to Ask for Recount in Duval County," *Florida Times-Union*, November 12, 2000, A1; Stafford's spokesperson said that Stafford thought Langton was asking about the number of votes that changed in Gore's favor after the automatic machine recount. Gore picked up 184 votes, while Bush gained 16. In another account, Stafford's spokesperson told a reporter that Stafford thought Langton was asking him about the total number of discarded absentee ballots, not overall ballots. See LaPeter, "Today Brings an Epilogue," 11A. Langton found out about the unusually high number of discarded ballots from a Jacksonville reporter who called on Friday, November 10, 2000, just hours before the midnight county deadline to request a manual recount. Langton was furious because he believed Stafford had sent a report about the high number of disqualified ballots to state elections officials the day after the election. "I don't have any reason to believe why he'd purposely mislead me, but he did," said Langton. Before he stopped talking to the press about what his spokesperson called a "miscommunication" between him and the Gore campaign, Stafford defended his actions. "We had a good ballot," he said, "very easy to understand. The voter needs to take some responsibility." See David DeCamp, "Heat Is On Elections Officials," *Florida Times-Union*, November 14, 2000, A1; Eric Boehlert, "The Disappearing Ballots of Duval County," *Salon.com*, November 13, 2000.

97. DeCamp, "Heat Is on Elections Officials," A1.

98. Steve Bousquet, "Voting Rights Lawsuits Might Only Prolong Furor," *St. Petersburg Times*, May 25, 2002, 1B.

99. U.S. District Court, Southern District of Florida, Case No. 01-120-

civ-Gold/Simonton; see also NAACP Legal Defense and Education Fund, "Florida Voting Rights Lawsuit Settled; NAACP/LDF to Monitor State's Implementation of Landmark Agreement," press release (n.d.), www.naacpldf .org/printable.aspx?article=80.

100. Proper implementation of the NVRA in Florida would not have prevented the various ballot design problems experienced by voters in a number of counties. But it would have reduced most of the problems associated with inaccurate voter registration records. See Monique L. Dixon, "Minority Disenfranchisement During the 2000 General Election: A Blast from the Past or a Blueprint for Reform," *Temple Political & Civil Rights Law Review* 11:2 (Spring 2002), 311–25.

101. Jim Sloan, "Ballot Woes Blamed on Punch Card Use," *Tampa Tribune*, November 10, 2000, 13. Jeffrey Toobin reports that privately, President Bill Clinton regarded what was happening in Florida as "the final chapter of a long siege" against him, yet another challenge to his legitimacy in office and an attempt to inflict punishment against his successor. He wanted demonstrators in the streets and thought the Democrats "should have been screaming about the treatment of black voters." This makes his attorney general's behavior all the more puzzling. See Toobin, *Too Close to Call*, 193–94.

102. See two reports by Allan J. Lichtman in *Voting Irregularities in Florida During the 2000 Presidential Election* (Washington, DC: U.S. Commission of Civil Rights, 2001): "Report on the Racial Impact of the Rejection of Ballots Cast in the 2000 Presidential Election in the State of Florida," appendix 7; and "Supplemental Report on the Racial Impact of the Rejection of Ballots Cast in Florida's 2000 Presidential Election and in Response to the Statement of the Dissenting Commissioners and Report by Dr. John R. Lott," appendix 10; see also Lichtman's reanalysis of the data presented to the U.S. Commission on Civil Rights confirming his original findings, "What Really Happened in Florida's 2000 Presidential Election," *Journal of Legal Studies* 32 (January 2003), 221–43.

103. Lichtman, "What Really Happened," 226.

104. Walters, *Freedom Is Not Enough*, 97.

105. After a wide-ranging investigation and testimony from over a hundred witnesses, including government officials subpoenaed and under oath, the commission's June 2001 report did not find "that the highest officials of the state conspired to disenfranchise voters. . . . Instead, the report concludes that officials ignored the mounting evidence of rising voter registration rates in communities. The state's highest officials responsible for ensuring efficiency, uniformity, and fairness in the election failed to fulfill their responsibilities and were subsequently unwilling to take responsibility." See

U.S. Commission on Civil Rights, *Voting Irregularities in Florida During the 2000 Presidential Election* (Washington, DC: U.S. Commission of Civil Rights, 2001), 2. A dissenting statement by Commissioners Russell G. Redenbaugh and Abigail Thernstrom challenging the final report's indictment of Florida election officials may be found in the report's appendix.

106. Advancement Project, "America's Modern Poll Tax: How Structural Disenfranchisement Erodes Democracy," November 7, 2001, 1.

107. Daniel P. Tokaji, "The New Vote Denial: Where Election Reform Meets the Voting Rights Act," *South Carolina Law Review* 57:4 (Summer 2006), 689–733; Deborah S. James, "Voter Registration: A Restriction on the Fundamental Right to Vote," *Yale Law Journal* 967: (June 1987), 1615–40.

108. Anne Kiehl Friedman, "Voter Disenfranchisement and Policy Toward Election Reforms," *Review of Policy Research* 22:6, 787. For accounts of voter intimidation in the form of Republican Party "ballot-security" programs see Davidson et al., "Republican Ballot Security Programs," September 2004; for other examples, see Ralph G. Neas and Julian Bond, "The Long Shadow of Jim Crow: Voter Intimidation and Suppression in America Today," Special Report to People for the American Way Foundation and National Association for the Advancement of Colored People (2004).

109. Some of the civil rights laws that could be violated apply only to racially discriminatory intimidation efforts; others apply regardless of motivation. For example, the most important voter intimidation law is the Voting Rights Act of 1965, which states that "no person . . . shall intimidate, threaten, or coerce, or attempt to intimidate, threaten, or coerce any person for voting or attempting to vote." See 42 U.S.C. § 1971 (1965).

110. The Civil Rights Project at Harvard University found that the residual ballot rate in the 2000 election varied widely from state to state, from as low as 1 percent in Maryland, Alabama, Louisiana, and Minnesota, to nearly 4 percent in Georgia and Illinois. Florida's problems were not anomalous, nor were they the worst case: seven states—New Jersey, North Carolina, South Carolina, Georgia, Illinois, Indiana, and Wyoming—all had residual ballot rates higher than Florida's and above the national average of about 2 percent. See the Civil Rights Project, "Democracy Spoiled: National, State, and County Disparities in Disenfranchisement Through Uncounted Ballots," http://www.civilrightsproject.ucla.edu/research/electoral_reform/ResidualBallot.pdf. (The Civil Rights Project moved to UCLA in 2006).

111. Caltech-MIT Voting Technology Project, *Voting: What Is, What Could Be*, Final Report (July 2001), http://web.mit.edu/voting/.

112. U.S. General Accounting Office, *Elections: Perspectives on Activities and Challenges Across the Nation*, Report to Congressional Requesters, GAO-02-3 (October 2001), 18.

113. Democratic Investigative Staff, House Committee on the Judiciary, "How to Make Over One Million Votes Disappear: Electoral Sleight of Hand in the 2000 Presidential Election," a Fifty-State Report Prepared for Rep. John Conyers, Jr., Ranking Member, House Committee on the Judiciary, Dean, Congressional Black Caucus (August 20, 2001); and Anita Miller, ed., *What Went Wrong in Ohio: The Conyers Report on the 2004 Presidential Election* (Chicago: Academy Chicago Publishers, 2005).

114. U.S. Congress, Joint Session of the House and Senate Held Pursuant to the Provisions of the Senate Concurrent Resolution 1, 107th Cong., 1st sess., *Congressional Record* 147:4 (January 6, 2001), House, 31–45.

115. Alison Mitchell, "Over Some Objections, Congress Certifies Electoral Vote," *New York Times*, January 7, 2001, 17; Larry Lipman, "Congress Certifies Bush as Winner," *Palm Beach Post*, January 7, 2001, 1A.

6. Keeping Down the Vote: The Contemporary Revival of Vote Suppression Tactics

1. Wayne Slater, "Democratic Activist 'Vindicated' by Outcome of Attorney General's Voter Fraud Probe," *Dallas Morning News*, June 13, 2008. www.dallasnews.com/sharedcontent/dws/news/texassouthwest/columnists /wslater/stories/060808dupolslater.d7735le.html.

2. C. Vann Woodward, *Origins of the New South, 1877–1913* (1951; Baton Rouge: University of Louisiana Press, 2005), 326.

3. Ibid., 327, citing *Richmond Virginia Sun*, June 14, 1893.

4. Ibid.

5. Ibid., citing Delegate William A. Handley, in *Proceedings of the Constitutional Convention of the State of Alabama, May 21st, 1901, to September 3d, 1901* (Wetumpka, AL, 1941), vol. 3, 2276–77.

6. Ibid., citing Delegate Albert P. Gillespie, in *Report of the Proceedings and Debates of the Constitutional Convention, State of Virginia . . . June 12, 1901, to June 26, 1902* (Richmond, 1906), vol. 2, 3014.

7. John Harwood, "Block the Vote: As a Final Gambit, Parties Are Trying to Damp Turnout," *Wall Street Journal*, October 27, 2004, A1.

8. Craig C. Donsanto and Nancy L. Simmons, *Federal Prosecution of Election Offenses*, 7th ed. (Washington, DC: GPO, 2007), 61.

9. Allen Raymond, *How to Rig in Election: Confessions of a Republican Operative* (New York: Simon & Schuster, 2008).

10. Lee Hockstader and Adam Nossiter, "GOP Outmaneuvered in La. Runoff," *Washington Post*, December 9, 2002, A4.

11. "Allegations Fly as Election Day Nears," *Baltimore Sun*, November 4, 2002.

12. Kweisi Mfume, "Voting Irregularities in the November 2000 Election and Proposals for Change," Testimony Before the Congressional Black Caucus, September 28, 2001.

13. Sherry A. Swirsky, "Minority Voter Intimidation: The Problem That Won't Go Away," Symposium on Constructive Disenfranchisement: The Problems of Access and Ambiguity, *Temple Political & Civil Rights Law Review* 11 (Spring 2002), 359.

14. The firefighters union, acting in a nonpartisan fashion, traditionally provided rides to the polls to the elderly and disabled who called in for assistance.

15. Court filings later suggested as many as eight hundred harassing calls were made in eighty-five minutes (or about one every six seconds) to six phone numbers used by the two organizations to coordinate rides and information for voters.

16. It is unlikely that John Sununu's victory in the U.S. Senate, which he won over Jeanne Shaheen by 19,751 votes, could be attributed to the Republicans' phone-jamming shenanigans, but other Democrats further down the ballot lost by only a few hundred votes, and it is reasonable to question whether some of them might have eked out victories.

17. Liberal bloggers Josh Marshall and Betsy Devine intensively covered the unfolding scandal. Marshall is credited with identifying James Tobin in October 2004 as the otherwise unnamed "official in a national political organization" who the government in its proceedings against one of the conspirators alleged played a role in rolling out the phone-jamming scheme. Both Marshall and Devine put together timeliness showing the glacial pace of the federal government's probe and the critical postelection timing of indictments. They echo the New Hampshire Democratic Party's concern, outlined in a letter to Senator Patrick Leahy of the Judiciary Committee and New Hampshire representative Paul Hodes, that throughout the criminal prosecution and the Democrats' civil suit against the Republicans in New Hampshire, "there were repeated actions of commission and omission on the part of the Department of Justice that give rise to serious questions as to whether or not there was political interference which operated to distort the judicial process." See Letter from Kathleen Sullivan, Chair, New Hampshire Democratic Party, and Paul Twomey, Attorney, to Senator Patrick Leahy and Congressman Paul Hodes, March 21, 2007, 1–2 (in authors' possession).

18. Tobin was serving as a Bush-Cheney New England campaign chair in October 2004 when it was publicly revealed that he was under investigation for his role in the 2002 phone-jamming episode.

19. Shaun Hansen, the smallest fish caught in the federal probe's

net, was the Sandpoint, Idaho, operator of a teleservices consulting firm that actually placed the harassing calls to the New Hampshire Democrats' get-out-the-vote phone lines. Hansen was indicted by information in April 2005; the government then withdrew the information against Hansen a month later after his attorney filed a motion indicating Hansen intended to defend himself by charging he had been entrapped by the government, acting under cover through the Republican National Committee. These intriguing claims of government involvement have gone unanswered. The next year, Hansen was indicted for conspiracy to commit telephone harassment, and he was scheduled to go to trial in December 2006. However, once the Democrats gained control of Congress in November, federal prosecutors hastily entered into a plea bargain in which Hansen traded a guilty plea for an agreement from federal prosecutors not to object to his appeal for leniency from the court. Hansen, thus, never testified at trial on the allegations of government involvement made in his July 2006 motion. Allen Raymond has since written a book about the case in which he claims, "The Bush White House had complete control of the RNC and there was no way someone like Tobin was going to try what he was proposing without first getting it vetted by his higher-ups." See Allen Raymond, *How to Rig an Election: Confessions of a Republican Operative* (New York: Simon & Schuster, 2008), 173.

20. Donsanto and Simmons, *Federal Prosecution of Election Offenses*, 61–63; R. Paul Margie, "Comment: Protecting the Right to Vote in State and Local Elections Under the Conspiracy Against Rights Act," *University of Chicago Legal Forum* (1995), 483.

21. *United States v. Tobin*, 480 F.3d 53 (1st Cir. 2007).

22. Greg Gordon, "Official: Justice Dept. Slowed Probe into Phone Jamming," McClatchy Newspapers, December 19, 2007.

23. Rehnquist's work coordinating Republican ballot-security programs is not in dispute; that he *personally* intimidated or harassed minority voters when challenging their credentials, a claim made by eyewitnesses, some of them lawyers who came forward during his 1986 Senate confirmation hearings, was first denied by Rehnquist in 1971 during his Senate confirmation hearings, and reiterated by him during the 1986 hearings. See George Lardner Jr. and Al Kamen, "1971 Rehnquist Account Is Challenged by 3 Men; 'Ballot Security' Role in '60s Called Active," *Washington Post*, July 25, 1986, A4; Al Kamen and George Lardner Jr., "Rehnquist Denies Challenging Voters; Nominee Stands by 1971 Statements to Panel," *Washington Post*, July 31, 1986, A1; see also Chandler Davidson, Tanya Dunlap, Gale Kenny, and Benjamin Wise, "Vote Caging as a Republican Ballot Security Technique," *William Mitchell Law Review* 34:2 (2008), 533–62.

24. John B. Judis, "Soft Sell: Can the GOP Convince Blacks Not to Vote?" *New Republic*, November 11, 2002, 12.

25. Judy Normand, "Controversy Greets Early Voting," *Pine Bluff Commercial*, October 22, 2002; Jack Whitsett, "Voting Quieter as Accusations Fly," *Pine Bluff Commercial*, October 23, 2002.

26. Interview with Tom Lindenfeld, quoted in Garance Franke-Ruta and Harold Meyerson, "The GOP Deploys," *American Prospect*, February 1, 2004, 29.

27. Clea Benson, Cynthia Burton, and Jacqueline Soteropoulos, "Chaotic Day Marks End of Tense Campaign," *Philadelphia Inquirer*, November 5, 2003, A1.

28. Davidson et al., "Republican Ballot Security Programs."

29. Ibid., 2; Sheldon S. Shafer, "GOP to Put Challengers in Black Voting Precincts," *Louisville Courier-Journal*, October 23, 2003.

30. Michael Janofsky, "Kentucky Elects a Republican Governor," *New York Times*, November 5, 2003, A22; Davidson et al., "Republican Ballot Security Programs," 5–6.

31. Robert J. Fitrakis, Steven Rosenfeld, and Harvey Wasserman, *What Happened in Ohio? A Documentary Record of Theft and Fraud in the 2004 Election* (New York: The New Press, 2006), 11–12.

32. At the time, Ohio voters were not required to show identification to vote; instead, they signed the poll book, and poll workers matched their signature to their registration. That law changed at the behest of the Republican Party in 2006, and now identification is required to vote. See Reginald Fields, "Voter ID Bill Gets Taft's Signature; Legislative Approval Follows Party Lines," *Cleveland Plain Dealer*, February 1, 2006, B3.

33. Fitrakis et al., *What Happened in Ohio?*, 16–17.

34. Jeffrey Toobin reports that the GOP minder sent to guide Florida secretary of state Katherine Harris toward rapid certification of Florida's 2000 election repeatedly urged her to "take the election in for a landing." See Toobin, *Too Close To Call: The Thirty-Six-Day Battle to Decide the 2000 Election* (New York: Random House, 2002), 69–70.

35. John Wooden, owner of a parody Web site, www.georgewbush.org, came into possession of the e-mails, whose subject lines were entitled "Caging.xls," when their authors at the Republican National Committee mistakenly sent them to Bush-Cheney campaign staff e-mail addresses using "@georgewbush.org" instead of "@georgewbush.com." Wooden forwarded e-mails containing two "caging lists" to Palast at the end of October 2004, and Palast reported on them for the BBC on October 26, 2004. See Palast's BBC *Newsnight* report, "New Florida Vote Scandal Feared," http://news.bbc.co.uk/2/hi/programmes/newsnight/3956129.stm; and

Palast's book *Armed Madhouse: From Baghdad to New Orleans—Sordid Secrets and Strange Tales of a White House Gone Wild* (New York: Penguin, 2006), 199–205.

36. The Census Bureau estimates there were 246,029 blacks in Duval County in 2004 out of a total population of 818,375. The data file is available at http://www.census.gov/popest/counties/asrh/files/cc-est2006-alldata-12.csv.

37. Mark Johnston, Standingup, and Aaron Barlow, "Palast, Progressives and Investigative Journalism," ePluribus Media, www.epluribusmedia.org/features/2007/20070704_palast_progressives_journalism.html (accessed July 17, 2007).

38. E-mail from Mindy Tucker Fletcher to Peter Barron, Editor, *Newsnight*, "Republican Response to Florida Vote Story," October 27, 2004, available at http://news.bbc.co.uk/2/hi/programmes/newsnight/3958475.stm.

39. "General Political News: Disfranchising Republicans; the Florida Democratic 'Plan' for Disposing of Republican Majorities—Thousands of Names Stricken from the Voting Lists Under a Misconstruction of a State Law," *New York Times*, October 25, 1878, 1.

40. Project Vote, "The Role of Challengers in Elections," *Issues in Election Administration: Policy Brief Number 10* (January 3, 2008).

41. Ibid., 4.

42. Ibid.; see also Advancement Project, "Report to State and Local Election Officials on the Urgent Need for Instructions for Partisan Poll Watchers," October 27, 2004, citing an 1850 law, 42. Rev. Stat. Ohio §§ 104–7.

43. O.R.C. Ann. § 3505.24; Michael Moss, "Big G.O.P. Bid to Challenge Voters at Polls in Key State," *New York Times*, October 23, 2004, A1.

44. O.R.C. Ann. § 3505.20.

45. Jim Dwyer, "Among Black Voters, a Fervor to Make Their Ballots Count," *New York Times*, October 11, 2004, A1.

46. Dan Balz and Thomas B. Edsall, "Unprecedented Efforts to Mobilize Voters Begin," *Washington Post*, November 1, 2004, A1.

47. Michael Moss, "Big G.O.P. Bid," A1.

48. James Dao and Adam Liptak, "G.O.P. in Ohio Can Challenge Voters at the Polls," *New York Times*, November 2, 2004, A1.

49. According to the U.S. Census Bureau, nearly one in five Americans of voting age moves annually. See Jason Schachter, "Geographical Mobility: Population Characteristics, March 1999 to March 2000," Current Population Reports, U.S. Department of Commerce, Economics and Statistics Administration, U.S. Census Bureau (May 2001), 1.

50. Steve Barber, Jim Halpert, Mimi Wright, and Frank Litwin, "The

Purging of Empowerment: Voter Purge Laws and the Voting Rights Act," *Harvard Civil Rights–Civil Liberties Law Review* 23 (1988), 499 and appendix A. The other states purging for failure to vote did so on an accelerated schedule, purging registered voters after two years of inactivity or for failure to vote in a single election. This was the law in Ohio in the 1960s when Carl Stokes ran for mayor of Cleveland.

51. Those states are Alabama, Connecticut, Kentucky, Maine, Massachusetts, Missouri, Nebraska, and Texas.

52. Christopher S. "Kit" Bond, " 'Motor Voter' Out of Control," *Washington Post*, June 27, 2001, A25.

53. Testimony of Deborah M. Phillips (Chairman, Voting Integrity Project), Senate Committee on Rules and Administration, *Hearing on Election Reform*, 107th Cong., 2nd sess., March 14, 2001.

54. Testimony of John Samples (Director, Center for Representative Government, Cato Institute), ibid.

55. Testimony of Todd F. Graziano (Senior Fellow in Legal Studies and Director, Center for Legal and Judicial Studies, Heritage Foundation), ibid.

56. David Scott, "Bond Calls for Investigation into St. Louis Voter Fraud Claims," Associated Press, November 9, 2000.

57. Safir Ahmed, "Slimin' the City," *Riverfront Times*, November 15, 2000.

58. Missouri Senator Christopher "Kit" Bond screamed the loudest. Bond was so certain the Democrats sued to keep the polls open so that they could steal the election, he later managed to get language into the Help America Vote Act that requires voters to cast provisional ballots where a court has extended voting hours. See 42 U.S.C. 15482(c).

59. Jo Mannies, "FBI Subpoenas Records from Election Board; Action Follows Charges of Vote Fraud in Recent Elections; Federal Grand Jury Will Get Documents," *St. Louis Post-Dispatch*, April 17, 2001, A1.

60. U.S. Congress, "Legislation to Facilitate Exercising the Right to Vote: Hearing Before the Subcommittee on Postal Operations and Services, July 30, 1985" (Washington, DC: GPO, 1985), 55.

61. See U.S. Department of Justice, Civil Rights Division, Voting Section Home Page, "Litigation Brought by the Voting Section: Cases Raising Claims Under the National Voter Registration Act," http://www.usdoj.gov/crt/voting/litigation/recent_nvra.html#nynvra (accessed June 2008). Jurisdictions sued for failing to purge their voter rolls include the states of Missouri, Indiana, and New Jersey, the city of Philadelphia, and Pulaski County, Arkansas.

62. The states receiving the Justice Department letter were Iowa, Mass-

achusetts, Mississippi, Nebraska, North Carolina, Rhode Island, South Dakota, Texas, Utah, and Vermont. See Steven Rosenfeld, "Voter Purging: A Legal Way for Republicans to Swing Elections?" *Alternet*, September 11, 2007, http://www.alternet.org/rights/62133/.

63. U.S. Department of Commerce, Bureau of the Census, *Current Population Survey: Voter Supplement File, November 2000* [Computer file] (Washington, DC: U.S. Dept. of Commerce, Bureau of the Census [producer], 2001), Ann Arbor, MI: Inter-university Consortium for Political and Social Research [distributor], 2001; U.S. Department of Commerce, Bureau of the Census, *Current Population Survey, November 2004: Voter Supplement File* [Computer file], ICPSR04272-v1 (Washington, DC: U.S. Dept. of Commerce, Bureau of the Census [producer], 2005), Ann Arbor, MI: Inter-university Consortium for Political and Social Research [distributor], 2006-01-16; U.S. Department of Commerce, Bureau of the Census, *Current Population Survey, November 2006: Voting and Registration Supplement* [machine-readable data file], 2007 (Washington, DC: U.S. Dept. of Commerce, Bureau of the Census [producer and distributor]). Authors' calculations.

64. Steven Rosenfeld, "Bush Government to Poor Voters: We Don't Want You to Vote," *Alternet*, July 17, 2007, www.alternet.org/rights/56957/bush_government_to_poor_voters%3A_we_don%27+_want_you_to_vote/.

65. It is not clear whether these states actually failed to conduct registration activities at poor- and disabled-serving agencies as required by law, or whether they simply did not provide the data to the EAC. Most had reported registration numbers from these agencies in previous years.

66. Dan Eggen and David A. Vise, "Ashcroft Takes On Voting Issues; Enforcement, Monitoring of Election Laws to Be Increased," *Washington Post*, March 8, 2001, A19.

67. Speech by Attorney General John Ashcroft, Voting Integrity Symposium, Washington, D.C., http://www.usdoj.gov/archive/ag/speeches/2002/100802ballotintegrity.htm (accessed June 2008).

68. Donsanto and Simmons, *Federal Prosecution of Election Offenses*, 10.

69. Paul Alexander, *Machiavelli's Shadow: The Rise and Fall of Karl Rove* (New York: Modern Times, 2008), 245–46.

70. Stan Bailey, "GOP Losers Want Probe into Voting; Democrats Win 4 Places Contested on High Court," *Birmingham News*, November 10, 1994, 101.

71. Tom Lindley and Stan Bailey, "Hornsby Claims Win; Hooper, Fraud Unofficial Figures Show Demo Leads by 304 Votes," *Birmingham News*, November 11, 1994, 1D.

72. Joshua Green, "Karl Rove in a Corner," *Atlantic Monthly*, November 2004, 92–102.

73. Ibid.

74. *Roe v. Sessions*, 676 So. 2d 1206 (Ala. 1995). In a case called *Wells v. Ellis* (551 So. 2d 382 [Ala. 1989]), the Alabama Supreme Court incorporated the Florida Supreme Court's well-known rationale in *Boardman v. Esteva*, 323 So. 2d 259 (Fla. 1975), holding that Florida's absentee-ballot law required only *substantial* compliance with regulatory requirements. As the court in *Boardman* put it, "The right to vote is the right to participate. . . . We must tread carefully on that right or risk the unnecessary and unjustified muting of the public voice. By refusing to recognize an otherwise valid exercise of the right of a citizen to vote for the sake of sacred, unyielding adherence to statutory scripture, we would in effect nullify that right."

75. The byzantine legal maneuvering began on November 11, 1994, when the Republicans asked the Shelby County Circuit Court to secure election records for an anticipated election dispute. Five days later, the Republicans filed suit in the U.S. District Court for the Southern District of Alabama alleging that election officials had violated Republican candidates' civil rights. Both courts issued temporary restraining orders enjoining election officials from taking any action to alter the ballots or any election records. On the same day, two voters sued in Montgomery County Circuit Court seeking an order that their un-notarized, un-witnessed absentee ballots be counted. Circuit Judge Eugene Reese ordered election officials to count absentee ballots that substantially complied with law by including the voter's residence, reason for voting by absentee ballot, and signature. The next day, a Republican voter brought suit in the U.S. District Court for the Northern District of Alabama seeking an injunction prohibiting election officials from following Judge Reese's order to count absentee ballots because it was a voting change requiring Justice Department pre-clearance under Section 5 of the Voting Rights Act. The state immediately asked for pre-clearance and three days later obtained it. The Republicans amended their federal court complaint in the Alabama Southern District and obtained another preliminary injunction prohibiting election officials from counting un-notarized, un-witnessed absentee ballots and ordering the secretary of state to certify the election for Hooper without them. One legal analyst observes, "To count or not to count, one thing was certain: if Secretary of State [James] Bennett followed the order of one court he would violate the order of the other." See Lori A. Tarle, "Comment: Statutory Interpretation and the Alabama Absentee Ballot Controversy," *Cumberland Law Review* 26 (1995–96), 203. The state appealed to the Eleventh Circuit Court of Appeals, which upheld the injunctive order and certified the question of the validity of the contested

ballots to the Alabama Supreme Court. That court reiterated previous lenient state court legal interpretations of Alabama's absentee ballot rule by holding that un-notarized, un-witnessed ballots met the requirements of the law. The Republicans took the case back to the Eleventh Circuit Court of Appeals and by October had obtained yet another ruling that the disputed ballots could not be counted. The Democrats appealed to the U.S. Supreme Court, which temporarily stayed the case, effectively delivering the election nearly one year later to Rove's candidate, Perry Hooper.

76. Green, "Karl Rove in a Corner," 94.

77. See Tarle, "Comment: Statutory Interpretation," 197–230.

78. Under the Bush administration, the Justice Department has piled up an impressive record of support for state election rules that make it harder for average Americans to register, vote, and have their votes counted. For example, the Justice Department has adopted a cramped view of voter list maintenance directives in the National Voter Registration Act of 1993 and threatened states with litigation where it believes election officials are not aggressively purging their lists to keep them up to date; it has strongly supported new restrictive voter identification rules adopted by several states, including Indiana and Georgia; and it has maintained that the Help America Vote Act of 2002 (HAVA) gives the states authority for determining whether provisional ballots must be cast in the proper voting precinct, despite an alternative interpretation favored by voting rights advocates that would define "jurisdiction" for these purposes in ways consistent with the National Voter Registration Act of 1993. Under the NVRA, jurisdiction refers to the "registrar's jurisdiction" that supervises election administration for the locality, usually understood as the county (see 42 U.S.C. 1973gg-6[j]). A couple of weeks before the 2004 presidential election, the Justice Department took the side of Republican secretaries of state in three swing states—Florida, Colorado, and Missouri—as federal judges endorsed some of the most restrictive provisional balloting rules in the nation. In Michigan, where the Republican secretary of state's rules requiring provisional ballots to be cast in the proper precinct were challenged by the Democratic Party, the Justice Department entered a friend-of-the-court brief arguing that, under HAVA, private parties had no standing to sue (the district court disagreed, but was reversed within days by the U.S. Sixth Circuit Court of Appeals). See Jordan Green, "DOJ Actions on Election Law Benefit Republicans," *Southern Exposure*, October/November 2004, 1–11.

79. This latter argument is explored more fully in a forthcoming book by Lorraine C. Minnite tentatively titled *The Politics of Voter Fraud*.

80. Cornell W. Clayton, *The Politics of Justice: The Attorney General and the Making of Legal Policy* (Armonk, NY: M.E. Sharpe, 1992).

81. Ibid., 146.

82. David Burnham, *Above the Law: Secret Deals, Political Fixes, and Other Misadventures of the U.S. Department of Justice* (New York: Scribner, 1996), 257.

83. Letter from Associate Attorney General D. Lowell Jensen to Rep. Peter W. Rodino, Jr., House Committee on the Judiciary, Subcommittee on Civil and Constitutional Rights, *Hearing on Civil Rights Implications of Federal Voting Fraud Prosecutions*, 99th Cong., 1st sess., September 26, 1985, 3–4.

84. Brian K. Landsberg, *Free at Last to Vote: The Alabama Origins of the 1965 Voting Rights Act* (Lawrence: University Press of Kansas, 2007), 115–25.

85. William E. Schmidt, "Selma, 20 Years After the Rights March," *New York Times*, March 1, 1985, A1; see also Frances M. Beal, "Black Political Power on Trial in Alabama," in Mike Davis, Steven Hiatt, Marie Kennedy, Susan Ruddick, and Michael Sprinker, eds., *Fire in the Hearth: The Radical Politics of Place in America* (New York: Verso, 1990), 237–49.

86. Quoted in Allen Tullos, "Voting Rights Activists Acquitted," *The Nation*, August 3–10, 1985, 79.

87. Quoting Wendell Paris, Sumter County Board of Education Chair, in Allen Tullos, "Crackdown in the Black Belt: Not-So-Simple Justice," *Southern Changes: The Journal of the Southern Regional Council* 7:2 (1985), 5.

88. Tullos, "Crackdown in the Black Belt," 4; see also Burnham, *Above the Law*, 257–58, citing U.S. Department of Justice press release, September 27, 1984; " 'Race-Based' Selective Prosecution of Voter Fraud by the Justice Department's Public Integrity Section," unpublished memorandum, n.d., 2–3 (in authors' possession).

89. Justice Department officials testified to Congress that approximately ten FBI agents were used in Perry County, but according to one of the lawyers involved in defending the black voter activists, Ira A. Burnim of the Southern Poverty Law Center in Montgomery, Alabama, "there were other FBI agents swarming over the county, going door to door with people's ballots and asking them if this was their ballot and asking them questions in who had assisted them and how it had been voted. So we are not talking about 10 FBI agents. We are . . . talking about just about every FBI agent in Alabama being detailed to this investigation." House Committee on the Judiciary, Subcommittee on Civil and Constitutional Rights, *Hearing on Civil Rights Implications of Federal Voting Fraud Prosecutions*, 128.

90. David Lawsky, "NAACP Fighting Vote Fraud Charges Against Southern Blacks," United Press International, April 20, 1985.

91. There were three grand jury sessions over the course of the investi-

gation, from October 1984 to January 1985, in which black witnesses were loaded up and transported to Mobile by bus.

92. House Committee on the Judiciary, Subcommittee on Civil and Constitutional Rights, *Hearing on Civil Rights Implications of Federal Voting Fraud Prosecutions*, 53.

93. Ibid., 36.

94. Ibid., 85.

95. Tullos, "Crackdown in the Black Belt," 10.

96. New scholarship on black electoral mobilization before the civil rights movement is turning up new evidence that black voter drives have long played an important role in the expansion of American democracy. See Paul Ortiz, *Emancipation Betrayed: The Hidden History of Black Organizing and White Violence in Florida from Reconstruction to the Bloody Election of 1920* (Berkeley: University of California Press, 2005) for an account of black electoral activity in Jim Crow–era Florida.

97. U.S. Department of Commerce, Bureau of the Census, Current Population Survey, November 2004: Voter Supplement File [Computer file], ICPSR04272-v1 (Washington, D.C.: U.S. Dept. of Commerce, Bureau of the Census [producer], 2005), Ann Arbor, MI: Inter-university Consortium for Political and Social Research [distributor], 2006-01-16.

98. Ibid. Approximately 9.2 million registered voters said they registered at a public-assistance agency, at an agency serving the disabled or unemployed, at a hospital, at a school, or on campus.

99. The National Commission on Election Reform Task Force on the Federal Election System notes that "the registration laws in force throughout the United States are among the world's most demanding . . . [and are] one reason why voter turnout in the United States is near the bottom of the developed world." National Election Commission, Report of the Task Force on the Federal Election System, chap. 2, "Voter Registration" (July 2001), 3; available online at http://www.tcf.org/Publications/Election Reform/NCFER/hansen_chap2_voter.pdf.

100. Michelle Malkin, September 29, 2004, blog entry; available online at http://michellemalkin.com/archives/000596.htm.

101. American Center for Voting Rights Legislative Fund, *Vote Fraud, Intimidation, and Suppression in the 2004 Presidential Election*, August 2, 2005, 35.

102. Several of these people technically were charged not with voter registration fraud, but with making false statements to government agencies (i.e., a driver's license bureau or the INS) regarding their citizenship status or eligibility to vote. We are casting the widest net possible in estimating these numbers, assuming, for example, that in those cases involving illegal

voting due to voter ineligibility, registration fraud was committed even if defendants weren't actually charged with registration crimes.

103. One of those convicted, Kimberly Prude, worked as an election inspector in Milwaukee. Prude lost her case on appeal. See *United States of America v. Kimberly E. Prude*, "Criminal Complaint," United States District Court, Eastern District of Wisconsin, Case No. 2:05-CR-00162-RTR, June 22, 2005.

104. In the ten cases of alleged illegal voting by felons in Milwaukee, one defendant was acquitted at trial and four had their charges dismissed. Among the dismissals evidence was presented that suggested defendants did not knowingly commit fraud. For example, the charges against Derek Little were dismissed when he was able to demonstrate to the court that he had registered to vote using his state offender identification card as proof of identity. See *United States of America v. Derek G. Little*, "Motion to Dismiss Indictment," United States District Court, Eastern District of Wisconsin, Case No. 05-CR-172 (LSA), March 14, 2006.

105. Western District of Louisiana, Press Release, "St. Martinville Woman Sentenced in Federal Court for Voter Fraud Charges," January 18, 2006; Richard Burgess, "Ex-Official Fined, Sentenced in Vote Fraud," *Baton Rouge Advocate*, January 19, 2006, 7B; U.S. Department of Justice, Criminal Division, Public Integrity Section, "Election Fraud Prosecutions and Convictions; Ballot Access and Voting Integrity Initiative, October 2002–September 2005."

106. See Lorraine C. Minnite, "The Politics of Voter Fraud," a Report to Project Vote, March 2007, 22–24.

107. *Mark Rubick et al. v. America Coming Together et al.*, Court of Common Pleas, Wood County, Ohio, Case No. 04-cv-650, 2004; see also Bob Fitrakis, "Fake Voting Rights Activists and Groups Linked to White House," *Columbus Free Press*, December 30, 2005.

108. See League of Women Voters of Ohio, "House Bill 3 Misses Target—Wrong Diagnosis, Wrong Remedy," HB3 Position Paper, n.d.; http://www.lwvohio.org/pdf/LWVO%20HB3%20Position%20Paper%201-03-06.pdf.

109. See court filings and other materials related to *League of Women Voters of Florida v. Cobb* and *Project Vote v. Blackwell*, available on the Brennan Center for Justice at New York University School of Law's Web site, www.brennancenter.org; see also Project Vote, "Restricting Voter Registration Drives," Issues in Election Administration: Policy Brief Number 5, January 9, 2006; and Steven Rosenfeld, "Are Voter Registration Drives Being Put Out of Business?" *Alternet*, July 25, 2007, http://www.alternet.org/story/57815/.

110. This is what the Web site says about the "National Mail Voter Registration Form": "If you are visiting or residing temporarily in Georgia, and you would like to register to vote in your home state, you may complete the *federal application for voter registration*. Note: the Georgia Secretary of State is unable to provide hard copies of the National Mail Voter Registration Form." See http://sos.georgia.gov/elections/voter_registration/voter_reg_app.htm. When we accessed the site in February 2008, the link to the federal form was dead.

111. Larry J. Sabato and Glenn R. Simpson, *Dirty Little Secrets: The Persistence of Corruption in American Politics* (New York: Times Books / Random House, 1996), 10.

112. See Tracy Campbell, *Deliver the Vote: A History of Election Fraud, an American Political Tradition—1742–2004* (New York: Carroll & Graf, 2005), and Andrew Gumbel, *Steal This Vote: Dirty Elections and the Rotten History of Democracy in America* (New York: Nation Books, 2005).

Epilogue

1. Political scientists do not by and large agree with these complaints. Consider for example this quote from Bruce Cain: "One of the ironies of contemporary politics is that even though American government is by any measurable standard more open, equal, and non-corrupt than it was 150 years ago, it does not always feel that way." Bruce E. Cain, "Reform Studies: Political Science on the Firing Line," *PS Political Science & Politics* 40:4 (October 2007), 635.

2. Hannah Fairfield and Griff Palmer, "Cashing In on Obama and McCain," *New York Times*, July 6, 2008, BU1.

3. See Nomi Prins, "Will Bush's Stimulus Package Work? It Depends on Who You Ask," *The WIP*, January 23, 2008, www.truthout.org/docs_2006/printer_0124081.shtml. Amaad Rivera, Brenda Cotto-Escalera, Anisha Desai, Jeannetee Huezo, and Dedrick Muhammad of the Institute for Policy Studies estimate the total lost wealth of blacks and Latinos to be between $164 billion and $213 billion. See *Foreclosed: State of the Dream 2008* (Boston: United for a Fair Economy, 2008).

4. See Michael B. Katz and Mark J. Stern, "Beyond Discrimination: Understanding African American Inequality in the Twenty-first Century," *Dissent* (Winter 2008), 61–65.

5. See Sigurd R. Nilson, "Poverty in America: Consequences for Individuals and the Economy," Testimony before the Chairman, Committee on Ways and Means, House of Representatives (Washington, D.C.: GAO, January 24, 2007).

6. In the 1950s and 1960s, the civil rights movement fought for integrated schools, and some integration occurred. Now school resegregation is proceeding apace. See Amanda Paulson, "Resegregation of U.S. Schools Deepening," *Christian Science Monitor*, January 25, 2008.

7. Julia B. Isaacs, "Economic Mobility of Black and White Families" (Washington, DC: Brookings Institution, November 2007), 10.

8. See Pew Research Center, "Optimism About Black Progress Declines: Blacks See Growing Values Gap Between Poor and Middle Class" (Washington, DC: Pew Research Center, November 13, 2007).

9. E.J. Dionne Jr., "Alien Nation," *New Republic*, December 10, 2007, www.thr.com/politics/story.html?id=e9ede3bf=3eb8=47bc=843f=6645c93 678ab.

10. The Southern Poverty Law Center reports a sharp increase in the number of hate groups since 2000, and the FBI reports a 35 percent increase in hate crimes since 2003. See Brentin Mock, "Immigration Backlash: Hate Crimes Against Latinos Flourish," *Southern Poverty Law Center Intelligence Report* (Winter 2007), http://www.splcenter.org/intel/intelreport/article .jsp?aid=845.

11. Myrna Pérez, "Proof of Citizenship Requirements; Chart of State Legislation," Brennan Center for Justice, New York University School of Law, June 19, 2008, http://www.brennancenter.org/content/resource/proof_of_ citizenship_requirements_chart_of_state_legislation/.

12. See Jennifer Bruner, Ohio Secretary of State, "Required Procedures in Administering Voter Challenge Statutes, R.C. 3503.24 and 3505.19," Directive 2009-79, September 5, 2008. Bruner concluded the Ohio law was unconstitutional, but the Republican National Lawyers Association disputed her ruling. See Ben Adler, "Ohio Secretary of State Prevents Vote Caging," *Politico*, September 13, 2008, http://www.politico.com/news/stories/0908/ 13415.html.

13. Kim Zetter, "Voter Database Glitches Could Disenfranchise Thousands," *Wired*, September 17, 2008, http://www.wired.com/politics/online rights/news/2008/09/voter_registration?currentPage=all.

14. Steven Rosenfeld, "2008 Season of Voting Meltdowns Begins," *AlterNet*, September 11, 2008, http://www.alternet.org/story/98369.

INDEX

Note: Tables and figures are represented by the letter "t" or "f" following a page number.